English for International
Tourism

Course Book

Miriam Jacob & Peter Strutt

Addison Wesley Longman Limited
Edinburgh Gate, Harlow, Essex, CM20 2JE, England
and Associated Companies throughout the world.

First published by Addison Wesley Longman Limited 1997

Set in Syntax 8.75/12pt

Printed in Spain by Gráficas Estella

ISBN 0 582 23753 X

Acknowledgements

The authors and publishers would like to thank the following
consultants and teachers for commenting on the manuscript: Sarah
Louise Moss, Joelle Bajolle, Ana Maria Peducci, Alison Gisvold, Susan
Karaska and especially Diane Conrad-Daubrah, who provided
inspiration as well as material for the book. Also students at the
University of Westminster and Hampstead Garden Suburb Institute
who piloted materials.

We are grateful to all those working in the travel business who gave
freely of their time and expertise and who agreed to be interviewed for
the book, in particular: Christopher Khoo of the Singapore Tourist
Board; Suzanne Bassett, Sales Executive, China Travel Service (UK) Ltd;
Miss Cumberbatch, Sales Manager, Barbados Tourist Authority;
Ludwig Szeiler, Prof Dr Dietrich Wildung, Curator, Ägyptisches
Museum, Berlin.

We would like to thank the following for providing help and
information: David Blair at the Welsh Office, Cardiff, Idwal Williams,
the planning officer for the Llanberis area, and Arfon County Council;
Elmeda Shelly of the Welsh Tourist Board; John Swarbrick; Bodo Hamel
of the Berlin Tourist Office; Jill Smillie at Conference Venues, and
Dawn Ellis and Pauline Thomas at Conference Contacts; Andrew
Rusack, Sales Manager for East of England, Going Places; Gary Lewis,
Senior Manager, Ground Operations, Air UK Ltd, Stansted Airport; Bill
Craig of American Express Training Dept; Emily F. Jacob.

Also: British Tourist Board; Egyptian State Tourist Office; Irish Tourist
Office; Intourist; New Hampshire Office of Travel and Tourism
Development, USA.

The authors would also like to thank the editorial team, Stephen
Nicholl, Sue Ullstein, David Riley and Janet Weller, and the publisher,
Gillian Rodrigues, for their dedication and commitment to the book.

We are grateful to the following for permission to reproduce copyright
material: Addison Wesley Longman for extracts from LONGMAN
ACTIVE STUDY DICTIONARY, © 1991 and INTERPERSONAL SKILLS
FOR TRAVEL AND TOURISM by Jane Lisa Burton © 1995; American
Express for an adapted training manual text, British Airways Holidays
Ltd for adapted extracts from a letter by Brian Eustace, Golf Manager
on behalf of British Airways and a British Airways Holiday feedback
questionnaire; British Tourist Authority/English Tourist Board for
adapted extracts from the articles 'Value of Tourism in the UK' &
'Tourist Spending Breakdown' from the leaflet NATIONAL FACTS OF
TOURISM, an adapted extract from BRITAIN'S STRENGTHS AND
WEAKNESSES: GUIDELINES FOR TOURISM TO BRITAIN 1991-1995
and an extract from the article 'Docklands turns its attention to tourism
growth' in TOURISM ENTERPRISE, January 1993; Commuter
Publishing Partnership for an adapted extract from the article 'How to
write a CV' by Eleni Kyriacou from MIDWEEK MAGAZINE, 1990;

Consumers Association for an adapted extract from the article
'Tourism the Destroyer - Plans for tourism development..' in HOLIDAY
WHICH? March, 1990; EMI Music Publishing Ltd trading as Elstree
Music, London WC2H 0EA for words to the song SUMMER
HOLIDAY Words and Music by Bruce Welch and Brian Bennett, ©
1963; The Financial Times Ltd for an extract from the article 'When it
pays to complain' by Diane Summers in FINANCIAL TIMES 28 July,
1994; The French Publishing Group for an adapted extract from YHR
GRAND LOUVRE GUIDEBOOK by Jerome Coignard, Joel Girard and
Christophe Lagrange, trans. Nigel Hollidge; Guardian Media Group plc
for a slightly adapted extract from the article 'A tale of two cities as
intrepid trio lose out on American dream' by John Mullin in THE
GUARDIAN, September, 1993;
Intourist Ltd for an adapted extract from 'Tailor-made booking
request form' in the brochure RUSSIA BEYOND 1994/1995; Lynton
Cooper Travel (London) Ltd for an adapted extract from the brochure
SKI THE AMERICAN DREAM - SKI AMERICA; Miller Freeman
Technical Ltd for extracts from articles 'Cut-and-thrust of contracting'
and 'Room at the top' in TRAVEL TRADE GAZETTE 14.6.90 & TRAVEL
TRADE GAZETTE EUROPA; Pergamon Museum/Accoustiguide GmbH
for extracts transcribed from PERGAMON ENGLISCH ACCOUSTI-
GUIDE (1991) by John Julius Norwich; Saga Studio for an adapted
extract from the 'Pacific Cruise Company' brochure SAGA CRUISE
COLLECTION - March 1994-February 1995; Times Newspapers Ltd
for an extract from the aritcle 'Promotion to the rank of flyer first class'
by David Churchill in THE SUNDAY TIMES, 21.11.93. © Times
Newspapers Ltd, 1993; United Nations Environment Programme for an
adapted extract from the article 'Safe Tourism - is it possible?' by Lelei
Lelaulu in the journal OUR PLANET, Vol 6, No 1 (1994).

We are grateful to the following for permission to use copyright
photographs: Alton Towers for page 18br; Clive Barda for page 35t;
Margarete Busing/Bildarchiv Preussischer Kulturbesitz for page 89t;
The Bridgeman Art Library for page 7bm, 89br, 89bm, 89bl, /Giraudon
for page 90; Capital Pictures for page 44ml; Going Places for page 30;
The Image Bank/Lisi Dennis for page 74, /Tom Owen Edmunds for
page 111b, /Renzo Mancini for page 9, /Andrea Pistolesi for page 46r;
The Kobal Collection for page 20; New Hampshire Tourist Board/Ralph
Morang for page 82t; Pepys Library, Magdelene College, Cambridge
for page 86l; Pictor International for page 7tr, 25, 38, 63, 73, 84;
Portsmouth City Council for page 87tl, 87tr; Ski the American Dream
for page 109m; The Slide File for page 23b; Steamboat Ski Corp/Larry
Pierce for page 109b, 109t; Tony Stone Images for page 7bl, /Michael
Busselle for page 11, /Richard Elliott for page 45, /Suzanne and Nick
Geary for page 87bl, /David Hanson for page 37tl, /Jeremy S Hibbert
for page 46l, /Simeone Huber for page 107, /David Madison for page
46m, /Hiroyuki Matsumoto for page 88br, /Kevin Morris for page 7tl,
/Jon Nicholson for page 37br, /Greg Pease for page 48l, /Lorne
Resnick for page 18ml, /Jon Riley for page 12m, 62; Strawbery Banke
Museum for page 82b; Telegraph Colour Library for page 6br, 6bm,
6bl, 7tm, 21, 23t, 24ml, 24tr, 24tm, 24tl, 24bl, 24bm, 24mr, 35r, 44b,
44tm, 50, 52, 56bl, 56tr, 56tl, 76, 77, 78, 86bm, 86br, 88tl, 88tr, 88bl,
111t, 114, /B & M Productions for page 12t, /Bavaria for page 7br,
/Bavaria-Bildagentur for page 22, /Colorific for page 18t, 44mr, 44tl,
/Colorific/Antonio Gusamo for page 6tm, /FPG for page 24m, 56br,
/James Kay Photography for page 12b, /Masterfile for page 6tl, 18mr,
44tr, /P Titmuss for page 87mr, /VCL for page 94, 104; Keith Tottem
Associates for page 70; Trip/Dinodia for page 37mr; Universal Press
Syndicate for page 50t; Elizabeth Whiting Associates for page 71.

Designed by Simon May, Sage Associates.

Illustrated by Kathy Baxendale, Richard Coggan, Michael A. Hill,
Biz Hull, Philip Mount (Tin Star), Caroline E. Porter, Debbie Ryder,
Michaela Stewart and Katherine Walker.

Cover photo by Andrew Hall.

To the learner

This book is for you if you work in the tourist industry or if you are studying tourism.

It provides excellent preparation for any of the major European examinations in English for Tourism including the London Chamber of Commerce and Industry English for the Tourist Industry exams.

What is in English for International Tourism?

The Course Book contains fifteen units and three scenarios, all based on themes from the tourist trade. It includes topics such as:

- the effects of tourism on the environment.
- how hotels are managed.
- how tour operators set their prices.
- how holiday destinations are selected and promoted.

What is in the units?

Every unit contains the sections below. We have used the same headings throughout the book so that you always know what kind of work you are going to do.

Preview

Each unit opens with a few questions, and often some pictures, to start you thinking about the theme you will be studying.

Speaking

Speaking activities present realistic and motivating situations where you can practise the language you have studied. You will make presentations, negotiate the terms of contracts, discuss key issues, give advice and information, deal with complaints and perform many other tourism-related tasks.

Listening

The cassette recordings include conversations and discussions between experts in the tourism trade. British, American, Australian and other international accents are featured, to help you understand how people speak English in different parts of the world. Tapescripts of the recordings are printed on pages 116–123 of the Course Book.

Language Focus

Here you will work on the key aspects of grammar that are essential for progress at this level. Language Focus sections include clear explanations and activities to help you understand and use the language effectively.

Vocabulary

The Vocabulary sections will help you to develop a richer vocabulary. These sections introduce and practise many words and expressions required in the tourist industry. A word list of more than 100 tourism terms included in the Course Book is printed on pages 124–127, along with translations into seven languages.

Speechwork

Good pronunciation will give you greater confidence, whether you are dealing with customers, taking part in discussions or guiding groups of visitors. The Speechwork sections will give you the systematic, regular practice which is the key to progress.

Reading

To help you improve your reading skills, we have chosen a variety of authentic texts from tourism publications, and have designed practical exercises to check your understanding.

Writing

In the Writing sections you will carry out real tasks from the tourism workplace. For example: writing letters, press releases, brochures and reports. There are model answers for all the writing activities in the Teacher's Resource Book.

Learning Tips

From time to time we include advice and information on how to improve your learning strategies and become more independent when you study.

Scenarios

After every five units there is a scenario. These are case studies which challenge you to use the English you have learned to deal with authentic situations in international tourism.

What about private study?

A Workbook with its own cassette accompanies the Course Book. This provides extra tasks for study at home or in class and includes three review sections where you can monitor your progress.

We very much hope you will enjoy using *English for International Tourism*.

Miriam Jacob

Peter Strutt

Itinerary

Unit	Setting	Professional activities	Language	Directory of texts

1
Types of Holiday
page 6
	Travel agencies and tour operators	• giving holiday information
		• talking about holiday experiences
		• writing and responding to letters of enquiry
			Language Focus: compound nouns
			Vocabulary: types of holiday
			               prices
			               compound adjectives
			               with numbers
			Speechwork: word stress
				Conversations with customers ⬡
				Letters about golfing holidays ▥

2
A Career in Tourism
page 12
	Recruitment and job hunting	• writing CVs and covering letters
		• taking part in job interviews
			Language Focus: simple/continuous
			               verb forms
			Vocabulary: remuneration
			               formal and informal
			               language
			Speechwork: stress in words ending
			               in -ate, -ic and -able
				Job descriptions ⬡
				How to write a CV ▥
				The write way to find a job ▥
				CVs ▥
				Recruitment advertisements ▥
				Letters of application ▥

3
Trends in Tourism
page 18
	Tourism organisations and tourist boards	• note-taking
		• writing a summary based on notes
		• giving a short presentation from notes
		• talking and writing about modern-day developments
			Language Focus: past simple/present
			               perfect simple
			Vocabulary: definitions of tourism
			               types and means of
			               travel
			Speechwork: past verb forms with
			               -ed
				Definitions of tourism ⬡
				Summer holiday ⬡
				Development of tourism in ⬡
				Singapore
				Summer holiday ▥

4
Where People Go
page 24
	Tourist boards, tour operators, Tourist Information Centres (TICs), and travel agents	• working with figures
		• designing a questionnaire and carrying out a survey
		• giving information from a chart
		• reporting on the nature and value of tourism in a country
			Language Focus: the definite article
			Vocabulary: British/American
			               usage
			Speechwork: the schwa / ə /
			               reading figures aloud
				Americans in Europe ⬡
				A tale of two cities ▥

5
Travel Agents
page 30
	Travel agencies	• telephoning
		• taking bookings and filling in booking forms
		• asking for and confirming information
		• writing letters of confirmation
		• writing a set of instructions: payment procedures
			Language Focus: asking questions
			               tag questions
			Vocabulary: phrasal verbs used in
			               phone calls
			               payment procedures
			Speechwork: the alphabet
			               intonation in questions
			               intonation in tag
			               questions
				Telephone calls ⬡
				A holiday booking ⬡
				Booking forms ▥
				Extract from a training manual ▥

Scenario 1 Advising a Client page 36	Travel agencies and tour operators	• reading brochures • giving information and advice • helping clients make choices • writing letters of recommendation	Revision	Goa, India ▥ Steamboat, Colorado, USA ▥

6
Tour Operators
page 38
	Tour operators and hoteliers	• writing reports
		• planning a package tour
		• negotiating an agreement
		• writing a letter of confirmation
			Language Focus: the passive
			Vocabulary: negotiations
			Speechwork: contracted forms of
			               modals and
			               auxiliaries
				A planning meeting ⬡
				Hotel contracting ▥
				When the welcome is frosty ▥

7
Promoting a Destination
page 44
	Tourist boards	• identifying strengths and weaknesses of a country
		• describing ways of promoting an area
		• writing promotional materials
		• describing an itinerary
		• presentations: reporting on a familiarisation trip
			Language Focus: referring to the
			               future
			Vocabulary: advertising and
			               publicity
			               countable/
			               uncountable nouns
			               brochure language
			Speechwork: pausing and rhythm
				Promoting Barbados as a ⬡
				tourist destination
				A "fam." trip to China ⬡
				Britain's strengths and ▥
				weaknesses

8 Responsible Tourism page 50	Ecological and economic issues National and local government Environmental and tourism agencies	• taking part in public meetings • writing press releases	Language Focus: reporting verbs Vocabulary: meetings – verb and noun collocations Speechwork: word boundaries	Overland Encounter ⬡ Safe tourism ▥

▥ = Reading text
⊙ = Listening text

5

1

Types
of Holiday

Dealing with trade and customer enquiries

Preview

1 **How many different kinds of holiday can you think of? Work with a partner and compare your lists.**

Vocabulary 1

2 **Put the words (1–9) into the appropriate spaces.**

1 winter sports	4 safari	7 adventure
2 self-catering	5 cruise	8 package tour
3 special interest	6 weekend break	9 homestay

a a relaxing ...... holiday with old-fashioned hospitality on a family farm

b a month's ...... holiday lost in the Amazon rain forest

c a fortnight's ...... holiday for the family in a rented Swiss chalet

d a ten-day ...... to Thailand, including flights, deluxe hotels and visits to the Sukhothai national park and the pagodas at Ayutthaya

e a two-week ...... in the Baltic Sea aboard the luxury liner Argenta

f a(n) ...... holiday skiing on the slopes of the Pyrenees

g a(n) ...... in Amsterdam to visit the Rijksmuseum and be back in time for work on Monday

h a stay in Mombasa combined with a(n) ...... in the famous Tsavo game park

i a(n) ...... holiday, excavating Aztec temples or learning English in London

3 **Join the phrases in the two sections a–g and 1–7 to make complete holiday descriptions.**

a A city break in Moscow

b A three-week expedition to Greenland

c A five-day stay in a purpose-built chalet

d Two weeks on an ocean liner

e A month's holiday in a mobile home

f A bed-and-breakfast stay

g A trip to Disney World

1 to study the geology, flora and fauna

2 in a caravan park in sunny Biarritz

3 at one of the Center Parcs holiday villages in Britain, France or Holland

4 with two nights at the Metropol hotel and tickets for the Bolshoi

5 including a three-day stopover in Tahiti

6 with free accommodation in a condo in Orlando

7 in a comfortable guest house near The Black Forest

4 **What types of holiday are those in exercise 3? Choose categories from the list in exercise 2 or add your own.**

5 **How would you describe the holidays in exercise 3? Choose from the list in the box below and justify your choice.**

frightening	relaxing	for the family
exhausting	cultural	once-in-a-lifetime
entertaining	romantic	adventurous

Listening

6 Listen to four conversations in a travel agency and match the customers to the advertisements.

CASABLANCA
Morocco

Get away from it all.
A luxury holiday at an affordable price.

VINTAGE SPAIN
Country cottages and fabulous fiestas at bargain prices

DISCOVER MOSCOW

The Red Square, the Kremlin,
St Basil's Cathedral... at give-away prices.

Places limited.

Renaissance
FLORENCE
A remarkable exhibition
"The Age of the Medici"

Book now for discount prices.
Details inside.

The World of Children's Fantasy
LAPLAND
IN SEARCH OF SANTA CLAUS
Flights by Boeing jets and Concorde at unbeatable prices

WEDDINGS *in* PARADISE
Tropical Island Holidays
Special rates for newly-weds
ENQUIRE WITHIN.

Vocabulary 2

Prices

7 Find the words in the advertisements that refer to the prices of the holidays. Then listen again and list the words that talk about price.

8 Write the words from the box along a line like the one below, going from the cheapest to the most expensive.

a bit pricey	reasonable	dear	exorbitant	prohibitive
at rock-bottom prices	economical	costly	free of charge	

cheap ←——————————————————————————————→ expensive

9 Work with a partner and discuss these questions.

a Where would you consider it economical/reasonable/exorbitant to go for a holiday?

b What kind of tourist activities in your area are free of charge?

c What are the disadvantages of holidays at rock-bottom prices?

d Which of the holidays in the travel agent's window would appeal to you?

e What would you consider to be the holiday of a lifetime?

Language Focus

Compound nouns

In English we can use nouns as adjectives. For example:

water sports   adventure holiday   caravan park

The first word functions as the adjective and answers the question *What kind of?*

The relationship between the two nouns can be of many kinds, including:

Place	**mountain slopes, city centre**
Time	**summer holiday, weekend break**
Function	**golf course, swimming pool**
Material	**paper bag, iron bridge**

Sometimes three or more words are combined:

Tourist Information Centre   air traffic control

business travel expenditure   winter sports holiday premium

Apostrophe *s*

The *'s or s'* can be used in expressions of time with numbers:

an hour's drive from the airport

a month's holiday in Hungary

two days' journey

five minutes' walk

BUT in expressions beginning with *a*, *the*, or a *possessive* and followed by a number, the first noun is singular. For example:

The tour includes a **two-day** expedition to the caves.

The **three-day** train journey was boring.

His **thirty-mile** hike over the mountains left him exhausted.

Practice

1 Match the nouns in A and B.

A	B
theme	city
hotel	book
boat	sports
incentive	resort
guide	travel
water	trip
capital	accommodation
health	park

2 Work in groups. How many compound nouns can you make using the word holiday? For example:

holiday accommodation   package holiday

3 Rewrite these sentences without changing the meaning. For example:

It takes five minutes to walk from the hotel to the beach.

It's a five-minute walk from the hotel to the beach.

A specialist lecturer accompanies each cruise which lasts seventeen days.

A specialist lecturer accompanies each seventeen-day cruise.

a It takes two hours to drive to the airport.

b The journey to the centre of London takes forty-five minutes.

c The excursion includes a meal with three courses at a gourmet restaurant.

d You can visit the vineyard, which extends over two hundred hectares.

e We stayed in a hotel with three stars.

f From Santiago to San Francisco there's a freeway with four lanes.

g A guide accompanies all tours scheduled for five days.

h They have produced a film, which lasts twenty minutes, on the Ammassalik region of East Greenland.

i Their expedition, which took six months, nearly met with disaster.

Speechwork

Word stress

10 Say these words.

1 ▪▫ costly

2 ▫▪ appeal

3 ▪▫▫ romantic

4 ▪▫▫▫ affordable

5 ▫▫▪▫ situation

Word stress is very important because if you place the stress on the wrong syllable, other people will find it difficult to understand you.

Read the following words aloud and classify them according to the stress patterns above.

adventure	enquire	expedition
relaxing	Japan	about
unbeatable	Britain	safari
Cairo	photographer	forest
again	prohibitive	cancellation
jungle	package	Arctic

Listen and check your pronunciation.

> **Learning Tip**
>
> When you note down a new word it's a good idea to include the stress:
>
> bargain ▪▫
>
> cathedral ▫▪▫
>
> exceptional ▫▪▫▫
>
> hospitality ▫▫▪▫▫

Speaking

11 Draw a grid like the one below.
Fill in the details of the best holiday you have ever had.
Then interview some other members of the class.
Who had the most exciting holiday? The best value for money?

Name	Me	Miriam	Gillian
Duration	2 weeks	2 weeks	3 weeks
Destination	N. Spain	Scotland	Cameroon
Type of holiday	Touring	Self-catering	Familiarisation trip
How organised	By myself	By us	Government
Means of transport	Car	Car + Boat	Plane, car, limousine
Activities	Sightseeing & eating	Sailing, eating, sightseeing, walking	Sightseeing, cultural visits
Value for money	Terrible!	Great	Excellent!

Reading

12 **Read these statements about business letters in English. Are they true or false? Do other people in the class agree with you? What other advice can you give about writing letters?**

a When you write a letter you put your name above your address.

b It is correct to write *Dear Mister* when beginning a letter.

c In the United States *1st April 1999* can be abbreviated to *4.1.99*.

d When writing a letter to the USA you can begin it with *Gentlemen:*.

e The abbreviation *Ms* is used to write to women when you do not know or do not want to refer to their marital status.

f It is rarely appropriate to use contractions (*I'll, don't, isn't*) when writing letters.

g If you begin a letter with *Dear Mr Grant* you should end with *Yours faithfully*.

13 **Read the letter on the left.**
Why is Mrs McSweeney writing? What information does she require?

44 Cedar Avenue
London
N3 1SR

Skyways Holidays
Publications Manager
Atlantic House
Hazelwick Avenue
Haywards Heath
West Sussex
HH10 1NP

30 October 199

Dear Sir or Madam

As an enthusiastic golfer I am very interested in combining a holiday abroad with the opportunity to receive expert tuition and improve my handicap.

I would be grateful if you could send me a brochure on special interest golfing holidays, together with details of transport, accommodation and any special out-of-season offers.

Thank you in advance. I look forward to hearing from you in the near future.

Yours faithfully

H. McSwny

Heather McSweeney (Mrs)

14 **Read the reply on the right.**
What information is missing?

Atlantic House, Hazelwick Avenue, Haywards Heath, West Sussex HH10 1NP

Mrs McSweeney
44 Cedar Avenue
London
N3 1SR

6 November 199

Dear Mrs McSweeney,

I am delighted to enclose a Skyways Holidays Golf brochure for next season.

This brochure offers the widest selection of golf holidays available today. Choose between a holiday near to home in Portugal, Spain or Madeira, or fly further afield to exotic destinations such as the Caribbean, the USA, Kenya or even Thailand.

Free Skyways UK Flights to Heathrow or Gatwick are available to connect with many holidays, and you will find a host of bonus offers at selected hotels throughout the brochure. With guaranteed no surcharges, you can be sure of real value for money. I do hope that this new brochure will help you find the holiday of your choice. Our specialist Golf Reservations Team on 01293 487725 will be delighted to help you with your booking, or alternatively visit your local ABTA Travel Agent or Skyways Travel Shop. If you have any specific questions, please call our Golf Advice Helpline on 01293 890572.
We look forward to welcoming you on a Skyways Holiday soon.

Yours sincerely,

Avril Sinclair

Avril Sinclair

Golf Manager

PS Our Golf Reservation Team on 01293 487725 will be happy to check availability on any holiday for you.

Writing

Letter of enquiry

15 **Read the instructions below and write a letter of enquiry. Give the letter to your teacher who will deliver it to another member of the class.**

You are American. You are planning a trip to Europe this summer and you are thinking of taking a touring holiday in France.

The French government tourist office has given you an address to write to:

EUROPA TOURS
74/1 Newbern Avenue
Medford
Massachusetts 02155

You would like to know what they can offer. You also want to know about prices, the type of transport, accommodation and any discounts that may be available.

Before you begin, decide on the following:

a who you are
b your age
c your marital status
d if you will be travelling alone or with others
e if with others, who they will be.

Your address is 611 E. Franklin Street, Richmond, Virginia 23219.

If necessary, refer to the Writing Tips below.

16 **When you receive a letter of enquiry use the information on page 102 to write the reply.**

Writing Tips

Making an enquiry

 KISS – **K**EEP **I**T **S**HORT AND **S**IMPLE.

- Explain clearly what information you wish to receive.
- Say why you need it.
- Use a separate paragraph for each request.
- Use simple rather than complex sentences.
- Delete unnecessary detail.

Useful language

I am writing to enquire about …
I was interested in your advertisement in …
I would be grateful if you could …
I look forward to hearing from you soon.

Replying to an enquiry

 KISS – **K**EEP **I**T **S**HORT AND **S**IMPLE.

- Answer all the questions.
- Give the client all the information he/she needs to make a booking.
- Be friendly and positive.
- Use a separate paragraph for each response to a question.
- Use simple rather than complex sentences.
- Delete unnecessary detail.

Useful language

Thank you for your letter/fax of (date) …
In reply to your letter/fax of (date) …
We specialise in catering for …
Please find enclosed …
If you need any further help or information please do not hesitate to contact us.
I look forward to hearing from you.

Follow-up

17 **If possible, look up the address of an English-speaking tourist board or a tour operator with offices in the UK, the USA, Canada, Australia, Ireland or New Zealand and write to them** requesting information about a holiday you might like to go on or promote.

2

A Career

in Tourism

1

Applying for jobs

Preview

1 Work in groups. Make a list of job titles in the tourism sector.
Compare your list with those of other groups.

2 Work with a partner. Choose two jobs and list the activities they involve.

2

Listening

3 Listen to six people talking about their jobs.
Match the people to their job titles.

a Product manager
b Conference coordinator
c Trainee hotel manager
d Travel consultant
e Cabin attendant
f Business travel consultant

3

Language Focus

Simple/continuous verb forms

Look at these pairs of sentences and answer the questions:

1 a I work for Exotic Tours.
    Is this a temporary or permanent situation?

  b I'm working for Exotic Tours.
    Is this a temporary or permanent situation?

2 a We fly to Dubai on Fridays.
    Is this a regular event or a plan?

  b We're flying to Dubai on Friday.
    Is this a regular event or a plan?

3 a The 4 p.m. shuttle is leaving.
    What time is it?

  b The next shuttle leaves at 4 p.m.
    What time is it?

4 a She's been working as a hostess.
    Does she still work as a hostess?

  b She's worked as a hostess.
    Does she still work as a hostess?

5 a When you phoned I was speaking to the manager.
    Did the phone call interrupt the conversation?

  b When you phoned I spoke to the manager.
    Did the phone call interrupt the conversation?

Practice

1 Read this extract from an interview in which a woman is talking about her career. Put the verbs in brackets into the correct tense. Then work with a partner and compare your choices.

> "I (have) ...... three jobs in my life so far. I (start) ...... as an Overseas Representative in Tunisia, Greece and Austria, and then I (work) ...... as an Assistant Resort Manager for two years in Turkey. I (head) ...... for promotion when I (decide) ...... to leave in order to start a family. Anyway, now I'm back in work and for the last six months I (work) ...... as a Contracts Executive so usually I (spend) ...... a lot of time with hotel managers and (negotiate) ...... contracts for hotel rooms and services. On top of that I (select)...... new resorts and locations.
> At the moment, I've got a trainee with me who (do) ...... some research into.,."

2 What is your occupation?
What does it involve?
Are you working on any particular project at the moment?

Speaking 1

Applying for Jobs

4 **Work in groups. Discuss these questions.**

a How do you find out about job vacancies?

b How do you apply?

c Have you ever applied for a job? What did you have to do?

5 **In order to apply for a job you usually have to send a curriculum vitae (CV) – in the USA called a resumé – and a covering letter. These documents are very important because they are the first impression you give.**

Work in groups. Read the statements about CVs and covering letters. On the basis of your knowledge and experience, decide if you agree with them.

a A curriculum vitae is more acceptable if it is hand-written.

b A covering letter should be hand-written.

c You should always include a photograph.

d The longer a CV is the better.

e A CV should list experience in chronological order.

f It's best to explain foreign qualifications and give an approximate equivalent in the country to which you are applying.

g There is no point in mentioning outside activities, hobbies, etc.

h Each CV should be customised for the job you are applying for.

i Perfect prose isn't expected; note form is perfectly acceptable.

j Use space constructively; don't mention failures or irrelevant experience.

k Don't include your previous salary or salary expectations, unless requested.

l You can lie on a CV: they'll never find out anyway.

m Any gaps in the dates should be explained.

n It's best not to send the CV by fax unless requested to do so.

o Always make a follow-up phone call a few days after sending off your CV.

Reading

CVs

6 **Work with a partner. Student A read the article "How to Write a CV" below, Student B read the article "The Write Way to Find a Job" on page 103.**

STUDENT A

Tell your partner what recommendations "How to Write a CV" makes about:

- personal information and experience.
- layout, language and style.

Which of the fifteen points (a–o) in exercise 5 are mentioned in the article?

HOW TO WRITE A CV

When applying for a job you'll be in competition with a number of other candidates. So your CV is important — interviewers will decide whether or not to see you on the strength of what you have written. Don't just think of it as a list of facts; it should sum up your personal, educational and career history, as well as being an indication of your strengths and weaknesses. Here are a few suggestions:

Presentation

- Always type your CV. Use a good typewriter or word processor.
  If a CV is hand-written, it goes into the wastepaper basket.
- Use good quality paper. Don't give the impression this is just another photocopy.
- Never send a CV without a covering letter explaining which vacancy you're applying for. If you're writing "on spec.", send a short letter explaining what kind of post you're looking for.
- Don't fax a CV unless you're asked to. It's a confidential document.

Content

- Write a list of important headings. These should include your name, date of birth, your address (and your e-mail address, if you have one), phone number (at work and at home), your work record and so on.
- Start with your most recent job and work backwards.
- Don't leave out any vital information. If you spent a year or two travelling, say so. Years that are unaccounted for will seem suspicious.
- Don't include any negative information, such as exam failures or lost jobs. Be positive about yourself, but don't lie or you will undermine yourself from the start.
- Don't ask for your CV to be returned; many companies keep CVs on file for future reference.

(adapted from an article by Eleni Kyriacou in *Midweek*)

7 Look at Mike Mortimer's CV and answer these questions.

a What was his first post?

b What is his most recent post?

c What kind of experience has he had?

d How has his career progressed?

e In your opinion, is his CV well written? If not, what changes would you make?

CURRICULUM VITAE

Name	Mike Mortimer
D.O.B.	12.06.72
Address	157 rue des Laboureurs, Moissy, 77550
Tel. No.	64886341
Marital status	Single

EDUCATION

- 09/93–02/94   Certificate of Theme Park Management: Miami University, Florida, USA
- 05/92–02/93   Diploma in Hospitality Management: Neath College, Wales
- 09/90–04/92   Higher National Diploma in Tourism and Recreation Management: Swansea Institute of Higher Education, Wales
- 09/88–06/90   BTEC National Diploma in Business and Finance: Fermanagh College of Further Education, Enniskillen, Northern Ireland
- 09/83–07/88   8 GCSEs – Grade B St Joseph's School, Enniskillen, Northern Ireland

LANGUAGES

- ENGLISH, mother tongue
- FRENCH, fluent
- SPANISH, elementary

EMPLOYMENT EXPERIENCE

BIENVENUE THEME PARK
Merville, France
12/96 – present
Attractions Lead Coordinator

- Pre-opening, supervised the personal development of staff on standards of customer care
- Compiled and arranged Safety Operating Procedures for Attractions
- Managed employees' daily schedule and delegation of tasks
- Monitored safe operation of major attractions in the Park
- Coordinated the show quality, ensured high standards of maintenance

SUPERWORLD THEME PARK
Miami, Florida
2/95–12/96
Intern Supervisor

- Implemented the Intern Program
- Planned and presided over Special VIP Events
- Supervised the training of new employees on operating procedures
- Participated in leadership development and trainer classes 03/94–02/95

International cultural representative

- Greeted guests and answered questions
- Took inventory of stock, organised shop displays
- Organised international cultural exchange events

THE NEWBERN GROTTO
Newbern, Northern Ireland
06/90–09/90
Tourist Information Assistant/Grotto Tour Guide

- Provided tourist information for local area
- Guided international parties in one of the largest caves in Europe
- Trained new employees on all aspects of cave guiding

INTERESTS

- Folk music, judo, water sports

ADDITIONAL INFORMATION

1990–1993	Sports club treasurer
1987–1990	Youth group leader

REFEREES

Christophe Allain
23, rue de la Paix
Moissy 77550
France

Anne Jones
Director, The Newbern Grotto
14 Rodney Drive
Newbern
Northern Ireland
BT74 8DF

Writing 1
CVs

8 **Choose one of the advertisements and imagine you are a candidate for the post. Make a list of the qualifications and personal qualities that are required to do the job. Design your CV.**

Wanted

Tour Operator Marketing Executive

Required by EXPLORE THE WORLD LTD, a well-established travel firm operating escorted tours of Europe (ranging from Inverness to Naples and from Budapest to Lisbon) for a primarily American clientele.

We seek resourceful, well-travelled applicants who not only have inbound tour-operating experience but also the ambition and ability to take on certain key management roles.

The ideal applicant must have WP skills, be literate and numerate, accurate and articulate, and have a real appetite for hard work.

A second (or third) language is essential.

Please write with full CV to:

The Managing Director, Explore the World Ltd., Priory Lane, Buxford, OX18 4DG

CABIN CREW

Skyways has opportunities for cabin crew who will be responsible for the safety, comfort and enjoyment of the passengers on board our aircraft, whilst maintaining our extremely high standard of in-flight service.

Are you aged 21–35, of between 160 cm and 180 cm in height, and of smart appearance?

Do you have a minimum of four GCSEs or equivalent (including Maths and English)?

Do you have a confident, outgoing personality and plenty of stamina?

Are you able to remain calm and level-headed even under stress?

Do you have experience in dealing with the general public?

If your answer is yes, then in return for your energy and commitment to quality of service, we offer:

• a competitive salary

• concessionary air travel

• excellent career prospects and training

• the opportunity to work for a dynamic, progressive organisation.

Interested? Then please write, quoting ref. DM3, with full CV, and enclose a good-quality, full-length photograph to us at the address below.

Claire Downing, Personnel Assistant, Skyways, Atlantic House, Hazelwick Avenue, Haywards Heath, West Sussex, HH10 1NP.

Closing date: 15 June.

Previous applicants currently on our files will automatically be considered. Please note that applicants will not receive a reply until after the closing date.

TRAVEL TRADE SALES EXECUTIVE

The responsibility you deserve. The freedom you'll enjoy.
Do you have at least two years' experience in a service-related industry – ideally gained in the travel trade?
Can you combine this with a fresh, enthusiastic approach, strong powers of initiative and outstanding interpersonal skills? If so, Monarch Hotels may have the ideal opportunity for you.
As a major international hotel group, we have 250 three-, four- and five-star hotels from Greenland to the Galapagos.
We are now seeking someone with these qualities to sell promotional packages to major tour operators. The role not only offers responsibility but freedom as well.

Based at our head office in Bern, you will be travelling extensively to visit our customers. By contributing to the development of promotional ideas you will have the chance to maximise your sales.
Sales experience is not essential. Natural enthusiasm and total commitment to success are more important. Demonstrate these and the rewards will be high. A competitive salary (according to age and experience) will be supported by benefits, including a fully expensed car and subsidised accommodation.
If this sounds like your kind of challenge, please write with full personal history to:
Karl Käser,
Jubilaeumstrasse 28, 3005 Bern, Switzerland

Writing 2
The covering letter: formal and informal language

9 The letters below do not contain any errors but the writers are very unlikely to be considered for a vacancy. Can you say why?

Dear Anthony Mayer,

I'm looking for a holiday job and I saw your ad in a newspaper and it looked as if it could be good because your company is very famous.

I don't have a lot of experience (in fact I haven't had a job before) but I've got lots of confidence and I get on pretty well with people in general.

I'm basically free in July but not August (because I'm going away then) but it would be really good if you could take me on because I need the money!

Hoping to get a reply from you soon.

Yours,

Mary Roe

Dear Sir,

In accordance with your esteemed request further to our telephone conversation of 25 November and the advertisement which appeared in The Times of 24 November inst., I have the honour to enclose herewith a copy of my curriculum vitae and would beseech you to acquaint yourself with the contents therein.

Trusting that I shall be favoured with an interview with a view to discussing my application in further detail, I beg to remain,

Yours faithfully,

Charles Fortescue Esq.

10 You have decided to help Mary Roe rewrite her covering letter. Work with a partner and complete the revised letter on the right. Invent any details about Mary's background that you feel would be relevant.

11 You have decided to apply for one of the jobs advertised on page 15 (either the same one for which you prepared a CV or a different one).
Write the covering letter to accompany your curriculum vitae.
Work with a partner and compare your letters.
Which creates the better impression and why?

(Address)

Mr Anthony Mayer
Personnel Manager
Travel Unlimited
Stansted
Essex CM24 1RY

(Date)

Dear ......

In reply to the advertisement ...... (state where it appeared), I would like to apply for the ...... (state what you are applying for).

As you will see from the enclosed CV, although I am relatively ...... I have successfully ...... (state what you have done).

I therefore feel I ...... (state what you can offer the firm).

I believe I am hard-working and reliable and would very much like to gain greater work experience.

I ...... interview whenever ...... and ...... near future.

_____

Mary Roe

Vocabulary

Word families: remuneration

12 Match the words in the box with the definitions.

salary	commission	tip
bonus	overtime	perks
wages	fee	

a the extra things, such as luncheon vouchers or free medical insurance, over and above the basic pay

b a small sum given to reward the services of people like waiters or taxi drivers

c money paid every month, but referred to as annual earnings paid to professional and managerial staff

d money paid to a professional person, e.g. a doctor or lawyer for advice given

e money paid to a manual worker, usually calculated hourly and paid weekly

f money added to pay, usually as a reward for good work

g money that is paid for extra hours of work

h money earned as a proportion of the goods or services sold by an individual

13 Replace the dollar sign in these sentences with a word from the box.

1 She left school without any qualifications then got a factory job, but the $ weren't very good.

2 The basic remuneration isn't high but she earns 15% $ on every tour she sells.

3 The salary is not exceptional but the $ include the use of a car and subsidised accommodation.

4 The consultants charged us a $ of £2,000 for an hour's work.

5 The starting $ is £35,000 per annum rising to £40,000 after two years.

6 We gave the guide a good $ because she made the visit so interesting.

7 The company paid each employee a £250 Christmas $ as profits had never been so high.

8 If they work on a Sunday they get $ which is double their usual rate of pay.

Speechwork

Word stress

14 An employer will probably want to take on someone who is:

articulate	considerate	accurate
numerate	computer-literate	dynamic
enthusiastic	optimistic	energetic
diplomatic		

Match the qualities above with these definitions:

a is able to use information technology

b thinks of other people's feelings

c is discreet and tactful in delicate situations

d shows a lot of enthusiasm and energy

e is good with figures

f can speak fluently

g is precise, pays attention to detail

h feels confident about the future

15 Underline the stressed syllable in each quality. What are the stress rules for words ending in -ate and -ic? Read the words aloud.

Listen and check your pronunciation.

16 Using the suffix -able, describe someone who:

- you can count on
- is friendly and likes mixing in society
- can start work at once
- corresponds to the job profile

Where is the stress in each word? Listen and check.

Speaking 2

Job interviews

17 Students A are interviewers; Students B are interviewees.

GROUP A

You are going to be interviewed for one of the jobs advertised on page 15 (your teacher will tell you which one).

Make a list of the qualities you think the successful candidate should have. Then make a list of your good points and be prepared to sell yourself at the interview. Think of the questions the interviewers will ask you and questions you will want to ask the interviewers.

18 An interview panel from Group B will interview you and other candidates for that job.

Follow-up

19 Type, word process or write your CV and show it to your teacher.

Trends
in Tourism

1

Describing patterns of change in tourism

Preview

1 Work with a partner. Look at these pictures and say what kinds of traveller they show.
Make a list of as many types of traveller as you can.
Compare your list with those of other people in the class.

2

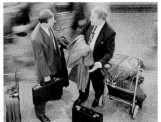
3

2 What do you think is the difference between a *traveller*, a *visitor* and a *tourist*? Write brief definitions of each word and discuss them with your partner.

Listening 1
Definitions of tourism

4

3 Listen to part of an interview with Dr Alberto Garcia, who works for the World Tourism Organisation. He is talking about how the WTO defines the words *traveller*, *tourist* and *visitor* when producing statistics on international travel. As you listen, write the words that are missing from the chart and from definitions (a) – (i) in the box below. You will need more than one word in some gaps.

```
                        TRAVELLERS
   ┌────────────────────────────┴────────────────────────────────┐
INCLUDED IN TOURISM STATISTICS                    NOT INCLUDED IN TOURISM STATISTICS
        VISITORS
   ┌───────┴───────┐                              ┌──────────────────────────────┐
 ┌────┐       ┌────┐                              │ 1 Temporary immigrants        │
 │ A  │       │ B  │                              │ 2                             │
 └────┘       └────┘                              │ 3 Nomads                      │
 ┌──────────────────────┐                         │ 4                             │
 │ MAIN PURPOSE OF VISIT │                         │ 5 Members of the armed forces │
 │ 1 Leisure and recreation                        └──────────────────────────────┘
 │ 2
 │ 3
 │ 4
 │ 5
 │ 6 Others
 └──────────────────────┘
```

The World Tourism Organisation's Classification of Tourism
Tourism comprises the activities of persons travelling to and (a) ...... in places outside their (b) ......
for not more than (c) ...... consecutive (d) ...... for (e) ...... , (f) ...... and other purposes.
- (g) ...... involves residents of a given country travelling only within their own country.
- (h) ...... involves non-residents travelling in the given country.
- (i) ...... involves residents of one country travelling to another country.

Vocabulary

Commonly confused words

4 Some words are very similar in meaning, and it is important to know exactly when, where and how you can use them. There are many ways of describing how we go from one place to another. Look at this entry from the *Longman Activator Language Dictionary* under the keyword heading of TRAVEL. Use the definitions to complete these sentences.

a If you're visiting Madrid, why not go on a day ...... to Toledo?

b The ...... was delayed because of air traffic congestion over Heathrow.

c The ...... on the ferry was very rough.

d The train ...... from Madras to Bangalore was uncomfortable.

e The Titanic sank on its maiden ....

f Why not hire a car and go for a ...... in the country?

g There's a volleyball team on ...... and they want hotel accommodation.

h The museum is a short bus ...... from the tourist information office.

Learning Tip

When recording vocabulary you can:

- use similar word networks or word trees.
- include grammatical information.
- use phonetic script or your own system.
- write a sample sentence to illustrate the meaning.
- make an accurate translation.
- draw a picture.

Word families

5 Work in groups. Add as many words as possible to this network and create new branches. Use a dictionary if necessary. Some words have been given to start you off.

---

8 a journey

journey	crossing
trip	drive
flight	ride
voyage	tour

journey /'dʒɜːʳni/ an act of travelling from one place to another, especially to a place that is far away [n C] *He had I've made you some sandwiches for your journey. | I've made you some sandwiches for your journey. | plenty of time to think of excuses during his journey to Tokyo.* | **make a journey** *We shall have to make the journey by boat.* | **bus/train/car etc journey** *We have a very long train journey ahead of us.* | **a 12 hour/five mile etc journey** (=that takes 12 hours, is five miles long etc) *It's a gruelling 12 hour journey to Kabul by road.*

trip /trɪp/ the act of travelling to a place and coming back, especially when you only stay in the place for a short time [n C] *Did you have a good trip? | I was feeling tired after my trip to New York. | It's a lovely day, how about going on a boat trip?* | **business/school/skiing etc trip** *a school trip to the seaside* | **go on a trip** *She's gone on a business trip and won't be back until Tuesday.*

flight /flaɪt/ a journey in a plane [n C] *I'd love to go to Australia but it's such a long flight. | Our flight was delayed, so we were stuck at the airport all night.* | **a 30 minute/12 hour etc flight** (=that takes 30 minutes,

12 hours etc) *Even when you get to Vancouver there's still a 90 minute flight up to the islands.*

voyage /'vɔɪ-ɪdʒ/ a long journey in a boat or ship [n C] *Valerie did not like long voyages because she suffered from seasickness. | The voyage from Europe was a hazardous undertaking, with heavy seas and strong winds.*

crossing /'krɒsɪŋ ‖ 'krɔː-/ a short journey in a boat or ship which goes from one side of a sea, lake, or other area of water to the other side [n C] *The ferry crossing was rough, but luckily none of us were seasick. | We boarded one of the tourist ferries for the crossing to Staten Island, home of the Statue of Liberty.*

drive /draɪv/ a journey in a car [n singular] *Lettie was expecting her at seven and the drive across town would be slower because of the rain.* | **a 12 hour/15 minute etc drive** (=that takes 12 hours, 15 minutes etc) *The six-hour drive was worth it to spend the weekend with him.* | **go for a drive** (=drive somewhere, just for enjoyment) *Anyone fancy going for a drive?*

ride /raɪd/ a short journey in a vehicle such as a car, or on a bicycle or a horse [n C] *He pretended to be asleep for the entire two hour ride.* | **bike/car/horse etc ride** *On the car ride back from the airport he told her all about his trip.* | **go for a ride** (=ride somewhere just for enjoyment) *It's a very fast bike. Do you want to go for a ride?*

tour /tʊəʳ/ a planned journey during which a politician, entertainer, or sports team visits several different places, usually within a fixed period of time [n C] *The King has left for a six-week tour of Australia and New Zealand. | We have had a request to include Lhasa as one of the cities visited on our tour. | Planning has already begun for next year's rugby tour by the Fijians.*

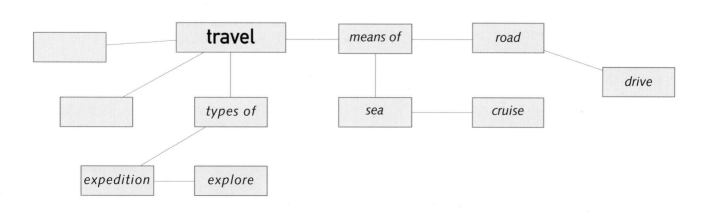

Listening 2

6 Listen to a song sung in 1963 by a British pop star called Cliff Richard. Put the line endings in the right order.

Line endings

holiday	holiday	holiday	holiday
two	two	brightly	you
true	blue	wanted to	you
true	movies		

Match the line endings with the lyrics.

We're all going ...... summer ......
No more working ...... week or ......
Fun ...... laughter ...... summer ......
No ...... worries ...... me or ......
...... week or ......

We're going ...... sun shines ......
We're going ...... sea ......
We've seen ...... the ......
Now let's see ....

...... summer ......
...... things they always ......
...... going on a summer ......
To make ...... come ......
...... me and ......

7 Listen again. Fill in the remaining gaps.

Reading

8 Work with a partner. Discuss the way holidays have changed during your lifetime.

9 Read the article about the way tourist destinations have developed over the last three decades and answer these questions.

a What was the film *Summer Holiday* about?
b How much did two weeks in Majorca cost in 1963?
c How much did it cost to go to Australia?
d What were package holidays like at that time?
e Why did package holidays have to last a long time?
f According to the article, which long-haul destinations have opened up since the 60s?
g How has Australia become a tourist destination?
h In what way has technology affected tourism?
i How has politics affected tourism?

SUMMER HOLIDAY

Peter Hughes looks at how our horizons have expanded and the world has shrunk since 1963

"We're all going on a summer holiday," sang a British pop star, Cliff Richard, way back in 1963, but he and his musicians never thought of going further than ex-Yugoslavia. Their adventure in the film Summer Holiday involved buying a London bus and driving through Europe.

The few package holidays available were to places such as the Costa Brava, Palma, Austria or Italy. Holidaymakers flew in a piston-engined aeroplane such as the Lockheed Constellation and paid about forty guineas* for 15 days in Majorca.

At that time package holidays were rarely shorter than two weeks. This was because the government wouldn't allow tour operators using charter flights to sell a holiday for less than the price of a return ticket on a scheduled airline to the same place. As a result, the number of people able to afford a holiday abroad was limited.

The expansion of popular travel has been explosive. Around 250,000 people took a package holiday in 1963; in 1992 the figure was 11 million. Increased prosperity, of course, has made this possible but the biggest influences have been politics and technology. Take Australia. In 1963 you would have spent your life savings getting there. Now you can go to Sydney on a two-week package and stay at a four-star hotel for a fraction of that price.

It was a mixture of politics and technology that brought the Great Barrier Reef and Sydney harbour within reach. For years the national airlines had opposed any competition from charters but, as the Australian economy declined and with the success of the bicentenary celebrations, revenue from tourism seemed more and more attractive. So the politicians changed their mind and charters started up in 1988.

The new technology was in the aircraft itself, the Boeing 767 two-engined jet with the range and economy to bring a whole catalogue of long-haul destinations into the package holiday domain. Thailand, India, Mexico, East Africa, the States and the Caribbean all have their place in the mass market brochures thanks to the new aircraft.

Politics with an even bigger "P" have opened up parts of the world that the most adventurous would have been reluctant to visit thirty years ago, even if they had been allowed in. Now several international airlines fly to Ho Chi Minh City, formerly Saigon, and the tourist can scramble through the Vietcong's secret network of tunnels which have been specially widened for broad-bottomed westerners. China now welcomes tourists who throng the Forbidden City, cruise up the Yangtze, and marvel at the Terracotta Warriors at Xian.

As for Eastern Europe, the Russians want tourists almost more than there are tourists to go there, and in the Czech state visitors stroll through the fairy-tale streets of Prague in their millions. In these cities a complete legacy of architecture has been handed down intact. St Petersburg would still be recognisable to Peter the Great; Prague is still much as Mozart knew it. Whatever else the communists did, their neglect of ancient buildings has proved to be an unexpected boon and has preserved the beauty of entire city centres.

{adapted from an article in *Expressions*}

* A guinea was worth £1.05.

Language Focus

The past simple and the present perfect simple

Here are some examples of the use of the *past simple* tense.

> Around 250,000 people **took** a package holiday in 1963.
>
> In 1992 the figure **was** 11 million.
>
> Prague is still much as Mozart **knew** it.

Here are some examples of the use of the *present perfect simple* tense.

> The expansion of popular travel **has been** explosive.
>
> It **has** now also **become** possible to cruise up the Yangtze.
>
> When they**'ve built** the new airport, they'll be able to accommodate more passengers.

1 **Decide if these statements are true or false.**

a The past simple can be used to describe past events or states.

b The past simple can be used with:
so far, up until now, over the last few years.

c The present perfect can be used with:
ago, last year, in 1994.

d The present perfect can be used to talk about past events whose effects are felt now.

e The present perfect can be used to refer to the future.

2 **Complete the definitions of these tenses using the words below:**

indefinite	definite	moment of speaking
unspecified	current	remote

The *past simple* refers to an event or state that is seen as ...... or ...... in time.

The *present perfect* is used to refer to events which are viewed as occurring at an ...... or ...... time in the past. The event is perceived as having ...... relevance and is connected to the ....

Practice

Complete the passage below by putting the words in brackets into either the past simple or the present perfect simple tense.

THE SPANISH TOURIST INDUSTRY

Tourism to Spain goes back to the 1930s, but package tourism really *(take off)* ...... in Spain during the late 1950s and 1960s. The post-war economic and population growth plus the increase in leisure time and disposable income in Northern Europe *(coincide)* ...... with Spain's policy to welcome tourism, offering a reliable climate, beaches, a different culture and low prices. The favourable exchange rate and competitive cost of living *(be)* ...... additional incentives.

Mass tourism *(begin)* ...... towards the end of the 1970s but the familiarity with Spain and falling standards *(lead)* ...... to a poor image of the country as a holiday destination. As a result, Spain *(face)* ...... competition in the late 1980s from other Mediterranean and long-haul destinations. At that time competitive airfares across the Atlantic to Florida and the low cost of living in America *(mean)* ...... that many people *(prefer)* ...... to go to the States rather than holiday in the Iberian peninsula. Even so, in 1993 Spain *(welcome)* ...... over 57 million visitors – 8 per cent of GNP – and *(account for)* ...... 24 per cent of all Britain's outbound tourism.

The Spanish tourism industry *(make)* ...... many mistakes in the early years with the building of high rise hotels and poor town planning. However, the situation is changing. Over the last few years the government *(restrict)* ...... building and is providing grants for organisations and training in the tourist sector. In addition, it *(implement)* ...... an investment programme to modernise public service facilities and infrastructure and to protect the environment. And with the help of soft loans which the government *(make)* ...... available for refurbishments, many hoteliers *(improve)* ...... the standard of accommodation provided in order to meet the new stricter guidelines.

Speechwork

Past verb forms with -ed

10 **There are three different pronunciations of *-ed* in regular past tense verbs.**

/ d /	/ t /	/ ɪd /
discovered	reached	exploited

How is the ending of each of these verbs pronounced?

created	opened	checked	developed
organised	visited	travelled	stayed
continued	received	asked	
jumped	delayed	lasted	

Listen and check your pronunciation.

Speaking 1

11 **Work in groups and discuss these questions.**

a What was your local area like fifty years ago?

b Was it attractive to tourists?

c What changes have there been since then?

d How have these changes affected tourism?

Writing 1

Taking notes in English

12 **Work with a partner and discuss these questions.**

a When listening to a talk *in your own language* how do you take notes?

b Do you write down everything the speaker says?

c How do you choose what to write down?

d What advice would you give to someone about taking notes in English?

13 **Here are a few tips to help you make notes.**

• Use recognised abbreviations:

e.g.	–	for example
∴	–	therefore
→	–	go to/lead to
asap	–	as soon as possible
<	–	less than/fewer than
>	–	more than

• Only write the CONTENT words; omit others, especially grammatical words:

~~The~~ train ~~will leave at~~ 16.45.

• You can also use your own invented abbreviations. For example:

The average noon temperature in Singapore is 31° C falling to 23° C at night all year round. Rain is frequent, often in the form of short downpours. Humidity is between 75 and 80 per cent.

Av. 12 p.m. temp. = 31° C

23° night. Freq. rain. Humid. 75–80%

14 **Look at the way this paragraph has been put into note form. Rewrite it in complete sentences.**

+ 20% visitors ➝ Hungary last year. Total no. = 41m (incl. approx. 23m on holiday) ➝ profit $440m ($592m prev. yr.). Profit ↓ because altho' no. tourists ↑ they stayed < nights than prev.

Listening 3

15 **Listen to Christopher Keoh talking about recent developments in Singapore. Take notes under these headings:**

ORIGINS OF TOURISM IN SINGAPORE

NUMBER OF TOURISTS

AVERAGE LENGTH OF STAY

BREAKDOWN OF ARRIVALS

Speaking 2

16 Work in groups of four. Within your group you will work in two teams of two people, Team A and Team B.
You are going to give short talks on tourism development in two different countries.
Team A look at the information on Ireland.
Team B look at the information on Egypt on page 104.

Team A
Read the Ireland fact file below.
Discuss tourism in Ireland.
Decide what you will tell Team B.
Make notes and plan your talk.
When you are ready, give your talk.

Ireland fact file

History	Recent developments	The present situation
beginnings of tourism unknown	real expansion over last 30 yrs	become 3rd largest export earner
1845: horse-drawn coach service operating round Ireland (4,000 miles/day)	govt. help	employs 91,000
C19: all visitors ◀— Britain	promotion of special interest hols, e.g. golfing, hiking, fishing	appeals to younger generation & independent travellers
1895: 1st package tour ◀— America	special purpose English language holidays	appeals to Irish Americans in search of roots
1920: 1st official tourism office		special attraction: the cultural holiday (Dublin, Blarney, Kilkenny)
1941–45: food scarcity in the UK —▶ US soldiers visit Ireland to eat better		visitors: 55% ◀— Britain 28.8% ◀— Europe
post 1945: plentiful food supply in Ireland —▶ British visitors		av. stay: holiday 11.1 days VFR 10.4 days

Writing 2

17 *Either* write up a full description of one of the fact files, *or* research an area of your choice and write an account of the development of tourism there.

Where
People Go

1   2   3   4   5   6   7   8

Describing the role of tourism in an economy
Working with figures

Preview

1 **Work in groups. Look at the pictures and answer these questions.**

a   Where are these places?
b   How long would it take you to get to each place from where you live?
c   How would you get there: by air, road or …?
d   What is the time difference:
    –   between these places and your country?
    –   between these places and GMT?

Reading

2 **This article is about three French women who set off on holiday and received an unpleasant surprise.**
Read the article and answer these questions.

a   What was their American dream?
b   Why is the article entitled "A Tale of Two Cities"?
c   Why weren't they suffering from time zone changes after eight hours' travel?
d   What was the "minor inconvenience"?
e   Who is *they* in "They simply had no idea"?

f   How did the policeman finally manage to explain the situation to them?
g   Why were they unwilling to take phone calls?

Has anything ever gone wrong for you or for one of your friends on holiday? What happened?

A tale of two cities as intrepid trio lose out on American dream

The three French women had set out bound for adventure. The hotel was booked. They had their holiday cash. They were looking forward to the autumnal scenes around Portsmouth, New Hampshire. It didn't seem that far away, the United States. Only eight hours on a ferry from Le Havre. They had preferred to take the boat, rather than fly. But even they were surprised at how little they were suffering from the time zone changes. There was only a minor inconvenience, it seemed. They stepped into a taxi, asking for the Sheraton. They had already booked for a three-day stay, and paid a $500 deposit. But those cabbies. They simply had no idea. Drive you about for hours, and still unable to find a luxury hotel as big as the Sheraton.

The police became involved when the cabbie turned in desperation to the Portsmouth constabulary. He was unable to trace the famous hotel. "They were adamant they had booked into the Sheraton in Portsmouth," PC David Crouch said. "They asked if they were in Portsmouth and I said 'Yes'.

Then they asked 'Is this Hampshire?' and I agreed. It was all a great mystery, so I asked if they had a brochure from the hotel and they produced a pamphlet. I spotted the word Portsmouth, then saw that it was in New Hampshire, USA. I pointed to the map on the leaflet and showed them Portsmouth, then ran my finger down about half an inch and said 'Look! New York!' I didn't know if they were going to laugh or cry when, in broken English, they asked 'Are we in the wrong country?' Fortunately, they saw the funny side and burst out laughing. I've been doing this job for 31 years and this is the first time I have come across anyone who accidentally came to the wrong country for a holiday." The three women, two in their twenties, one a little older, were taken to the two-star Arcade hotel in Portsmouth. They plan to return home this morning, according to the receptionist, Sara de Bathe. They were fighting shy of all telephone calls. Particularly long-distance ones.

(from *The***Guardian**)

Vocabulary

British and American usage

3 **If the French women had managed to get to the USA, they would have heard people using American English words and expressions.**
Match the words in A and B which have the same meaning. Which words are British and which American?

A	B
autumn	a bill
a check	a closet
a cupboard	fall
an elevator	ground floor
a faucet	a lift
first floor	a one-way ticket
a fortnight	a round trip
a restroom	a tap
a return	a toilet
a single	two weeks

Listening 1

Americans in Europe

4 Listen to an American family talking about their holiday in Europe and take notes on the comments they make about each of these topics:

PARIS AND FLORENCE

SWISS CHOCOLATE

CHEESE

ICE CUBES

SHOPPING

Speechwork 1

The schwa sound

5 **In exercise 4 Penny says:**

"I would've kind of liked to stay longer at a couple of places."
/ə wəd ə kaɪnd ə laɪk tə steɪ lɒŋər ət ə kʌpəl ə pleɪsɪz/
Which sound occurs most frequently?
This sound is the most common sound in English but it is spelt in many different ways.

6 **Listen and write down the words you hear. Underline the letter that corresponds to the / ə / sound in each word.**

7 **Read the sentences and phrases below. Where are the / ə / sounds?**

- twenty per cent   • for instance   • not at all
- sooner or later   • there and back   • as soon as possible
- Her itinerary was totally unacceptable.
- I've been given a brochure for Singapore.
- We went to Great Britain and managed to visit London, Oxford, Stratford-on-Avon, and Yorkshire.
- I'd like to look at the figures for South-East Asia. I want to do an analysis of all the data to see if we're meeting our targets.

8 **Listen and compare your pronunciation with that on the tape.**

CONCORDE INTERNATIONAL
BUSINESS SCHOOL
ARNETT HOUSE
HAWKS LANE
CANTERBURY
KENT
ENGLAND
CT1 2NU

Language Focus

The definite article

1 Look at the following and put them into logical groups.

Africa	the Himalayas	Everest	the Seychelles
the Alps	Italy	the Gobi Desert	Napoleon
Asia	Kilimanjaro	the Nile	Count Dracula
Australia	Lake Michigan	the Pacific	the temples of Bangkok
the beaches of Goa	Lake Ontario	the Parthenon	the Thames
Buenos Aires	Lenin's Mausoleum	the Mediterranean	the Uffizi
the Czech Republic	the Louvre	the Sahara	the United Kingdom
Japan	Madame Tussaud's	Saigon	the United States of America
Geneva	the Mayan ruins of Yucatan	St Basil's Cathedral	the West Indies
			the Yangtze

2 Look at the examples and write rules for the use of *the* in each case.

Rule 1: the Uffizi, the Prado, the Victoria and Albert

Rule 2: the Nile, the Thames, the Atlantic

Rule 3: the Seychelles, the West Indies, the Philippines

Rule 4: the Sahara, the Alps, the Rockies

Rule 5: the Czech Republic, the USA, the UK

Rule 6: Innsbruck, Switzerland, Europe

Rule 7: Napoleon, Count Dracula, Prince Charles

Rule 8: Lake Ontario, Everest, Lake Garda

Rule 9: the beaches of Goa, the Tower of London, the Mayan ruins of Yucatan

Rule 10: Madame Tussaud's, St Basil's Cathedral, Lenin's Mausoleum

Practice

The word *the* has been deleted from this article.
Put it back whenever necessary. The first paragraph has been done for you.

Seventy per cent of Britons believe visiting London is more dangerous than going abroad, while in Scotland this rises to 80 per cent. These findings come despite a number of tourist killings in Florida, Egypt and elsewhere in Africa, according to Lunn Poly, **the** travel firm which polled a random sample of 1,030 adults about their holiday intentions.

Trips to Florida from Britain fell by 20 per cent last summer and nearly half of people who were polled said they would not go there next year. That is bad news for Disney World in Orlando, top American attraction for British tourists, and bookings are also down to Disneyland near Paris. British fear of London is not shared by nine million foreigners who visited capital last year – London's attractions, such as Changing of Guard being main reason why Britain was world's sixth tourist destination. At least 25 per cent of British families are expected to holiday abroad next year, and a record nine million are forecast to book a foreign package holiday.

It looks as if biggest beneficiary will be cheapest country, Spain, where bookings are up by 50 per cent – not least because peseta has fallen faster than pound.

Language Tip

Other uses of *the*

a We use *the* in superlative expressions:
   The biggest influences on tourism have been politics and technology.

b When the identity of the thing referred to is clear from the context:
   I'll meet you in **the** lobby. (It is obvious which lobby.)

c When the identity is made clear by a following clause:
   The price (that) you gave me was wrong.

d When a noun or adjective is used to create a category:
   The Russians want as many tourists as possible.
   The dollar is wanted everywhere.

e When the noun referred to has been previously mentioned:
   She bought a map and a guidebook but took **the** map back. It wasn't detailed enough.

Other omissions of *the*

a Before nationalities, when referring to an individual:
   She's British but her husband is Greek.

b When referring to an ability to speak a language:
   He's very gifted at languages. He can speak French, Russian, German, Spanish and Arabic.

c Before nouns used in a general sense:
   Ask here for information.
   Tourism earns foreign currency.

Speaking 1

9 Work in two groups. Group A look at the grid below. Group B look at the grid on page 105.

GROUP A

Discuss what should go in the gaps. Then work with a partner from Group B to check your answers.

COUNTRY	CAPITAL	LANGUAGE	CURRENCY
Argentina			Peso
	Vienna	German	
Brazil	Brasilia		
		Czech	Crown
Egypt		Arabic	
		Greek	Drachma
Hungary			Forint
	Rome	Italian	
Japan			Yen
Kenya		Swahili, English	
	Kuala Lumpur	Bahasa Malay, Chinese, English	
	Madrid		Peseta
Switzerland			Swiss Franc
Tunisia	Tunis		
Turkey			Lira
	Kiev	Ukrainian	

10 In many cases the nationality is the same word as the language (*French – French*); but sometimes they are different (*British – English*). Do you know any others that are different?

Listening 2

Figures

🔘 11 **Listen and write down the figures that you hear.**

Language Tip

Working with figures

a We say *9 million* (NOT *9 millions).
We say *9 million foreigners* (NOT *9 million of …*)
BUT we say *millions of foreigners, thousands of tourists*, etc.

b For figures over 100, British English uses *and* between the hundreds and the tens:

257	**two hundred and fifty-seven**	USA: **two hundred fifty-seven**
983	**nine hundred and eighty-three**	USA: **nine hundred eighty-three**
1,000	**a thousand** or **one thousand**	

We use *and* when there are no hundreds:

1,030   **one/a thousand and thirty**;

but we say *one thousand* before a number of hundreds:

1, 548   **one thousand five hundred and forty-eight** (NOT *one thousand and five hundred…*)

c If we use a decimal we say *point*. Each figure is said separately:

	0.35	0.5	8.75
UK/USA	zero **point** three five	zero **point** five	eight **point** seven five
UK	nought **point** three five	nought **point** five	eight **point** seven five

d Fractions are expressed using ordinal numbers:
a third $1/3$ a quarter $1/4$ a half $1/2$ two fifths $2/5$ three quarters $3/4$

e Note these mathematical terms:

18 x 34 = 612   eighteen **multiplied by/times** thirty-four **equals/makes/is** six hundred and twelve

27 ÷ 3 = 9 $\frac{27}{3} = 9$ twenty-seven **divided by** three is nine

f Many figures are pronounced individually:

A Boeing 757	**seven five seven**
Flight BA 818	**eight one eight**
Your reference number is 995.	**nine nine five**
My room number is 631.	**six three one**
My telephone number is 205478.	**two oh five four seven eight**

g *From, to,* and *by* are used to indicate changes in figures:
The price has risen **by** 5%, **from** $100 **to** $105.

h When speaking about money we say the currency unit *after* the figure:

| £55 | **fifty-five pounds** |
| C$800 | **eight hundred Canadian dollars** |

Speaking 2

Calculations

12 **Read these calculations aloud.**

5 coaches @ £1,550 each =
£7,750 with 10% discount
£7,750 -
£775
= £6,975

cost of coach hire = £500
breakeven = 30 PAX
$\frac{500}{30}$ = £16.66 a head

Total no. of visitors to Singapore
= 6,400,000
$2/5$ were holidaymakers = 2,560,000
$1/6$ were on business = 1,066,666

Describing tables and pie charts

13 Work with a partner. Student A look at the statistics in the exercises below. Student B look at page 105.

STUDENT A

Ask your partner for the information which is missing from the table and answer his/her questions.

THE MOST VISITED MONUMENTS AND MUSEUMS IN THE EU (NUMBERS PER YEAR)		
RANK	PLACE	NO. OF VISITORS
1	The Pompidou Centre	7.9m
2		
3	The British Museum	3.8m
4		
5		
6	Versailles	2.6m

Present the figures in this pie chart to your partner. Then listen to your partner talking about tourist spending in the UK and complete the information on the pie chart opposite.

Writing

Questionnaires

14 Write a questionnaire and, if possible, interview some foreign visitors to your town or city. Not everybody speaks English of course, but you should be able to find some people who can. It is probably best to do this outside a local tourist attraction.

Ask the visitors about:

- the places they have visited.
- the reasons for their travel.
- the type of transport used.
- where they are staying and for how long.
- what special purchases they have made.

Compare your findings with those of other members of your class and write up the findings of your survey using charts and statistics where appropriate.

15 You work for the market research department of the UK tourist board. You have been asked to write a short report on the nature and value of tourism to the UK. Use the information from Speaking 2.

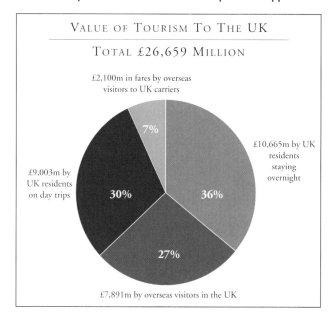

VALUE OF TOURISM TO THE UK

TOTAL £26,659 MILLION

£2,100m in fares by overseas visitors to UK carriers — 7%
£9,003m by UK residents on day trips — 30%
£7,891m by overseas visitors in the UK — 27%
£10,665m by UK residents staying overnight — 36%

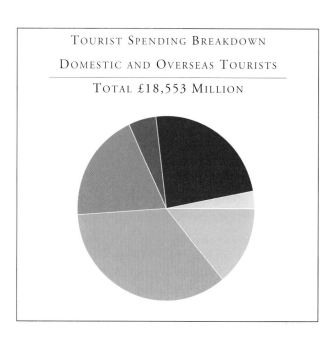

TOURIST SPENDING BREAKDOWN

DOMESTIC AND OVERSEAS TOURISTS

TOTAL £18,553 MILLION

5

Travel
Agents

Taking and making holiday bookings

Preview

The alphabet

1 How are these letters pronounced?

   A E I O U

   G J Y

Make sure you know how to say the English alphabet.

2 Work with a partner. Student A look at the card below. Student B look at the one on page 106.

STUDENT A
Tell your partner your name, address and phone number (on the business card), and write down your partner's name, address and phone number.

E I K O   H A M A C H I

3 - 7 - 5 2 C H I Y O G A O K A

K A S U K A B E

S A I T A M A

J A P A N

T E L : { 8 1 } 4 8 6 2 3 6 2 3 4

⚙3 Listen and check your pronunciation.

Vocabulary 1
Two-part verbs

4 The verbs in the box are often used when making telephone calls. Use them to fill in the gaps.

hold on	hang up	put someone through
cut off	get through	ring up
get back (to someone)		

a Sorry, I don't know what happened. We got ....
b I'll ...... you ...... to her extension.
c The line is constantly busy – I never seem to be able to ....
d Could you ...... a minute and I'll see if she's in her office.
e Would you ...... Sky Air and ask if they have any seats on this Saturday's flight to Delhi?
f I'll make some enquiries and ...... to you by eleven.
g Don't ...... yet; the call may be diverted to another number.

5 **What would you say in these situations?**

a Someone phones but the call is for a colleague who works on the second floor.
b The line went dead. The person you were speaking to rings back.
c You're on the phone but need to get a file from the office next door.
d You're on the phone but haven't got all the information to hand. You need about an hour to get it together.
e The number is constantly engaged.
f You want someone else to call Global Tours for you.

Language Tip

Talking on the phone
Here are a number of expressions that you may find useful when making a phone call:

May I speak to/with ...
I'm returning your call.
Sorry, could you repeat that?
I'm afraid he/she's not in at the moment.

I'm afraid she's not answering her phone.
I'm sorry, there's no reply.
Can I take a message?
Shall I get him/her to call you back?
Mrs X will get back to you.

Hold on a moment, please.
I'll just put you on hold.
I'm sorry, you've got the wrong number.
Sorry to keep you waiting.

Language Focus

Asking questions

In formal situations it is more polite to ask questions indirectly, especially at the beginning of a conversation. For example, when asking a customer for information, it can be better to use an indirect form such as *Could you tell me when you were born?* rather than *When were you born?*

1 Look at the questions below. What do you notice about the way indirect questions are formed?

Direct questions	Indirect questions
How far is it?	Can you tell me how far it is?
How much does it cost?	Could you tell me how much it costs?
How long does the journey take?	Do you know how long the journey takes?

2 Which of these is correct? How would you reply?

Would you mind spelling that for me?

Do you mind if I sit here?

Would you mind to spell that for me?

Do you mind if I'm sitting here?

3 Study the way these tag questions are made.

A visa is compulsory, **isn't it?**

You're not leaving until next month, **are you?**

They haven't confirmed the booking yet, **have they?**

You won't forget to fax me the details, **will you?**

Tanya, pass me the brochure, **will you?**

Let's have a look at the schedule, **shall we?**

You had a single room last year, **didn't you?**

What are the rules for the formation of tag questions?

Why do we use tag questions? What is their function in the examples?

4 Sometimes a question doesn't really function as a question. For example:

Why don't you try a holiday in Scandinavia?

Let's have a look at the schedule, shall we?

How would you categorise the following?

Shall I look after the paperwork for you?

Would you like me to make the visa arrangements?

Would you care for a cup of coffee?

Practice

The following questions have been jumbled. Put them in the right order.

For example: spell   you   could   me   for   Linares ?

Could you spell Linares for me?

a   details   if   the   you   I   mind   do   check ?
b   sharing   mind   twin   you   a   would   bedroom ?
c   me   you   is   can   what   tell   fax   your   number ?
d   for   I   necessary   shall   the   make   arrangements   you ?
e   you   in   mind   filling   would   this   form   me   for ?
f   want   many   you   how   could   you   me   tell   to   with   go   people ?
g   you   like   would   to   me   hold   put   you   on ?
h   you   won't   sharing   be   twin   a   bedded   room   you   will ?   (2 answers)
i   requirements   your   entry   draw   the   I   may   attention   to ?
j   again   on   they   are   aren't   strike   the   traffic   controllers   air ?

Speaking 1

Telephone skills

6 Discuss with your partner:

a The impression you would like clients to have of you.
b The impression they should receive of your firm.
c How you can give this impression over the telephone.

Listening 1

7 Listen to six telephone calls and answer these questions.

a Who made a good impression and why?
b Who *didn't* make a good impression? Why not?

Think of an adjective to describe each speaker.

Speaking 2

8 Work with a partner. Student A look at the text below; Student B look at page 106.

STUDENT A

1 You work on the switchboard of Skyways Holidays. Take the telephone call. No one is available in the sales department at present. Offer to take the name and telephone number so that the caller can be contacted.

2 You work in the sales department of Skways Holidays. Return Ms Penelope McBain's call. Find out what she requires and take down the relevant details.

Speechwork

Intonation in questions

9 Listen. You will hear the same question twice, with different intonation. Which sounds friendlier? Why?

If your voice is flat and has little expression in it, you may sound bored and uninterested. This often provokes a negative response in the listener. So, when you want to ask a question beginning with a verb raise your pitch on the last stressed word. This helps to make you sound more polite and interested.

10 Read these questions aloud. Then listen and compare your intonation with that on the tape.

a Can I help you at all?
b Would you mind spelling that for me?
c Can you tell me your number at work?
d Sorry, could you repeat that for me?
e Could you please give me your passport number?

f Do you have any idea how long it takes?
g Could you tell me what the price includes?
h Can I get back in touch with you later?
i Can you tell me when you wish to return?
j Do you mind if I ask you how old you are?

Intonation in tag questions

11 Tag questions can be said in two ways. The intonation either rises or falls:

a She isn't going, is she?
You haven't paid yet, have you?

b She isn't going, is she?
You haven't paid yet, have you?

If we use falling intonation (as in *a*) we are looking for confirmation or agreement.
If our voice rises (as in *b*) then we don't know the answer and we want to know.
Listen. Which are real questions, which are requests for confirmation?

12 Work with a partner and complete this conversation.

A Good morning. (a) ...... some help or are you just (b) ......?
B Good morning. Well, I was considering taking a short skiing trip. You don't happen to have any bargain packages, (c) ......?
A Ah well. As it so happens, yes. But could you first give me some idea of where and when (d) ......?
B Anytime between now and mid-March really, but the sooner the better.
A Would (e) ...... ski in Europe or America?
B I was thinking of Switzerland or Austria but it's more a question of cost and good skiing. Could you suggest where (f) ...... good intermediate to advanced ski runs?
A Mm, well... We have a seven-night self-catering deal to Verbier in Switzerland and that's £259, and one to Alpach in Austria for £169. Both leave this Saturday. That's not too short notice, (g) ......?

B No, that's fine. Um, my partner prefers Switzerland so I guess I'll take that one. Er, could (h) ...... airport (i) ......?
A Yes, Gatwick.
B And the plane comes back to Gatwick, (j) ......?
A That's right.
B Fine.
A Right, well, let me take a few particulars. Could you (k) ...... name (l) ...... ?
B Yes, Bogdan Kominowski.
A Um... yes... , er, would you mind spelling that for me?

13 Listen and compare your answers. Then act out the conversation.

ⓘⓃ T O U R I S T

PLEASE USE BLOCK CAPITALS

BOOKING REFERENCE	UKR 352.JP
TOUR NUMBER	_____
DEPARTURE DATE	_____
DEPARTURE AIRPORT	_____
TOTAL HOLIDAY PRICE	_____

Mr / Mrs / Ms / Miss	First name	Surname	Address	Tel. No.	Nationality

INSURANCE

Insurance is compulsory on an Intourist Travel Limited holiday.

We assume you require our Insurance UNLESS you have made alternative arrangements for greater or comparable cover.

PAYMENT

Deposit of £100 per fare-paying passenger or full payment when travel is within 8 weeks.

Insurance premium per person	£ _____
Visa per person	£ _____
Deposit per person	£ _____

If payment is made by credit card, the credit card charge form must be completed.

TOTAL

VISA SERVICE

A visa is compulsory. The visa charge will automatically be added to the invoice. Please fill in the standard application form.

I warrant that I am authorised to make this booking. I have read and agree to abide by the booking conditions and other information set out in the brochure relevant to my holiday.

SIGNATURE:

Reading 1

Booking forms

14 Look at the booking form for holidays in Russia and say whether these statements are true or false.

a The customer has to purchase an Intourist travel insurance policy.

b Clients do not need a visa.

c If you make a reservation for four people ten weeks before departure, you have to make a deposit of £400.

d Deposits cannot be made by credit card.

e Full payment is due two months before departure.

Listening 2

🔘 **15** Listen to someone make a holiday booking over the telephone. Note the details of the travellers, their trip and payments. After you have listened work out the sum of money the caller will write on the cheque.

Speaking 3

16 Work with a partner. Take turns to be Student A and Student B. Student A works for a travel agency taking bookings. Student B wants to go on holiday (choose a destination).

Act out the beginning of the conversation. Student A should note down information about :

– the holiday
– the dates
– the customer's name.

Reading 2

17 Read the extract from a travel agency training manual.
Then copy and complete the flow chart.

BOOKING PROCEDURE

ONCE THE client has signed the booking form, you must collect the appropriate deposit payment. If the client pays in cash or by cheque, you should issue a receipt according to office procedure and then forward this payment to the tour operator concerned.

However, if the client pays with a credit card, you should make sure he or she has completed and signed the credit card section on the booking form. You may find also that from time to time the operator may want the client to sign a Standard Sales Voucher instead.

Of course, it is important for the client to take out insurance. If the tour operator's insurance is chosen, make sure the booking form is correctly completed and then add the premium to the deposit.

Should the client decide on an alternative insurance policy or perhaps no insurance at all (not to be advised), make sure this is properly noted on the booking form. Remember that if you sell our own group's travel insurance, you can earn up to 45 per cent commission.

Once the booking form has been signed, it should be sent to the tour operator immediately. If the option expiry date is coming up soon, it is best to telephone and make arrangements to extend the option so as to avoid any risk of the booking arriving too late. When the tour operator receives the booking form, all the details such as flight reservations or hotel rooms will be confirmed.

It is a good idea to note the date by which you should get the confirmation or the invoice back – usually two to three weeks after the booking. It is also a good idea to make a note of the date by which the client must make full payment (usually about six to ten weeks before departure). When confirmation is received you should check the details to make sure they are the same as those in your file and on the photocopy of the booking form. Finally, the confirmation should be sent to your client, highlighting the latest date for payment.

adapted from ***American Express Training Manual***

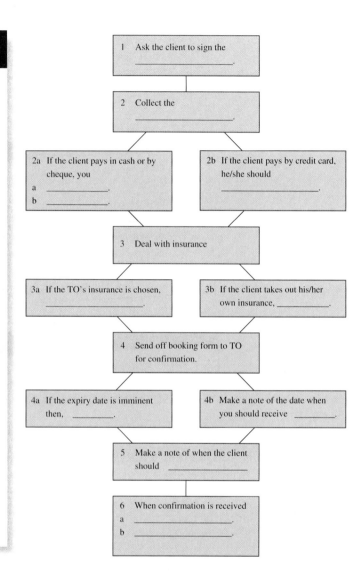

1 Ask the client to sign the _____ .

2 Collect the _____ .

2a If the client pays in cash or by cheque, you
a _____ .
b _____ .

2b If the client pays by credit card, he/she should _____ .

3 Deal with insurance

3a If the TO's insurance is chosen, _____ .

3b If the client takes out his/her own insurance, _____ .

4 Send off booking form to TO for confirmation.

4a If the expiry date is imminent then, _____ .

4b Make a note of the date when you should receive _____ .

5 Make a note of when the client should _____ .

6 When confirmation is received
a _____ .
b _____ .

Vocabulary 2

18 The extract on the right also comes from the travel agency training manual and completes the description of the booking procedure. Fill in the gaps with words from the box.

settle	file
option	expiry
come	liability
due	departure
issue	confirm

PAYMENT OF BALANCE

ABOUT EIGHT WEEKS before the client is due to travel, full payment for the holiday must be collected. Make sure YOU check each booking form to see *exactly when* payment is (a) ...... and make a note on your (b) .... If the client cancels *after* the (c) ...... date for final payment, hefty cancellation charges apply. You must safeguard yourself against (d) ...... for these charges by ensuring you are holding full payment before the date that cancellation charges (e) ...... into force.

As far as tour operators are concerned, late bookings are bookings made after the date when full payment was expected. So usually a late booking is one made less than eight weeks before (f) ....

Since cancellation charges would apply immediately in this case, it is essential that you should collect full payment at the time of booking. If the client is unable to pay at once, take out a(n) (g) ...... on the holiday and (h) ...... it when they return to pay by an agreed date, at which time the client must (i) ...... in full.

When payment has been finalised you are then ready to (j) ...... the travel documents.

Writing 1

19 Write a checklist of points for newly-trained staff to remember when making a booking.

Speaking 4

20 Making a holiday booking by telephone

Work with a partner. Take turns to make and take a telephone booking for a holiday. Before you begin, list the sort of information you will need in order to fill in a holiday booking form. Student A look at the information below. Student B look at page 107.

STUDENT A
You want to go on holiday to Cefalù in Sicily. Ring up to make a booking and check the details.

Cefalù, Sicily

Dates?

Things to see and do?

Accommodation?

Insurance?

Cost?

Credit Card ⊗

4773 0978 6337 2451

Expiry date:
03/2005
M. FIGUEREIDO

M. FIGUEREIDO

Portuguese/English
Translations

29 Fitzroy Square
London
WC1 5CD
Tel: 0171 923 5000

You will receive a phone call from a client interested in a tour called "Venice and the Verona Opera".
Reply to his/her enquiries and take down the details. Charge the full amount of the holiday to his/her credit card.

Venice and the Verona Opera

Departures:

15 July   25 August: 7 days

Programme:

Performances of *La Bohème*, *Norma*, *Nabucco*, *Aida* and *Otello* to choose from (tickets for two performances in the second sector of the Arena in Verona).
Plus a full tour of Venice and the Venetian villas of the Brenta River and a stay in Venice.

Price: from £795. Insurance £18.

Includes flight from LGW, three nights' HB accommodation in Verona at the Hotel Borghetti in en-suite rooms. Three nights' bed and breakfast in Venice at the Grand Hotel Principe on the Grand Canal. Waterbuses to St. Mark's Square depart from the main station just a few metres away. All transfers between the hotels and the airports, plus the services of local hosts and guides.

Writing 2

STUDENT A

21 Write a letter of confirmation to J. Wilkes, enclosing the tickets
and the details of the holiday in Venice and Verona.

Scenario 1
Advising a Client

Giving information and advice on specific holiday destinations

Work in two groups. Group A look at the text below. Group B look at page 108.

GROUP A

Activity 1

You are trainee tour operator sales staff for Paradise Holidays plc. Today you are attending a training session. You are learning about the amenities and facilities at a new resort.

Work with a partner from your group. Read the brochure extracts about Goa on page 37 and follow the instructions below.

1 **Answer these questions.**

a Where is the resort?

b How long is each holiday?

c At what time of year can you go?

2 **Note the important facts about the resort and the hotel under these headings.**

THE RESORT	THE HOTEL
• location	• facilities
• amenities	• cuisine
• climate	• rates
• transport	• discounts
• activities	
• souvenirs	

3 **Discuss these questions.**

a Which are the most popular weeks?

b What type of client is attracted to this type of holiday?

Activity 2

Work with someone from Group B. He/She is a travel consultant.

You are at your desk at Paradise Holidays plc. A travel consultant contacts you by phone. Use your notes to answer the caller's enquiries.

Activity 3

Now change roles, but keep your partner from Activity 2. You are an independent travel consultant. Your partner works for Dream Holidays Inc.

You work on behalf of the social committee of a large car manufacturer. The chairman of this committee has asked you to give him some information about skiing in the USA. Approximately forty adults are thinking of going, plus twenty-eight children. The chairman himself will be going with his wife and four children aged 5, 8, 12 and 14. They all realise that skiing in the States is a bit pricey but they are looking for value for money.

You have recently received advance information about a package. You think it's called the Sheraton Colorado but can't be sure. Ring up the agent at Dream Holidays Inc. and find out about the hotel and the resort.

In particular, you want to find out about:

THE HOTEL/PACKAGE	THE RESORT
• the precise location	• transport to and from the resort
• its size	• skiing and equipment hire
• hotel amenities	• eating out
• facilities	• shopping
• rates and discounts	• climate
• cuisine	

It is important to find out whether the children will be catered for as well as the adults in the party.

Activity 4

Work with other people from your group.

You have now gone back to your consultancy offices. Were you impressed by Dream Holiday's description of the package? On the basis of what you have heard, will you want to recommend this American hotel and the resort?

Discuss your recommendations with your colleagues. What will you want to tell your client?

Activity 5

Write to your client to give your opinion of the hotel and the resort.

GOA

The Garden of Eden Hotel ★★★★

Set in lush tropical gardens leading on to the beach this modern hotel offers a good standard of accommodation in the main building or in garden cottages. All rooms are en suite, with air-conditioning, patio or balcony, TV, telephone and mini-bar. Regular entertainment includes beach barbecues, folk dances and live music.

Hotel Amenities

- 2 swimming pools
- coffee shop, shopping arcade
- 2 restaurants: traditional Hindi and Portuguese Indian
- 2 garden bars
- health spa
- beauty parlour
- gymnasium
- evening entertainment

On the beach

- windsurfing
- water-skiing
- paragliding
- boat cruises can be arranged

Flights

Scheduled from Gatwick to Dabolim. Transfer to hotel approximately 50 mins.

Transport

Courtesy buses to the cities of Old Goa and Panaji.

Value Plus

SINGLE SAVERS   No supplements
FREE UPGRADE   For honeymooners
CHILD REDUCTIONS £100.00

Climate

Month	Temperature	Hours of sunshine
Nov	33ºC	8
Dec	33ºC	9
Jan	31ºC	9
Feb	32ºC	9
Mar	32ºC	10
Apr	33ºC	9

Sinquerim Beach

Relax on Goa's golden beaches or swim in the luxuriant sea under the protection of Aguada Fort, built by the Portuguese to guard against intruders.
Visit the unspoilt ecosystems of the Western Ghats and the habitat of the King Cobra.
But no journey to Goa is complete without viewing the treasures of the ancient Hindu city of Goa which now lies in ruins. Nor should the Portuguese old city with its fine churches and temples, in particular the sixteenth-century Basilica of Bom Jesus and the Se Cathedral be missed.
Finally, you'll love shopping in the colourful markets where vendors in traditional costume sell everything from fabrics, jewellery and spices to a variety of souvenirs.

Holiday code IND 309		
Room type	twin/shower or bath/patio or balcony	
Board basis	bed & breakfast	
No. of nights	7	14
from 01 Nov to 17 Dec	456	516
from 18 Dec to 23 Jan	548	688
from 24 Jan to 02 Mar	634	844
from 03 Mar to 24 Mar	548	688
from 25 Mar to 05 Apr	612	822
from 06 Apr to 30 Apr	456	516

6

Tour
Operators

Planning and negotiating holiday packages
Writing letters of confirmation and reports

Preview

1 **Work in groups and discuss these questions.**

a What do you think a foreign tour operator wants from a hotelier?
b What do you think a local hotelier wants from a foreign tour operator?
c Who is in a better position to negotiate?
d What problems do you think there might be?

Reading

2 **Work with a partner. Student A read the text below. Student B read the text on page 110.**

STUDENT A

Before you read the article below, check you know the words in the box. Use a dictionary if necessary.

| crucial | to bluff | a hike (prices) | (room) allocation | to bargain |
| to feature (in a brochure) | to brief | to barter | an upgrade | a shortfall |

Read "Hotel Contracting" and answer these questions.

a Who is Gary David?
b What does his job involve?
c In his opinion, how cooperative are the hoteliers he has been working with?

Tell your partner about Gary's job. Make notes before you begin.

HOTEL CONTRACTING

Hotel contracting is one of the most crucial activities of any holiday company's business – it is also one of the most demanding with an endless round of resorts and hotels and the inevitable negotiations of next season's rates.

"We need hoteliers as much as they need us," said Cadogan Travel's tour operations general manager Gary David, who has made thirty-four visits to nine destinations featured in the winter brochure. "But they play games; there's a lot of bluffing going on."

He claims this year to have toured 170 hotel and self-catering properties, viewed 500 bedrooms and visited sixty-five handling agents. This is in addition to briefing couriers, inspecting hotel noticeboards to make sure material is well displayed (it often isn't), visiting the tourist offices for each destination and dealing with forty airlines that serve the resorts.

"There are all sorts of politics," said Mr David. "It is a question of attitude as well because some hoteliers like bigger operators while others do not."

At Gibraltar's Rock Hotel, the manager agreed to contributions for advertising and brochures, whereas in Tangier, the Rif Hotel manager refused to move from his 20 per cent hike in rates.

However, bartering for room rates is only one aspect of Gary David's work. Others cover increases in room allocations, upgrades, added extras such as wine, fruit or flowers, afternoon tea, improved child reductions, long-stay deals and contributions towards advertising, which are all used to improve the overall deal.

Another way of getting a better deal from hoteliers is to introduce a new section to the brochure which promotes a top hotel in each resort, and use this as a bargaining tool, or give out awards to tempt them to give better discounts.

"In Gibraltar I've had to drop two hotels because of poor standards so I've got a shortfall in capacity. I've got now to push for increased room allocation, but I'm dealing with hoteliers who don't need me because most cater for business traffic."

(adapted from *Travel Trade Gazette*)

Vocabulary

3 Work with a partner. Choose five new words from the text you read. Explain their meanings to your partner.

Writing 1

4 Work with a partner. You are research assistants for a tour operator called Exotic Destinations. Write a report on the relationship between your management and resort hoteliers. Use the two articles "Hotel Contracting" and "When the welcome is frosty", your own ideas and the headings below as the basis for your report.

1   TERMS OF REFERENCE

At the request of the MD, to carry out a survey on the relationship between our management and resort hoteliers.

2   PROCEDURE

- A questionnaire was designed in consultation with senior marketing staff.
- Our hoteliers and our Tour Operations Department were approached and asked to complete the questionnaire.
- The findings were analysed.

3   FINDINGS

3.1   Tour Operations outlined the following difficulties:

3.2   Hoteliers tended to focus mainly on money and methods of payment.

4   CONCLUSIONS AND RECOMMENDATIONS

Name:
Research Assistant   Date

Learning Tip

When you read a text in English you may notice that some of the vocabulary can be grouped around a topic. For example, in the two texts, there are many words which can be grouped around the topic of money.

Report-writing Tips

Most short formal reports have a format similar to this:

- Title page or heading – this should be clear but short.
- Terms of reference/Objective – this states why the report is being written.
- Procedure – the method used to collect information.
- Findings – what was discovered.
- Conclusions and recommendations – a summary of your report and suggestions for the future.

After drafting your report, check it:

- Does it have clear headings and a numbering system?
- Is all the information relevant and necessary?
- Is it logically organised?
- Is the language in the right style for the intended readership?
- Is it easy to read?
- Is the English correct?

Listening

5 Listen to part of a meeting between Maria Rodrigues, the MD of Exotic Destinations, and members of the Planning Committee. They are discussing a new package tour to Cuba. Then answer these questions

a Why are Exotic Destinations interested in starting a package to Cuba?
b Why do they think they will be competitive?
c What load factor will they be working on?
d What kind of overheads are mentioned?
e What are they going to charge for a two-week package?
f How will they compensate for their low profit margin?
g What is the difference between their rates and those of their competitors?
h Why does Richard want the final package prices?

Speechwork

Contractions

6 Listen to David talking at the meeting. What words are missing from the gaps? (There is more than one word in each gap.)

> *"Well, (a) ...... us their seat rates and (b) ...... a discount by taking a time slot (c) ...... been able to fill. So (d) ...... 270 seats at approximately £250 each for twenty-five weeks in rotation.*
>
> *And (e) ...... by the marketing people (f) ...... probably be working on load factors of about 80 per cent – so we should be doing OK."*

7 Decide if contractions are possible in these sentences. Then listen and check your answers.

a What will it be like?
b She has been working there for six months.
c She has to do a really difficult job.
d There is a lot of bluffing going on.
e There are all sorts of politics involved.

f I have had to drop two hotels.
g She was in Majorca last week.
h You should not have told them our profit margin.
i She cannot have finished by now.
j Pass me the ashtray, will you?

8 Read the phone conversation that took place the following day between Maria and Simon, the Assistant Managing Director. Underline all the auxiliary verbs, the forms of *be* and *have*, and the negatives. Decide if they could be contracted. Practise the dialogue with a partner.

Simon Hello, Maria. I am sorry I could not make the meeting. I should have been there but my plane was delayed and you know what it is like getting back from the airport. There are never any taxis when you need them. Anyway, what was it like?

Maria Well, my secretary has typed up the minutes and you should have got a copy on your desk. Can you see it?

Simon No.

Maria She must have forgotten then. Anyway, I will fill you in with what we discussed. Um, you know, do not you, that I have negotiated a site at Guardalavaca. Well, we have now been able to squeeze some very competitive rates from the hoteliers.

Simon Good! And did you discuss how much we are charging the punters?

Maria £550 for two weeks.

Simon You cannot go as low as that!

Maria We can! I mean we have to otherwise the competition will take away our custom. It is very tight but we have got no alternative!

Simon I see what you mean but I think we had better think again. I wish I had been there because I really do not agree that the price is right.

Listen and compare your pronunciation with that on the tape.

Language Focus

The passive

1 **Read these groups of sentences and decide which are in the active and which are in the passive.**

a We've been approached by Sky Air.
b Sky Air has approached us.
c I'm told by the marketing people that we'll probably be working on load factors of about 80 per cent.
d The marketing people tell me that we will probably be working on load factors of about 80 per cent.
e The brochures should be sent to the travel agents in October.
f They should send the brochures to the travel agents in October.
g All expenses must be authorised in advance.
h You must get authorisation for all expenses in advance.
i The managing director was given the information.
j The information was given to the managing director.
k He gave the managing director the information.
l It was stipulated that the agreement would allow for increases in the cost of aviation fuel.
m Sky Air stipulated that the agreement would allow for increases in the cost of aviation fuel.
n It is said that an influx of tourists will destroy the plant life.
o Environmentalists say that an influx of tourists will destroy the plant life.
p She was paid $2,000.
q The tour operators paid her $2,000.

2 **Answer these questions.**

a When do we use the passive rather than the active voice?
b How is it formed?

3 **Match the following statements about the passive to the examples in 1 above.**

a Sometimes it is appropriate to say who carried out the action.
b Modal forms can be used.
c Verbs with two objects can be made passive in two ways.
d Passive constructions beginning with *it* are used to make a statement more formal or impersonal.

Practice

Complete this letter to Mrs Marinelli by expanding the following notes.

Dear Mrs Marinelli,

This is to confirm our recent discussions. At the meeting / hold / 25 January / it / agree that:

1 500 rooms with sea view / make available / Grand Canyon hotel / 30 March – 25 November / weekly basis.

2 We, Global Tours, / require / inform the hotelier / 4 weeks advance / if we wish our allocation / cancel. The account settle / 1 month after close / of the holiday period i.e. by or before 25 December.

3 All payments / make / US$. The rates for this year / fix / advance / $1 = 1650 lire.

4 It bring / attention / tour information / not display / last year. Therefore suitable space / must provide / for our company leaflets and notices / display.

We trust we are in agreement on all these points. I remain / disposal / raise / further points.

It has also come notice / your copy of the contract / never return. / I grateful / complete / without delay / return to our Head Office.

It note / this agreement / valid / 2 years. / 6 months' notice / require in writing / in order it / terminate.

Yours sincerely,

Speaking

Putting Together a Package

9 **Work in groups. Look at the following steps in planning a new tour programme, and put them into a logical order. Add any stages which you feel are missing.**

- Resort representatives are recruited and trained.
- Exchange rates and a selling price are fixed.
- The final destination is chosen.
- Economic factors are investigated; patterns of demand are identified.
- The brochure is designed.

- Bulk hotel accommodation and airline seat rates are negotiated.
- The brochure is printed.
- The first holidaymakers arrive.
- New potential sites are compared.
- A trial costing is drawn up.

Are there any stages that could be done at the same time? How long do you think the whole process takes? At what stage are Exotic Destinations in their planning of tours to Cuba (page 39)? What else do they have to do?

Re-opening for the summer

10 **Work in groups. You are re-opening your hotel for the summer season. Decide what needs to be done.**

Negotiating an Agreement

11 Work in groups of four. Within your group you will work in two teams of two people. Team A consists of the Marketing Manager and the Chief Negotiator for GETAWAY, a tour operator. Team B consists of the Commercial Relations Manager and the Chief Negotiator for VISTAS, a chain of travel agents. Team A look at the text below. Team B look at the text on page 111.

TEAM A: GETAWAY

Look at the agenda on the right. You have just finished discussing item 2. Read and discuss your negotiating position.

Item 3
You usually give agents 11%. The highest you have ever offered is 12.5 per cent.
Item 4
You would like to have guaranteed eye-level racking in all agencies.
Item 5
If they ask for incentives, offer 80p to the person confirming the booking. You would make this payment monthly, working from the departure date. If they pay quarterly (like all your other clients), you can offer £1.10.
Item 6
Your policy is to acknowledge complaints within five days and where possible to give a full explanation within three weeks. Often a lot of time is needed to check up on all the facts .
Item 7
You can offer an educational for the travel agency staff which this year will be to India.

Agenda 12/03
Sales of GETAWAY Tours
1 Minutes ✔
2 Review of forecasts for next season ✔
3 Commission levels
4 Racking
5 Incentives
6 Policy on complaints
7 Educationals

Before you start negotiating with VISTAS you should decide:

- what you want to achieve.
- your order of priorities.
- what you think VISTAS will want.
- how much you are prepared to accept.
- what you think VISTAS will be prepared to accept.

Decide who will say what. Then negotiate with the VISTAS representatives.

Language Tip

Useful negotiating language

Making a proposal	**Disagreeing**
I suggest we …	*Yes, but …*
Our position is that …	*I'm afraid that's out of the question.*
We're sure you'll agree …	*We appreciate your position but …*
Agreeing	*I see your point but …*
I'd go along with that.	*Let's be realistic.*
Point taken.	*As we see it …*

Writing 2

12 After your negotiations between GETAWAY and VISTAS, write a letter to confirm your agreement. Use this outline as a model. If you haven't reached agreement, you will have to modify some of the wording.

Dear

This is a summary of the points we covered during our meeting of (date)

1 **Commissions**
It was agreed …

2 **Sales, Display and Racking Policy**
The policy on this will be …

3 **Incentives**
After discussion, it was decided …

4 **Customer complaints**
It was agreed …

5 **Educationals**
These will …

With best regards

Yours sincerely

7

Promoting a Destination

Identifying the strengths and weaknesses of tourist destinations
Giving presentations
Writing brochure texts

Preview

1 **The photographs show some popular aspects of Britain. Work in groups and discuss these questions.**

a Why do people come to your country?
b What do they do when they are there?
c Is it the perfect place to come to or are there some disadvantages?
d Why do you think people want to visit Britain?
e What do you think are the negative features of Britain?

Reading

2 **The table lists some of the positive and negative features of Britain as a tourist destination.**
Does this correspond to what *you* think Britain is like?
Is there anything you would like to add to the table or take away?

Product strengths	Product weaknesses
• Friendly people	• Lack of foreign language skills especially good-quality, on-site interpretation in other languages
• Historic cities/pleasant countryside • Attractive coastline • Good shopping facilities	• Litter and pollution, particularly in London and on some polluted beaches
• Many types of accommodation • Good network of Tourist Information Centres	• Limited supply of modern budget accommodation in urban areas and on transit routes • Limited booking services for some types of accommodation (e.g. self-catering and farmhouses)
• Channel Tunnel • Toll-free motorways • Widespread availability of lead-free petrol	• Insufficient investment in connecting road/rail transport links • High rail/tube fares • Perceived difficulty of driving on the left
• Wide variety of good cuisine	• Perceived high costs • Perceived low quality by some visitors
• Good choice of language schools	• Variable standards
• High standards of health and hygiene • Free press/media • Politically stable	• Poverty and violence in a number of inner cities
• Attraction of the Royal family/historical traditions/ceremonies	

Writing 1

3 Think of the strengths and weaknesses of your own country as a tourist destination and produce a similar table for it.

Listening 1

4 Does your country have a government organisation which is responsible for the development of tourism? If so, what does it do?

Listen to Ann Trevor talking about the way the Barbados Tourist Authority promotes the Caribbean island within the trade and answer these questions.

a What is the Barbados Tourist Authority's marketing strategy for Barbados?

b What does Ann do at trade fairs?

c How does the BTA work with tour operators?

d Why does she mention Almond Beach Village?

Is her work the same as the work of the tourist authority in your country?

Vocabulary 1

Advertising and publicity

5 Ann talks about promoting and marketing a destination. Make three networks round the headings *advertising*, *public relations* and *promotions*.

Use the words and expressions in the box and add as many words as you can.

stickers	brochures	leaflets
lobbying	trade fairs	competitions
receptions	sponsorship	billboards
commercials	exhibitions	publicity
special offers	press releases	discounts
posters	promotional videos	talks and presentations

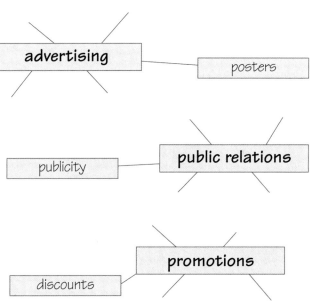

6 Work with a partner and compare your networks. Then discuss which strategies are the most and least effective and under what circumstances.

7 Nouns in English can be countable (like a *trip*) or uncountable (like *travel*). Match the uncountable nouns on the left with the countable nouns on the right which are associated with them.

A	B
Uncountable	Countable
advice	a fact
advertising	a close watch
progress	a recommendation
research	a coin
monitoring	an advertisement
baggage	a study
information	a step forward
money	a suitcase

45

Listening 2

Describing itineraries

⚙ 8 Tour operators, airlines and national tourist boards often run "educationals" (also called "familiarisation trips") for people in the travel trade who are in a position to promote a particular destination.

Listen to Helen Lee describing a familiarisation trip to China and follow the itinerary on the map. Then listen again. Which of these places are mentioned as part of the tour?

- the Forbidden City
- the Summer Palace
- the Jingshan Park
- the Temple of Heaven
- the Potola Palace

- the Terracotta Warriors
- the Banpo Village
- Shanghai River Tour by night
- the Yangshuo Orchid Garden

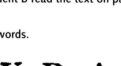

Speaking 1

Familiarisation trips

9 Work with a partner. Student A read the text below. Student B read the text on page 111.

STUDENT A
Tell your partner about the itinerary below in your own words.

CUBA

O U T L I N E   I T I N E R A R Y

DAY 1

Depart London mid-morning Tuesday on VIASA via Caracas. Arrival late evening in Havana. Direct to the Hotel Plaza, opposite Central Park in old Havana, the area famed for its old Spanish Days.

DAYS 2 – 3

Explore Havana. Visit to a handicraft centre and the Guanabacoa museum on the outskirts of Havana, which has rooms dedicated to the influence of African cultures on Cuba. Free time to wander the streets of old Havana and appreciate the city's fine architecture. Visit to The Museum of the Revolution, the old fort and the Cathedral.

DAY 4

Visit to a cigar factory. Transfer to the airport for flight to Santiago de Cuba in the east of the island, famed for its buildings and beautiful settings. Overnight stay in Las Americas hotel.

DAY 5

City tour, including the Moncada barracks which Fidel Castro and a group of followers failed to storm in 1953 in an early abortive attempt to seize power. Good museums in Santiago include the Casa Velazquez dating back to the 16th Century and the Museo Bacardi. (Optional).

DAY 6

Excursion to the Basilica in El Cobre, a village 18 miles northwest of Santiago. Transfer to airport and return to Havana. Accommodation in the Plaza Hotel.

DAY 7

Return home

Language Focus

Referring to the future

During her talk Helen Lee used a number of verb forms when referring to the future itinerary.

1   I'm **going to** describe the itinerary to you.

2   You**'ll be visiting** most of the famous places.

3   From Beijing we **go** by coach to a smaller city in the North.

4   The guide **will take** you on a sightseeing tour.

5   We**'re flying** there the following day.

6   By the end of the tour hopefully you**'ll have learnt** a lot about China.

Match each of the verb forms above with a description (a–d) on the right. There may be more than one answer.

a   She is referring to a schedule which is programmed in advance and possibly difficult to change.

b   She is talking about an event that will be completed at a given future time.

c   She is announcing her intention to do something.

d   She is describing arrangements that have been made.

As you can see, it is sometimes possible to use more than one future form although there might be a slight change in emphasis. What is important to remember is that **will** is only one way of referring to the future.

Practice

1   **Study the following sentences, and say which verb form is appropriate in each case and why.**

a   Could you ring the airport and ask what time the first flight to Brussels *shall leave/leaves?*

b   (*The telephone rings – it is 10.55.*). Oh, that*'ll be/is to be* Rosa. She said she'd ring at 11.

c   We'd better hurry up – it looks as if it*'s going to rain/will be raining.*

d   The Antarctic *will certainly become/will certainly be becoming* an important tourist destination.

e   You haven't got a car *I'll give/I'm giving* you a lift if you like.

f   It's not surprising he *won't do/is not to do* any work for you – you don't pay him!

g   Don't panic! I*'ll have finished/'ll be finishing* the report by Wednesday afternoon.

h   I *won't have/am not having* time to see you – I*'ll have finished /'ll be finishing* the report on Wednesday afternoon.

i   Ricardo says he *doesn't attend/won't be attending* the meeting – he thinks it *will be/is to be* a waste of time.

j   The Prince of Wales *is to open/will have been opening* the new theme park on April 1st.

k   We *will have/are having* an office party on Friday after work for Justyna. She *will work/will have been working* for us for twenty years.

l   I'm fed up with working here. I*'m going to try/will try* to get a better job somewhere else.

m   On the second night of the programme everyone *will be going/will have been going* to a cabaret show.

2   **Using what you have learnt from the previous activity, read these grammar notes and write your own sample sentences to illustrate their use.**

a   The *present simple* can be used for a programme or regular schedule which is unlikely to change.

b   The *present continuous* can be used to refer to arrangements.

c   **will** can be used to make a deduction, or to make a factual prediction.

d   **will** or **'ll** can also be used to make spontaneous offers.

e   **won't**, as well as predicting that something will not happen, can also be used to indicate a refusal, or lack of willingness.

f   **going to** can be used to predict future events based on a present evaluation of circumstances.

g   **going to** is also used for a personal decision or intention.

h   **is/are to** refers to events which (*Complete the rule.*) …

i   *The future continuous* (**will be** + **verb -ing**) can be used for:
   i   arrangements
   ii events which (*Complete the rule.*) …

j   *The future perfect* (**will have** + **past participle**) can be used for an event that will be completed at a given future time.

k   *The future perfect continuous* (**will have been** + **verb -ing**) can be used (*Complete the rule.*) …

Vocabulary 2

Brochure language

10 The brochure is probably one of the most important documents used in the promotion of a destination. Brochures use very descriptive language to make holiday destinations sound attractive.
Read this description of Salou in Spain and pay particular attention to the highlighted words.

Salou has all the ingredients for a perfect seaside holiday. Its major attraction is a long, wide beach of soft, gently-shelving sands, backed by a fine, tree-lined promenade. East of the beach you will find uncrowded streets alongside a picturesque coastline with pretty wooded areas and several smaller bays.

West of Salou is the attractive fishing village of Cambrils.

With its marvellous beach, idyllic harbour and many magnificent seafood restaurants it is a resort in its own right. But wherever you stay in the Salou area you'll have access to a whole host of pleasures: superb bathing, every kind of watersport and, by night, plenty of excitement in countless bars and discos. Another impressive attraction is the truly amazing Aquapark at La Pineda, a short bus ride from Salou itself.

Descriptive adjectives

11 Each of the groups of three adjectives below can be used to describe one of the nouns in the box. Match each noun with a set of adjectives. Can you add an appropriate adjective to each set?
Use a dictionary to help you.

beach	village	hills	mountains
hotels	views	city	atmosphere

1 rolling	2 low-rise	3 quaint	4 relaxed	5 spectacular	6 unspoilt	7 ruined	8 secluded
gentle	spacious	old-world	carefree	soaring	striking	medieval	safe
undulating	well-appointed	charming	welcoming	majestic	panoramic	bustling	uncrowded

Writing 2

12 This text about a holiday complex is informative but not very descriptive. Decide where the words in the box may be placed in the text to make the holiday complex sound more appealing.

A STAY IN PARADISE

This holiday complex is within reach of the bay and the sea. There are four tennis courts available to guests and the Sandy Lane Golf Club is just a bus ride away.
Hole Town exudes an atmosphere with its streets and houses. Watch the world go by from the café terraces or sample dishes in the restaurants.

easy	easy-going
floodlit	many welcoming
whitewashed	ideally situated
secluded, rocky	short
cobbled	mouth-watering
free-of-charge	

13 Work with a partner. Add descriptive words to the following passage, but this time choose the words you want to insert. Then compare your text with one written by another pair of students.

TANGIER

Tangier with its bazaars and architecture provides a taste of the Orient. It has sporting facilities, including golf, tennis and sailing. Watersports can be enjoyed along its coasts which have beaches. You can try your luck in the casino or window-shop down the boulevards of the quarter. The Mendoubia Gardens, a palace and antiquities are just some of the attractions that Tangier has to offer.

Speechwork

Pausing and rhythm

14 You work for a major tour operator and have recently been involved in setting up Cuba as a new destination. You are preparing the soundtrack for a promotional video praising the attractions of the island. Below is the text you will have to read. Your text will have to synchronise with the video images and you should therefore be careful to respect the pause boundaries (/), the stress markers, the intonation patterns and the speed of delivery. Record your soundtrack in a language laboratory or, as homework, on to an audio cassette. Then compare your recording with the tape.

> If I mention <u>Cuba</u> to you, / what are the <u>three</u> things / that <u>immediately</u> / come to <u>mind</u>? / <u>Castro</u> / <u>Communism</u> / and <u>cigars</u> /. Maybe it's not <u>your</u> idea / of the <u>perfect</u> holiday. / Well, you're <u>wrong</u>! / Because in <u>fact</u> / Cuba has <u>changed</u> / and it's <u>changed</u> / for the <u>better</u>. / And so why do <u>many</u> more people / <u>now</u> decide / to have a <u>fantastic</u> holiday in Cuba? / Well, the <u>first</u> reason / is that <u>Cuba</u> / is an <u>affordable</u> tropical destination / with fan<u>tastic</u> <u>beaches</u> / and <u>watersports</u> / as good as <u>anywhere</u>. / The <u>second</u> reason / is the <u>people</u> / and their <u>music</u> / <u>reflecting</u> as they do / such a <u>variety</u> of ethnic origins. / And <u>last</u> / but not <u>least</u>, / the history of <u>Havana</u>, / <u>especially</u> / its association with two <u>great</u> / twentieth-century <u>writers</u>, / Graham <u>Greene</u> / and Ernest <u>Hemingway</u>.

15 Write your own commentary for a video about a place you like visiting.

Speaking 2

Making a presentation

16 You have recently returned from a familiarisation trip to a holiday resort and now have to report back on your visit. Decide which resort you went to and which tour operator paid for your holiday. Prepare a presentation. Talk about the resort itself and also about those facilities offered by the tour operator. Include the following:

- TRANSPORT TO AND FROM THE RESORT
- THE CLIMATE
- THE ACCOMMODATION
- THE LOCAL ATTRACTIONS
- THE FOOD
- TRANSPORT IN THE RESORT
- THE PRICE AND VALUE FOR MONEY
- THE KEY SELLING POINTS

After the presentation, work in groups and discuss these questions:

a Could everyone hear you?

b Did they understand you?

c Did they think you sounded confident?

Language Tip

The language of presentations

- **Introduction**
  Good evening, everyone.
  Thank you for inviting me to speak on …
  Tonight I am going to talk about …

- **Introducing your talk**
  I would like to start by …
  I shall begin by …
  Then I will speak about …
  Thirdly I will talk about …
  And lastly …

- **The main part of the talk**
  Let us begin with …
  However …
  As far as (the accommodation) is concerned …
  Moving on to …
  My third point deals with …
  And last but not least …

- **Summing up/conclusion**
  So, in conclusion, you can see that …

- **Saying thank you and ending your talk**
  Thank you all for listening so attentively.
  I hope I have been able to tell you a little about …
  Before I sit down I would first like to thank … for …
  Does anyone have any questions?

8

Responsible
Tourism

Considering environmental issues
Taking part in meetings
Writing press releases

Preview

1 **Work in groups and discuss these questions.**

a What could be the negative impact of
tourism on the following?

- historic sites
- beaches and the coastline
- the countryside
- wildlife
- the host community's culture

b What kinds of initiatives have been taken to counteract some of these adverse effects?

Calvin and Hobbes   by Bill Watterson

CALVIN AND HOBBES © 1993 Watterson. Dist. by UNIVERSAL PRESS SYNDICATE.

Reading

2 This article was written for a magazine called *Our Planet* and, using the example of Waikiki,
describes ways in which small island states can develop sustainable tourism. As you read,
make a note of the things that a developer should and should not do.

Safe Tourism

MOST RESOURCE-POOR island states trying to manage to
survive in the global economy cannot afford to
neglect the economic opportunities tourism offers. As
they suffer from the continuing slide of international
commodity prices, many have no alternative but to offer their
natural beauty – and cheap labour costs – to attract the
tourist industry. Following the rules for sustainable tourism –
while tough – could reduce the risks to the environment.

SO, WHAT RULES keep you profitably safe and sustainably
beautiful? The first rule is: keep tourists all in one place for as
long as you can during their visit to your island. Leaving aside
the thorny issues of foreign ownership and oversaturation,
Hawaii can teach us a few things about safe tourism. The
world's most recognised tourist destination is Waikiki. Now
Waikiki was not always a beach – it was a swamp before
developers trucked in white sand to create the fabled strand.
The hotels on Waikiki all rose out of the same swamp and
reclaimed lands. Which neatly encapsulates your second rule
of safe tourism: do not displace any existing destinations.

WAIKIKI ITSELF, WITH some 30,000 hotel rooms, covers little
more than seventeen city blocks. Despite its small area, the
great majority of the five million tourists who visit Hawaii
every year do not venture beyond this luxurious ghetto, much
to the delight of the indigenous communities. Have you ever
tried to get an hotel room outside of Waikiki on the island of
Oahu? It is tough to find an hotel. And there are no plans to

approve any more, say aides to Governor John Waihe'e, Hawaii's first Polynesian governor. Governor Waihe'e seems proud of the fact that he has not approved a major tourist development since he took office.

ANOTHER RULE: TAKE fewer tourists who will stay longer and spend more. A report commissioned by the (former) Hawaii governor's office found that the four million people who visited the islands in 1984 spent an average of ten days and unloaded $1,000 per head. Not a good sign, because infrastructural construction and maintenance costs, already hovering around one billion dollars a year, rise to keep up with such huge numbers of visitors to an island state with a total population of about a million. And do not forget that close to 60 per cent of the tourist receipts are immediately repatriated off island.

WITH THE CONCENTRATION on volume, massive hotels had to be built to cope with the millions of bodies that the airlines were dumping on the island – with competitive fares designed to put bottoms on the much larger numbers of seats in the huge 747s. In many cases the bigger hotels were relying on package tours for half their occupancy rates.

AND WHAT IS wrong with big hotels? You can imagine the amount of water, energy, personnel, roads and the like which have to be diverted to such large constructions – paid for by local tax-payers. Building huge hotels requires enormous amounts of money which are available only in the metropolitan countries, which in turn means handing ownership over to off-island corporations. Owners from distant places have a history of tying their continued presence abroad to the amount of incentives offered by the authorities, which are already saddled with the infrastructural costs, while the vast majority of revenues from tourism are repatriated off-island.

HAWAII HAS REDIRECTED its efforts to attract fewer visitors of a higher calibre. By so doing, the resorts are smaller, less costly, and much more pleasant places to visit. It was ironic that the most successful, and expensive, resorts in Hawaii were the smaller ones like Hana Maui Ranch, which had neither television nor air-conditioning. Hana Maui Ranch did have a cultural show, but it did not feature professional entertainers – those dancing for the guests were the maids, gardeners, accountants and managers of the hotel, all of whom were local Polynesians. Yet it continues to enjoy some of the highest return rates anywhere.

THAT LEADS ME to another rule: involve the local community. Ensure your success is shared by them. Offer local farmers and business folk the first opportunity to provide your resort with food. A letter from your resort to a grower guaranteeing to buy all they can grow of certain vegetables can be used by the farmer to get a favourable loan from the local bank. Instead of importing, for example, an artist-in-residence, which is fashionable in the top resorts, appoint local artists, and import a coastal-botanist-in-residence, and give the findings to the local authorities, thereby increasing the knowledge the community has of its own natural resources. Also consider marine biologists, musicologists, agronomists, and for the really confident and savvy, mythologists. In other words try to improve the lot of the locals. If you do not, then you are sentencing yourself to eventual failure which will manifest itself in surly workers and insults hurled at your hotel guests. When you first notice these signs – find a buyer, quick.

(article by Lelei Lelaulu in *Our Planet*)

---

3 Work in groups and discuss these questions.
a What advice would you give to a developing country trying to enlarge its tourist industry?
b Which of these points could an overdeveloped tourist area take note of?

Speechwork 1

Word boundaries

4 **The word sequences in the box occur in the article you have just read (lines 14–18). How would you say them aloud? What happens when one word ends in a consonant and the following word begins with another consonant? Listen and check.**

recognised tourist destinations	fabled strand
reclaimed lands	second rule

5 **These phrases are also taken from the article. Practise saying them aloud and compare your pronunciation with the tape.**

tried to	visit to	cheap labour costs	the great majority
tourist development	neither television nor air-conditioning	own natural resources	island states

Listening

Protecting the environment

6 Michael Leech is Managing Director of a company called Overland Encounter, which organises adventure holidays to remote destinations. He is very concerned to protect the sites he visits and talks about the way he thinks the environment can be protected.

What steps would you take to make sure that no damage is done to the environment?

Listen and answer the questions.

a Michael mentions patterns of behaviour which an operator can encourage among tourists. What are they?

b What, according to Michael, is a "key factor"?

c In what way is tourism now putting things back into the environment?

7 What guidelines would you give to tourists about:

- clothes?
- religion?
- photography?
- begging?

Would these be the same wherever they travelled?

Speechwork 2

Word boundaries: linkage

8 Read these expressions aloud.
What happens when a consonant sound is followed by a vowel sound?
Listen and check.

global economy   tourist industry   foreign ownership
a small area   economic opportunity

9 Listen again to this extract from the interview with Michael Leech. Write the words that are missing from each gap. Are these words pronounced separately or are they run together?

"I know you're very (a) ...... environmental issues at Overland Encounter but, in practical terms, what can a tour operator do to make sure that tourists don't destroy the beauty of the thing they came to see?"

"Well I think you have to get involved in what we call '(b) ......' tourism. You can't deprive people of their interest in wanting to travel. But what you can do is to (c) ...... patterns of behaviour which will introduce them to a country in a responsible way. That means, for example, making sure that, on an adventure holiday, no detergents are used in springs or streams and that no (d) ...... left behind after camps. It means, if you're visiting a (e) ...... like the Antarctic, that people must respect the rules and not damage (f) ...... or go too near the penguins. It means providing travellers with a pack with (g) ...... how to behave and what to do to best preserve the cultures and places visited."

10 Work with a partner. Take turns to be A and B. Read this conversation aloud.

A OK, so tourism can have a beneficial effect by generating income and creating employment, but what about its effect on the environment?

B Well, if you're not careful it can cause serious problems.

A You mean allowing tourists to go to Antarctica, then letting them trample all over rare plants?

B Yes, but it's not only in remote areas where this ecological damage is being done but also in modern, highly technological countries like Britain.

A What do you mean?

B In areas of natural beauty such as Snowdonia; first, the footpaths have been eroded away. Secondly, where the tourists have strayed off the paths the vegetation has not only been killed but the soil is now unfit for cultivation.

A Mm – this is what's happening in mountain areas where there are too many ski slopes, isn't it?

Listen and check your pronunciation.

Language Focus

Reporting verbs

These verbs are often used to report what someone has said. Do you know them all?

acknowledge	concede	insist	remark
accept	confirm	maintain	reply
agree	deny	observe	reveal
announce	explain	point out	state
claim	imply	promise	suggest

They can be followed by a clause beginning with *that*. For example:

The protest movement **claimed that** the environment would suffer but the chairman of the planning committee **guaranteed that** it would be protected.

These verbs can be followed directly by *to*.

accept	agree	claim	promise	threaten

The hotel has **agreed to** reduce noise levels after midnight.
The protest movement has **threatened to** blow up the planned development.

Some reporting verbs are followed by a person then *to*. These include:

advise	instruct	order	remind	urge
ask	invite	persuade	tell	warn

They **persuaded** the operator **to** drop the project.
She **warned** them **not to** go ahead.

Practice

Choose suitable verbs to complete the extract. (Often more than one answer is possible.)

IN A STRONGLY-WORDED article published two weeks ago, Vanessa Gardner, editor of *Tourism Alert* (a) ...... that "Green Tourism" is just another marketing gimmick to lure even more tourists to new destinations and make even more bucks for the operators. She (b) ...... that tourism brings foreign income to developing countries but (c) ...... that all the local population get out of tourism is the privilege of making our beds and shining our shoes. And she (d) ...... that the marketing people are wrong to (e) ...... that a holiday can only be Green if it takes place in an undiscovered part of the world and costs the earth. She (f) ...... that you only need twenty rich foreigners descending on an Amazonian village to create more environmental and cultural damage than 10,000 ordinary holidaymakers enjoying themselves in a resort where there is no fragile ecosystem or culture left to ruin.

But in another article which appeared in last week's *Travel Gazette*, Antony Jay of Outreach Adventures plc disagreed. He (g) ...... that Green tourism was just a fashion and (h) ...... that operators did care about the future. And to prove it he (i) ...... to donate $100 per person to the Worldwide Fund for Nature. How many businessmen would do that?

Vocabulary

Meetings

11 Match the verbs in A with the noun phrases in B to make expressions which are often used in meetings.

A	B
find	round in circles
face	comments
put	to a decision
invite	agreement
reach	the proposal
second	facts
raise	(something) to the vote
go	the subject
come	common ground

12 This is an extract from a meeting about tourism in Goa.
Fill in the gaps with expressions from exercise 1.

The chairman (a) ...... *from the audience.*

Mr Singh *I would like to (b) ...... of cost – who is going to pay to clean up the beach?*

Mrs Patel *Mr Chairman, we've already debated these issues – we must now (c) .... I know we hold opposing views but perhaps we can (d) .... But if you want my opinion, we must (e) ...... – either we encourage tourism or we remain poor.*

Mr Dahar *But look, we're (f) ...... ; if we don't (g) ...... now we'll be here all night.*

Mrs Devi *I think we have discussed the matter enough. We must now (h) ....*

Mrs Patel *I (i) ...... ; it's an excellent idea.*

13 Match the adjectives in A with the nouns in B. Use a dictionary if necessary.

A	B
a foregone	argument
a fruitful	arrangement
a heated	block
a key	collaboration
a stumbling	conclusion
a vested	interest
a workable	issue

14 What is missing from these sentences? Use the expressions from exercise 13.

a Perhaps the main ...... to responsible tourism is the profit motive.

b There's been a very ...... between local pressure groups and the Ministry of Tourism and most of the problems have been resolved.

c There's no point in holding the meeting – the result's a ......

d He owns a number of hotels in the area so he has a ...... in promoting the growth of tourism.

e It's not the best solution but it's a ...... for the time being.

f There was a ...... on the proposal to build a new motorway and some people got very angry.

g Although the effect of tourism on the environment is a ...... some people still don't want to measure the effects.

Speaking

Holding a public meeting

15 You are going to take the roles of different people and debate the
pros and cons of a major tourism development in an area of outstanding
natural beauty. First read this newspaper article and summarise the main points.

Ambitious plans to spend £100 million on a disused slate mine in north Wales are causing a fierce dispute among locals. The tourist development is planned to centre around a "Quarrytorium", with a guided visit down the mine, and a residential complex built around eight dry ski slopes, a tropical park with illuminated waterfalls, lasers and holograms and an adventure playground.

The disused mine is at Glyn Rhonwy, less than a mile from the village of Llanberis, on the northern edge of the Snowdonia National Park. It has been bought by Arfon Borough Council which has asked several developers to come up with plans for redeveloping the site.

Recently a company called LeisureLand has come up with a project which, besides the Quarrytorium, also includes hotels, conference facilities, shops and restaurants, and a sports centre. Most controversially, there are also plans for thirty "holiday farmsteads", each consisting of about twenty farm-type cottages.

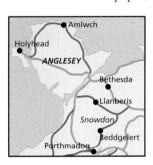

However, since the proposals were published in the local paper, people have started objecting. A protest group has been formed, headed by Gwynneth Jones, whose house overlooks Glyn Rhonwy. Although careful to give credit to the council for buying and trying to develop the area, the protest group feels that the scheme would overwhelm the village and be alien to the natural beauty of the region.

The matter is now being debated at an extraordinary council meeting in the town hall at which a decision on the future of Arfon must be reached. Representatives of all the viewpoints of the local community have been invited.

(extract from *Holiday Which?*)

16 Work in groups. Your teacher will choose a chairperson who should use the role card below. Your teacher will tell the other
people where to find their role cards. You can add your own ideas to the suggestions on the cards.

The chairperson

Your role is to make the meeting go smoothly and let everyone have their say. Discussions can get heated and you
may have to remind participants to remain polite, not interrupt, not monopolise the discussions and so on.
Here is some useful language:

Opening a meeting	*Right, shall we get started?* *The first thing we have to discuss / decide is …*		*Could we stick to the subject under discussion, please?* *Perhaps we could come back to that later.* *I'll come to you in a minute.*
Inviting comments	*I'd like to give the floor to …* *Mrs Olsen, is there anything you would like to say?* *Does anyone have any further comments?* *Would you like to come in here?*	Closing the meeting	*Are there any further points anyone wishes to make?* *To sum up, …* *Are we all agreed on this?* *Shall we take a vote? All those in favour? All those against?* *I declare this meeting closed.*
Directing the proceedings	*We seem to be losing sight of the main issues.* *With respect, I don't think that is entirely relevant.*		

Meetings Tip

Writing

17 Write a 250-word press release reporting what was said at the public meeting about the development at Glyn Rhonwy.

9

Transport

Analysing transport requirements
Planning a transport network

Preview

1 **Work in groups and list some different means of transport. Then discuss these questions.**

a What are the advantages and disadvantages of each one for long or short distances?

b How do you prefer to travel? Why?

Listening 1

2 **Susan recently went to the USA for three weeks. The map below shows the places she stayed in or visited during her trip. Listen to Susan making the final arrangements for her trip and answer these questions.**

a What is an open-jaw ticket?

b Why doesn't Susan want to use the Greyhound bus?

c Why doesn't she want accommodation booked in Las Vegas or LA?

3 **Listen again and follow Susan's route. Write the dates, times and means of transport.**

Language Focus

Two-part verbs (Phrasal verbs)

1 Two-part verbs are formed by combining a verb with a preposition (or particle) to change its meaning:

I **get up** at six o'clock.
The plane **takes off** at 7.30.

2 A verb can be used in the same sentence as a preposition without changing its meaning:

I **took** the book **off** the table.

In this case, **take** and **off** do not make a two-part verb.

3 The same combination of verb and particle can have more than one meaning:

The plane **took off**. (leave the ground)
He **took off** his jacket. (remove)
I can **take** 5 per cent **off** the price of a ticket. (discount)

We are going to look at three types of two-part verbs:

TYPE 1 TRANSITIVE TWO-PART VERBS

1 Transitive verbs take an object:

He **took off** his jacket,

In this sentence *his jacket* is the object of the verb.

2 Transitive phrasal verbs are separable. The object can be placed between the verb and the particle:

The travel agent **sorted out** her itinerary. *(sort out = organise)*
The travel agent **sorted** her itinerary **out**.

3 If the object is replaced with a pronoun (*it, him, me*) the verb is always separated:

The travel agent **sorted** it **out**.

Which of these sentences are correct?

a Susan's uncle put her up.

b Alicia saw off him at the airport.

c She took up the option.

d A: Can I have the bill?

B: Sure, I'll make it out now.

e The board of directors set up a meeting for 4 p.m.

TYPE 2 PREPOSITIONAL VERBS

These verbs take an object, but are inseparable. The object always goes at the end:

A tour guide will **look after** the group.
A tour guide will **look after** them.

Put the words in italics into the right order:

a *around / Chicago / looked / she.*

b There are new airline safety regulations: *can't / get / tour / operators / them / round.*

c *for / made / nearest / taxi / stand / the / we.*

d *the / chance / she / at / jumped /* to visit the Himalayas.

e *old / an / he / into / ran / friend /* at the airport.

TYPE 3 INTRANSITIVE TWO-PART VERBS

Intransitive verbs cannot take an object and cannot be separated.

The bus **broke down**.
We had to **hang around** for three hours while they mended it.

Put the words in the right order to make correct sentences:

a checked in/before the flight/forty-five minutes/we

b in Dubai/flights to Hong Kong/stop over

c fell through/their trip/at the last minute

d backed out/but/we had a deal/the hotel chain/we thought

e after/broke even/finally/the hotel/three years of losses

Phrasal/prepositional verbs

Some verbs have three parts:
The holiday didn't **live up to** our expectations.

Practice

Replace the words in italics with a suitable phrasal verb. Do as many as you can, then listen to the tape (Listening 1) again to check or complete your answers.

a I've pretty well *planned and formulated* what I'll be able to do while I'm there...

b So I'll be *departing* on 1st September...

c My uncle will be *collecting* me from the airport and *accommodating* me for a few days...

d You can *travel* quite easily on the subway and if you want to *sightsee*...

e Are you sure your budget will *cover* that?

f I've been *economising* for this and I really don't want to *lose the opportunity* of seeing the Niagara Falls...

g *Wait* a minute...

h The only problem is that you'll have to *wait with nothing to do* in Chicago...

i I really need to *reduce* costs so I'm hoping to be able to *locate and see again* some old friends...

j I'll *write* the itinerary for you...

Vocabulary 1

Connections

4 These words are all connected with transport.
Put them into logical sets.

liner	sail	long-haul	platform	cruise
toll	runway	compartment	make for	stopover
registration number	break down	see off	jet lag	run out of
stand-by	station wagon	crossing	roundabout	ticket collector
track	set off	drop off	highway	starboard
press on	self-drive	guard	harbour	gangway

Add two more words to each set and compare
your sets with those of other students.

5 Imagine that you recently accompanied a group of travellers on a trip involving several means of transport.
Write a short account of the trip using as many of the words in the box above as you can. For example:

*At 6.13p.m. we **set off** from Victoria Station aboard the Orient Express in our first-class **compartment** ...*

Listening 2

Understanding rapid speech: announcements

6 It can often be difficult to understand announcements made
in public places, especially if the public-address system is
poor. Listen to the messages.

Which would you hear:
a on a train/at a railway station?
b on board ship?
c at an airport/on a plane?
d on a bus?

Listen again and note the information.

Speechwork

Word boundaries

7 Listen and notice what happens to the sounds at the word
boundaries in these examples:

The next time.
Mind the doors.

**Now try saying these sentences. Which sounds disappear?
Which sounds run together?**

a Here in the main square, on your right, is the famous Leaning
Tower.

b Passengers are advised not to leave their luggage unattended.

c We're now approaching Pigeon Point, Tobago, where
passengers can disembark.

d Would Miss Andreas please report to the Purser's Office?

e Captain Nolan would like to welcome you on board.

Listen to the tape and check.

Speaking 1

Making announcements

8 Your teacher will give you a number of messages which have
to be given out over a public-address system. Record the
messages and play them to the rest of the class. Did
everyone understand? If not, what was the problem?

Vocabulary 2

Synonyms: British and American English

9 When she went on her trip Susan had to understand some of
the words and expressions which are used in the USA but
not in the UK. The ones in the box below are all to do with
travel.

**Find the pairs of synonyms and put them under the correct
headings.**

For example:

BRITISH ENGLISH   AMERICAN ENGLISH
driving licence   *driver's license*

puncture	hood	driving licence	pavement
city centre	sidewalk	flat	underground
line	car park	motorway	downtown
queue	gas	estate car	subway
freeway	petrol	station wagon	bonnet
parking lot	driver's license		

**Do you know any other words that are different in British
and American English?**

Reading

Passenger care

10 Travelling can often be tiring and uncomfortable. What kinds of things can be done to make the journey more agreeable for the passenger travelling by these means of transport?

- air
- rail
- sea
- coach

11 This article describes how Gatwick Airport in the UK has made travelling easier for business passengers.
Decide which of the extracts A–G match the numbered gaps in the text. There is one additional extract which does not belong in any of the gaps.

> **A** Looking at what London Gatwick Airport has done, the solution now, in hindsight, seems obvious.

> **B** But Fast Track has other benefits for the business traveller.

> **C** The best ideas in business are quite often the most obvious.

> **D** Even at the busiest times of the day, it now takes business passengers only a minute or two to pass through the barriers to go airside.

> **E** Many airlines offer attractive incentives such as free limousine and helicopter transfers, advance seat reservations and priority baggage handling.

> **F** For the busy executive, it is not so much that time means money, rather that he or she usually cuts it fine when getting to the airport.

> **G** This system, called Fast Track, enables First and Business Class passengers from all airlines using North and South Terminals to use a special dedicated route through passport control and security checks.

1 = **C**

For example, business travellers passing through Europe's airports have constantly bemoaned the fact that however much their ticket cost, or however much they were pampered in-flight the real hold-ups always came when passing through passport control and security, or waiting in duty free.

2

That last-minute report to finish, or taking just one more phone call, has spelt disaster for many business travellers suddenly finding themselves at passport control behind a plane-load of holidaymakers who are quite happy to take their time – after all they are going on holiday.

3

However, it is a simple fact that no other airport appeared to have tackled the problem successfully until London Gatwick became the first airport in the UK or Europe to implement a "red carpet" priority system especially for First and Business Class travellers.

4

A pass is given to eligible passengers at check-in.

5

The special entry gates to the departure lounges, however, only operate up until 2 p.m. The airport's research has shown that the bulk of business travel flights were before this time, with only a handful afterwards when the regular control points had no queues. However, it is a position that is regularly reviewed by the airport.

6

For instance, those who have hurried to the airport without the time to pick up any foreign currency can collect pre-ordered currency from a special Fast Track desk at the airport's bureaux de change. Or if they travel to the airport via the Gatwick Express, they can use the credit-card phone on the train to order the currency on the way from Victoria. Forgotten to buy a present for that important contact you are going to meet on arrival? Instead of queuing up with the leisure travellers at the duty free counters, Fast Track pass-holders can take advantages of their own check-out.

Not surprisingly, Fast Track has been a smash hit with London Gatwick passengers (numbers using it have increased from 40, 000 a month when it first started, to 65, 000 a month at present). Perhaps the fact that other European airports are looking at emulating the Fast Track idea shows how big a step forward it is in taking the hassle out of business travel.

Writing

Dealing with complaints

12 Unfortunately, not everything runs as
smoothly as in the previous article!
You work at an airport in your country
and have received this fax from Gary
Richards, Ground Operations
Manager at Skyways.
Work with a partner. Read the fax and
discuss Gary's complaints.
Then write a reply to explain how you
are dealing with each complaint.

FAX

To: L. Atienza, Airport Administration
From: G. Richards, Skyways
Date: 05/06
No. of pages inc. this one: 1

Dear Mr Atienza,

Thank you for your hospitality offered to Peter Forster, John Carlyle and myself earlier this month.

Since my visit, our Chairman, Francis Parker, has visited and on his return reported certain items which he considers need improvement:

1   The delivery and installation of two additional sets of scales for check-in should be dealt with asap.

2   All bags should be presented at check-in. There is no excuse for bags not being weighed, subjected to security screening and proper excess baggage payments not being collected.

3   I hope that, with greater experience, your new aircraft cleaning teams will speed up and be able to complete the job in less than thirty minutes.

4   Representations should be made urgently and strongly to the authorities which at present allow boarding to take place at one set of steps only. We have two sets of steps to the aircraft and they should be used.

5   Only one piece of cabin baggage per passenger is allowed onto the aircraft. Can you please make sure that this ruling is implemented.

6   Finally, on arrival the Chairman had to wait some fifty minutes for his baggage to come off the plane. This speed of delivery is entirely unacceptable.

Many thanks for your help in these matters, and I look forward to hearing from you soon.

Yours sincerely,
Gary Richards
Senior Manager, Ground Operations

Speaking 2

Making recommendations

13 Peakland is a mountainous country which has few natural resources. Sixty per cent of the
population is employed in agriculture but there is a rural exodus towards Sommerton, the
capital, and the coastal ports. However, the situation is slowly changing and will certainly be
accelerated by some recent developments.
Read this newspaper article about Peakland and discuss this question. Do you think foreign
investors will be willing to invest in tourism developments in Peakland?

Following the astonishing discovery last year of the world's largest dinosaur graveyard – hundreds of skeletons unearthed in near-perfect condition – the Peakland government yesterday announced its decision to go ahead with the creation of Tyrannosaurus Park, a huge open-air dinosaur museum and leisure complex eighty kilometres from the capital city, Sommerton.

It is hoped that this attraction will draw tourists away from the troubled DinoWorld theme park in Westland and attract foreign currency.

However, despite the enthusiasm of both national and foreign investors, the eventual success of the venture very much depends on the ability of the government to revitalise its transport network which, like much else in Peakland, has suffered from years of under-investment and neglect. Fear of its neighbours, travel restrictions and, until recently, a limitation on private car ownership had left the country with poorly-maintained roads and an inadequate rail and telecommunications network.

Despite this heritage, Prime Minister and leader of the Republican Movement, Richard Hardcastle is convinced that the find represents an opportunity for the country to become a major player in the tourist industry. At a press conference last night, Hardcastle declared, "Until recently, Peakland was one of the most isolated countries in the world, with an unconvertible currency and few political, trade or transport links to the outside world. Now the moment has come to create the wealth and prosperity that will take our country into the twenty-first century."

It is true that the situation has begun to change. Hotel projects on the unspoilt western coast already represent the largest single source of foreign investment, accounting for an estimated $275 million. And Arab-world investors are building a second business hotel in the heart of Sommerton.

Much will depend on the government's capacity to finance the transport infrastructure that is lacking. Already overtures have been made to the International Investment Fund and the Central Bank for Reconstruction and Development.

14 Work in groups.

You are members of a think tank for the Peakland Tourist Board. Study the map of Peakland and the summaries of the various transport infrastructure projects that have been suggested. Which would you recommend to the Tourist Board?

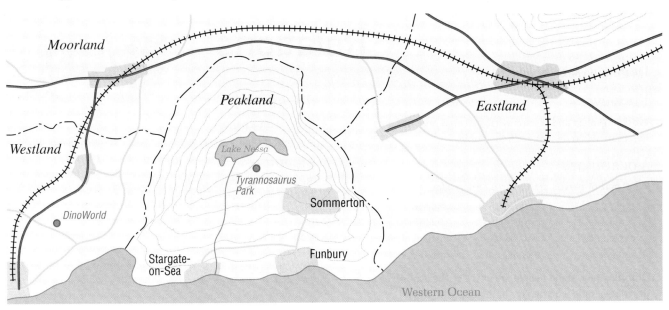

Air

Peakland airlines believe that the future lies in the development of air transport both national and international. If tourism is to develop in a big way it can only do so by attracting visitors on long-haul flights from the developed world. They therefore advocate the construction of a major airport to the west of Sommerton which would enable swift transfer to the Park.

In addition, Peakland engineers have come up with a revolutionary Super Helicopter which is able to transport fifty people at a time. A network of helipads around the country close to resort developments is, in their opinion, bound to be a success.

Rail

The SNCF (the French national railways) has tendered for the construction of a high-speed train network linking Sommerton with the capitals of other countries.

They point to the success of the *tren alta velocidad* in Spain and the *train à grande vitesse* in France. They propose to adapt the rolling stock to the varying needs of passengers, for example, family compartments and on-train activities such as hi-fi music, video entertainment, telecommunications services and catering arrangements to suit international tastes.

The SNCF points out that tourists visiting Tyrannosaurus Park are unlikely to come by car. The chances are they will be more interested in a short all-inclusive break with rapid through trains taking them door-to-door.

Road

McKenzie and White, the British construction company, has put in a bid to build a motorway network which would link key towns and cities with border countries.

They argue that road transport accounts for 77 per cent of all world international arrivals. It is flexible as the driver can control every aspect of the journey: the speed, the duration, the route taken and the destination.

In addition, Peakland roads are uncongested and would provide great scenic variety.

McKenzie and White are sceptical of the value of a rail network, feeling that, in all probability, it would damage the environment and be unsuited to the terrain of the country.

Sea

The Peakland ferry operators and the naval shipyard at Stargate-on-Sea are anxious to see a substantial development in cruise holidays. They point to the potential of Lake Nessa as an attraction with its spectacular shoreline and the tales of fantastic monsters that may have lain in the hidden depths of the lake. They also highlight the potential popularity of longer cruises from Funbury on the Western Ocean.

They remain sceptical about the future of Tyrannosaurus Park and doubt very much whether it would be as successful as claimed. Last year, DinoWorld, despite government intervention, made record losses and saw its share prices plummet from $77 to $13.

Customer
Relations

Dealing with complaints

Preview

1 Work in groups and discuss what personal qualities are necessary when dealing with the public.

Vocabulary

2 What sort of person are you? You are no doubt:

tidy	organised	efficient
sympathetic	professional	polite
experienced	responsible	patient
capable	friendly	motivated

Unfortunately, some people are not. Use these prefixes to describe people who behave in the opposite way:

un-	im-	ir-	in-	dis-

3 What prefix is used to form the opposite of all these verbs?

behave	interpret	direct	hear	calculate
interpret	manage	quote	treat	understand

Reading 1

4 Work with a partner.
Student A read the text below. Student B turn to page 112.

STUDENT A

Read this case study about an unfortunate incident in a travel agency and answer the questions below.

A number of years ago I was working in a retail travel agency, where one of the employees, a young woman of sixteen, was coming to the end of her first week at work. She was well dressed and well groomed, made good eye contact with those who entered the agency, and looked in every way a pleasant trainee travel agent.

At this time, she was not expected to sell travel products, but had been instructed to carry out a few simple administration tasks and to sit with the assistant manager to observe how the customers were dealt with, and how the paperwork was processed. At this early stage in her career she was not expected to deal with a customer herself.

On one particular afternoon, a regular customer came in to pay a balance. He was a valued customer who would book several fairly expensive tours in the course of a year. He was a very pleasant man who was quite friendly, but who liked to feel special, in that he was always treated well and received the best service from staff. He talked with the assistant manager for some time, and then asked a few questions of the new travel assistant – how she liked the job and how she was getting on. He then turned his attention back to the assistant manager and started to write a cheque for his holiday balance. "What is the date today?" he asked. "It's the thirteenth," replied the assistant manager. "Oh, Friday the thirteenth," he said. "Unlucky for some!" "Yes," said the new trainee. "You never know, your cheque might bounce!"

a Who was involved?
b Were the travel agency staff experienced?
c What kind of mistake did the staff make?
d How do you think the customer felt?
e How would you describe the staff and their behaviour?

Tell your partner what happened.
What lessons can be learnt from the two situations?

Listening

5 You will hear Melanie Flowers talking about a flight she made from London to Dallas. Decide if these statements are true or false. Correct any false statements.

a They were late checking in.

b The airline staff tried to hide from the passengers.

c The couple were given preferential treatment because of their children.

d They were content to be able to go to Houston.

e The hotel in Houston turned out to be much better than they'd expected.

f In San Francisco the airline staff were extremely rude.

g Melanie has learnt to be firm without being rude.

Have you heard any stories about unfortunate travelling incidents? Tell your partner how they were dealt with.

Speechwork

Contrastive stress

6 We often place the stress on a particular word in order to compare or contrast it with another word. For example, on the tape you heard:

The plane would leave in two hours and, instead of flying direct to **Dallas**, would take us to **Houston**.

Listen to Melanie again and find other examples of contrastive stress.

7 Read these sentences aloud. Which words are stressed?

a Did you want to travel by charter flight or scheduled?

b It wasn't so much the lack of comfort as the level of noise in the hotel.

c You can't go on a visitor's passport. You need a full British passport.

d She said she wanted a room at the front of the hotel not at the back.

e The flight wasn't delayed – it didn't even exist.

f Was it you who booked the holiday or your wife?

g I wanted to know where they were travelling from not where they were travelling to.

Listen and check your answers.

Language Focus

Infinitive (*to*) or gerund (*-ing*)?

1 **Look at these examples:**

> I **wish to claim** compensation.
> (NOT *I wish claiming compensation.)

> I **suggest writing** to the manager.
> (NOT *I suggest to write to the manager.)

Put the following verbs into two groups: those that are followed by an infinitive and those followed by the gerund.

admit	afford	anticipate	arrange	avoid
choose	claim	consider	decide	delay
demand	deny	expect	fail	hope
involve	justify	manage	mind	miss
offer	plan	postpone	promise	recommend
refuse	risk	save	suggest	undertake

2 **Some verbs can take both the infinitive and the gerund but with a change of meaning.**

Can you explain how the meaning of the verb changes in each of these pairs?

1 a They **stopped** to take extra passengers on board.
  b They **stopped** taking extra passengers on board.

2 a You must **remember** to write to them.
  b You must **remember** writing to them.

3 a I'll **try** to phone her when the meeting finishes.
  b I'll **try** phoning her when the meeting finishes.

4 a If you want any compensation it will **mean** taking them to court.
  b Sorry, I didn't **mean** to take your seat.

5 a He **went on** complaining about his holiday for at least half an hour.
  b After describing the terrible journey he **went on** to complain about the state of the accommodation.

Practice

Rewrite the following sentences without changing their meaning. Use a second verb in the infinitive or the gerund each time.

For example:

> She hasn't got enough money to travel first class.
> She **can't afford to travel** first class.

> If you don't pay the invoice soon there may be a 10 per cent penalty charge.
> If you **delay paying** the invoice there may be a 10 per cent penalty charge.

a I think it would be a good idea to write to the tour operator.
  I suggest …

b Would it be inconvenient for you to wait a little longer?
  Would you mind …

c OK, yes, I made a mistake about the time but not the date.
  I admit …

d I'll do my best to have an answer within a week.
  I promise …

e If I were you, I would make a strongly-worded complaint.
  I recommend …

f The guide said she certainly did not turn up late.
  The guide denied …

g It would require us to make a change in the schedule.
  It would mean …

Reading 2
Handling a complaint

8 **In the Listening section on page 63 you heard how an airline treated a customer who had a complaint. Think about situations when you have complained and answer these questions.**

a How did the person you spoke to react to your comments?
b What action was taken to solve your problem?
c How satisfied were you with the result?

9 **Read the article on the right and decide if these statements are true or false.**
Correct any false statements.

a A dissatisfied customer who makes a complaint will usually fly again with British Airways.
b About one sixth of BA's satisfied customers defect to other airlines.
c Both satisfied and dissatisfied customers will fly with BA again in about the same proportions.
d BA gives money to customers if they complain.
e Customers are anxious to find out who was responsible for things going wrong.
f It is not a good idea to admit to being in the wrong.

Speaking 1

10 **Work with a partner.**

Take turns to make/deal with a complaint in four different situations. Student A read the text below. Student B turn to page 112.

STUDENT A
Situation 1 You have just checked into a hotel and you have noticed that there are no towels in the bathroom. You go down to reception.

Situation 2 You are the manager of a hotel and feeling pleased with yourself because you have a 100 per cent occupancy rate for this week. A customer has just asked to speak to you.

Situation 3 You arrived at the resort yesterday on a fifteen-day package but the courier failed to turn up in the morning. You are angry because you feel you have lost half a day you had paid for.

Situation 4 You work in a travel agency. A customer has just come through the door and is looking angry.

When it pays to complain

A dissatisfied customer who complains is just as likely to remain loyal as a completely satisfied customer. This surprising state of affairs has been observed by British Airways, which has turned the handling of complaints into something of a science.

Charles Weiser, BA's head of customer relations, calculates that about 13 per cent of customers who are completely satisfied with BA's service may not fly with the airline again. "Perhaps they changed jobs, found a frequent flyer programme which better suited their needs, or maybe they felt it was time for a change of airline," he says, writing in the July issue of *Consumer Policy Review*, the journal published by the UK's Consumers' Association.

Half of all customers who experience problems but do not complain, do not intend to use the airline again. This contrasts with the customers who are dissatisfied but do complain – just 13 per cent of this group will defect, the identical rate of defection as the "satisfied" group, says Weiser.

Clearly, it pays to encourage customers to complain, and to encourage complaints departments to turn themselves from "blame" to "customer retention" departments, he says. Weiser's guide to satisfying complaints includes the following points:
• Apologise and "own" the problem. Customers do not care whose fault it was – they want someone to say sorry and champion their cause.
• Do it quickly – customer satisfaction with the handling of a complaint dips after five days.
• Assure customers the problem is being fixed. Complaints departments need to know their company inside out and work with front-line departments.
• Do it by phone. Many departments are frightened of the emotion customers often show when things go wrong, but customers appreciate a personal apology and reassurance the problem will be solved.

(from **THE FINANCIAL TIMES**)

Language for handling complaints
Introducing your complaint
I'm not one to make a fuss, but …
I don't want to complain, but …
I'm sorry, but I really feel I have to make a complaint about …

Handling a complaint
I'm sorry to hear that.
Let me take the full particulars.
I fully understand.
I'll do my best to sort it out.

Language Tip

Writing

Letters of apology

11 Do you agree or disagree with the following statements?

a You should thank the person for having made the complaint.
b You should avoid making an apology unless it is requested.
c You should never say anything was your fault.
d You should never blame a member of staff who works in the same organisation as yourself.
e You should always explain the cause of the problem.
f You should say that the error was exceptional.
g You should say what action is being/has been taken.
h You should make some sort of special offer as compensation.

12 You are the General Manager of a catering firm which has been subcontracted to provide food, drinks and table service to a famous museum. You have recently received this letter of complaint.

Before you read the letter, think of some of the reasons someone might have for wanting to complain about the catering. Then read the letter, see if your predictions were right and answer these questions.

a What is your reaction to the letter?
b How do you explain the poor services she accuses you of?
c What would you do?

13 You want to apologise to Ms Shapur and have made some notes. Expand them into a letter of apology.

> THANK YOU + SORRY
> UNTYPICAL
> MAIN REASONS - SHORTAGE OF STAFF
> (SICKNESS & HOLIDAYS)
> VERY BUSY PERIOD
> ACTION TAKEN (SPECIFY WHAT)
> ENCLOSE VOUCHER (FREE MEAL & WINE)
> HOPE FOR IMPROVEMENT

14 "Send" your letter to a partner. Is he/she satisfied with your response?

---

7 July

Dear Sir,

I am writing to complain about the appalling standard of service I received yesterday at the Heritage Museum Coffee Shop.

On entering the self-service restaurant at three o'clock my friend and I found a very long queue. We had to reject two trays before finding a clean one. Once at the counter we found most of the food had gone except for three, tired man-handled open sandwiches and the odd cake. There was no one to serve us – a girl rushed up only when a man started to help himself to soup. The girl obviously had no training; she knew neither what the soup was made of nor whether there were any more sandwiches available. (Ten minutes later she appeared with a big cardboard box and threw some sandwich packets on the counter.)

The two girls at the drinks counter were also slow and sloppy. I had a ten-minute wait for a coffee half spilled across my tray and there was a further wait for the one cash till in operation.

I was disgusted to find the cutlery covered with dried blobs of food and grease. The table we occupied was dirty, and finally the soup I bought was greasy, heavy and over-spiced. I regret to say that I was sick in the museum toilets shortly afterwards.

None of this is an exaggeration. I cannot believe that such atrocious service could exist in a world-famous institution. I was embarrassed and furious not only for myself but on behalf of all the visitors who come to this otherwise beautiful country.

I am a regular visitor and, as an employee in the travel industry, in a position to recommend that visitors boycott this restaurant unless I receive a letter indicating what measures you intend to take to improve the level of service.

Yours faithfully,

Mira Shapur

Letter-writing Tip

Letters of apology: useful expressions

I was sorry to hear that …

Please accept my sincere apologies for …

I have thoroughly investigated your complaint …

I apologise for the inconvenience.

… due to circumstances beyond our control.

I will personally make sure …

I can assure you this will not happen again.

Speaking 2

A feedback questionnaire

15 You recently went on a Skyways holiday and you weren't very satisfied about some aspects of it.
Use the questionnaire below to help you think about what could have gone wrong with your holiday.
Then work with a partner and take turns to phone the Skyways representative (your partner) to complain.

The Skyways rep should:
- try to establish the exact nature of your complaint
- say what action will now be taken
- write a letter outlining what has been agreed.

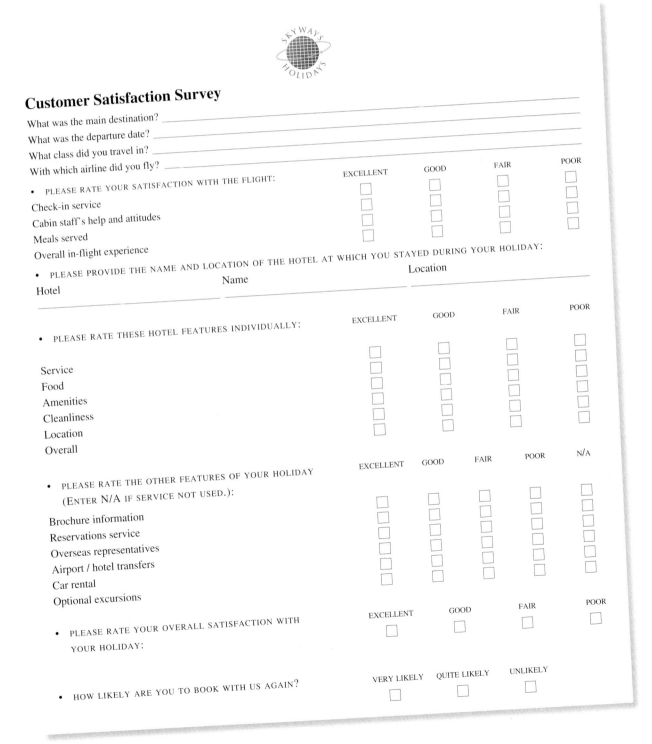

Customer Satisfaction Survey

What was the main destination? _____

What was the departure date? _____

What class did you travel in? _____

With which airline did you fly? _____

	EXCELLENT	GOOD	FAIR	POOR
• PLEASE RATE YOUR SATISFACTION WITH THE FLIGHT:	☐	☐	☐	☐
Check-in service	☐	☐	☐	☐
Cabin staff's help and attitudes	☐	☐	☐	☐
Meals served	☐	☐	☐	☐
Overall in-flight experience	☐			

• PLEASE PROVIDE THE NAME AND LOCATION OF THE HOTEL AT WHICH YOU STAYED DURING YOUR HOLIDAY:

Name   Location

Hotel

	EXCELLENT	GOOD	FAIR	POOR
• PLEASE RATE THESE HOTEL FEATURES INDIVIDUALLY:	☐	☐	☐	☐
Service	☐	☐	☐	☐
Food	☐	☐	☐	☐
Amenities	☐	☐	☐	☐
Cleanliness	☐	☐	☐	☐
Location	☐	☐	☐	
Overall				

	EXCELLENT	GOOD	FAIR	POOR	N/A
• PLEASE RATE THE OTHER FEATURES OF YOUR HOLIDAY (ENTER N/A IF SERVICE NOT USED.):	☐	☐	☐	☐	☐
Brochure information	☐	☐	☐	☐	☐
Reservations service	☐	☐	☐	☐	☐
Overseas representatives	☐	☐	☐	☐	☐
Airport / hotel transfers	☐	☐	☐	☐	☐
Car rental	☐	☐	☐	☐	☐
Optional excursions					

	EXCELLENT	GOOD	FAIR	POOR
• PLEASE RATE YOUR OVERALL SATISFACTION WITH YOUR HOLIDAY:	☐	☐	☐	☐

	VERY LIKELY	QUITE LIKELY	UNLIKELY
• HOW LIKELY ARE YOU TO BOOK WITH US AGAIN?	☐	☐	☐

Scenario 2
Handling a Complaint

Dealing with correspondence about an unsatisfactory holiday

1 Mr and Mrs Austin recently went to Turkey on a holiday organised by a company called Cheapside Tours, whose Customer Relations Manager is Mr Massey.

Unfortunately, they felt they had to complain about their holiday to the local representatives and to Mr Massey. Here is a record of their correspondence.

Read it and arrange the letters, memos and faxes in chronological order.

A

CLARKE, MURDOCH & WHITNEY
Solicitors
CHANCERY LANE

Mr G. Massey
Manager
Customer Relations Dept
Cheapside Tours
345 Hall Lane
London WC2 1ET

Dear Sirs,

Breach of contract claim

We are acting on behalf of Mr and Mrs J. Austin who have instructed us to seek recovery for losses sustained through your failure to apply the terms and conditions relating to the purchase of a holiday advertised in your brochure CHEAPSIDE TOURS LTD in accordance with the requirements of the legislation in force.

The extent of our client's loss is set out in the schedule below and we will be pleased to have your proposals for an amiable settlement within a week.

Yours faithfully,

C. W. Whitney

Details of loss

Expenses	
Telephone calls	£47
Facsimile transmissions	£34
Additional food costs at the Hamada	£190
Room upgrade charge at the Scimitar	£235
Total	**£506**

B

Hotel Scimitar
Bodrum
Tel: + 90 024 87394857
Fax: + 90 024 87394858

To: Customer Relations Dept., Cheapside Tours
Fax no.: 44 932 880552
From: J. Austin, of 75, Silver Birch Lane, Newton, Essex, CM34 9AD
Fax no.: 90 024 87394858

Date:

Dear Sir/Madam

Booking Reference No. 690202/S93

We arrived last night at the Hotel Scimitar, having booked a villa room.

The villa room accommodation was basic, the floor was uncarpeted and dirty. Worse, water was dripping through a green stain on the bathroom ceiling and the bathroom stank.

After much discussion with the staff (consisting entirely, it seems, of trainees) we persuaded them on deposit of a cash sum to allow us to move into a sea-view room in the building. This room is simple but barely adequate.

However, it can never justify the description in your brochure of 'luxury accommodation'. The air conditioning is broken (the temperature is 40°C) and the television does not work. The room is noisy with continuous music from the disco at night and the swimming pool by day.

We have tried many times today to contact your local representatives but to no avail.

We are treating this matter very seriously and require you to move us to another hotel that matches the statements in your brochure and to do so today.

Would you please telephone us on receipt of this fax.

J. Austin

C

Facsimile cover sheet
To: Mary D., Mr Massey's secretary
Company: Cheapside Tours
Fax: 44 932 880552

From: J. Austin
Company: 75, Silver Birch Lane, Newton,
Essex CM34 9AD

Date
pages including this cover page : 1

Dear Mr Massey

Further to our two faxes sent to you from Turkey at the
beginning of August we note that you have not had the
courtesy to contact us in any way. As you know this is a
breach of the tour operator's code of conduct and we are
referring it to ABTA and our solicitor.

Yours sincerely

J. Austin

D

CHEAPSIDE**TOURS**

MEMO

To: Mr Massey, Manager Customer Relations
From: Pamela Watson, Area Manager, Turkey
Re: Mr and Mrs Austin
Date:

Helena Leary has passed on a request to deal with the
case of Mr and Mrs Austin who have been making life
difficult for us.

After having been moved to the Hamada they now find
the catering inadequate. I've spoken to Patrice
Visseyre, the food and beverage manager, who has done
his best to cater for their strict vegetarian habits.
They are complaining that they have had to pay an
extra $8 on the à la carte menu but this is normal
practice.

They have instructed their bank not to honour the
cheque which was made out when they transferred to
the Hamada.

They are now threatening legal action. In my opinion
they do not have a leg to stand on. It is true that
the air conditioning was not functioning but this was
rectified shortly after their arrival and we have
done everything we can to meet them halfway.

E

Hotel Hamada, Bodrum, Turkey
Fax: 90 024 8647382

Facsimile cover sheet
To: Mr Massey
Company: Cheapside Tours
Fax: 44 932 880552
From: J. Austin of 75, Silver Birch Lane, Newton, Essex CM34 9AD
at present at: Hotel Hamada, Bodrum, Turkey
Fax: 90 024 8647382

Date
pages including this cover page: 1

Dear Mr Massey

*Your local representatives and so-called customer relations department
are either incompetent or unconcerned.*

*Ms Leary could not be bothered to inspect the Scimitar Hotel despite its
being only a five-minute walk from her offices. Nor would she supervise
our transfer to the Hotel Hamada.*

*Given this behaviour we were not surprised that your senior management
failed to telephone as promised by your secretary*

*The Hamada is marginally better than The Scimitar but the standard of
service is poor. It is certainly not 'a superbly appointed hotel, the perfect
choice for discerning guests who seek deluxe comfort in a tranquil setting'
as described so misleadingly in your brochure.*

*I am about to fax my bank to stop the cheque which I was required to
make out to cover the more expensive rates at The Hamada*

*We have no intention of letting this matter drop until we have received
full compensation for a ruined holiday in circumstances which at best are
negligent and at worst fraudulent.*

Yours sincerely

J. Austin

F

CHEAPSIDE**TOURS**

MEMO

To: Mr Massey, Manager Customer Relations
From: Helena Leary, Tour Representative, Bodrum
Re: Mr and Mrs Austin
Date:

I have recently spoken with two irate clients who feel
that the Hotel Scimitar is substandard. I have not been
able to deal with the matter myself due to pressure of
work but they were given a sea-view room after making
their initial complaint and have now been moved to the
Hamada.

They have mentioned noise levels but this is the first
time we've received any complaints. The vast majority
of guests seem to enjoy the nightlife when on holiday.
As the Hamada is more expensive I asked them to make a
payment of 50% of the excess rate.

I've informed Pamela Watson, the Area Manager.

2 **Who are the following?**
   CLARKE, MURDOCH & WHITNEY
   Pamela Watson
   Patrice Visseyre
   Helena Leary

**What are Mr and Mrs Austin complaining about? To what
extent do you think they are justified?**

3 **You are the Managing Director of Cheapside Tours and
anxious to maintain your reputation but, at the same time,
you have confidence in your staff. On the basis of the above
correspondence, decide what to do next and then write to
the couple to tell them your decision.**

11

Hotel
Facilities

Describing hotel facilities
Making and answering enquiries
Setting rates

Preview

1 **Work in groups and discuss these questions.**

a What do you expect from a good hotel?

b Which of these do you consider the most important?

- price   - facilities   - service   - location

Reading 1

2 **Work with a partner. You are going to read about the organisation of two hotels, as described by their respective managing directors. Student A read the opinions of Tommaso Zanzotto, Chairman and Chief Executive of Hilton International on the right.**

Student B read the views of Richard Williams, General Manager of Sandy Lane, Barbados, on pages 112–113.

STUDENT A

When you have finished reading your text, ask your partner questions to find out about:

- the good features of Richard Williams's hotel.
- the staff.
- the room-pricing policy.
- his favourite stay at a hotel.
- what he dislikes at a hotel.
- what he would like to see happen in the industry.

Answer your partner's questions about Tommaso Zanzotto.

Speaking 1

3 **Discuss these questions with your partner.**

a Where would you prefer to stay – at Sandy Lane or at one of the Hilton hotels?

b What are your best and worst experiences at a hotel?

TOMMASO ZANZOTTO TALKS ABOUT HILTON INTERNATIONAL...

HIS HOTELS: What is absolutely essential is the core – a well-equipped room with all the facilities expected by the customer. That must be perfect. Then what I expect of a hotel is the circle around this room such as meeting facilities, banquet facilities, bar and relaxation areas which form the first circle around the core. What I expect after that is the ambience, the quality of service and what I call the intangibles. The customer goes from the outside ring into the core because he expects the core to be there. I do not think people start with the core. They start at the intangible and the advantage of Hilton is it does have an intangible element around the core.

STAFF: I think the most important thing for staff is attitude. Attitude assumes you have the right tools behind you. For instance, there must be the right check-in system at reception and room service must have the right back-up. So to me, attitude is the first ingredient but not the only ingredient. I started my career in a travel agency in Milan when I was seventeen. When you go into the agency you like the staff to ask how you are even if they have already done that 150 times that day because it is a unique experience to you. It is a tough job. I recognise it is not easy. The human touch – particularly in the hotel business, that is one place computers will never take over.

RATES: Pricing must be a local strategy in terms of what the hotel is. I am against discounting just for the sake of keeping the customer. There is a price for a product and the customer must pay that in order for the quality of service to be maintained. I do not believe in giving customers an impression which is different from reality. For instance mileage programmes – somebody is paying for these somewhere and that is not fair on the customer, but competition makes you do things which you do not think are necessarily right. If I find a solution I will do that. I do not have a magic solution. But I believe that all the zillions of miles which exist all over the world, somebody will pay for them and it will not be the shareholders. The cost will pass through the system through different pricing mechanisms. There is no such thing as a free lunch. Loyalty must be built on true relations rather than the fact you have a few miles from me.

FAVOURITE STAY AT A HOTEL: Club Med in Bali. A combination of events contributed to this recent stay. One was the fact I was changing jobs so I was very relaxed and it was also my twenty-fifth wedding anniversary. What was particularly good was the ambience and the pleasant attitude of the staff.

DISLIKES: The hotels I do not like are the ones with no personality or flavour or anything local. If there are some hotels in our group which need to move along that route we will do something.

ONE WISH FOR THE INDUSTRY: That government and society realise travel and tourism is such a powerful economic driver. It has to be taken into serious planning consideration in all countries.

(from Travel Trade Gazette)

Vocabulary 1

4 Which of these facilities would you expect to find in a deluxe hotel such as Sandy Lane or a Hilton International hotel? Are there any you would add to the list? Is this the same for all countries?

trouser press	lift	air conditioning	floodlit tennis court
cable television in room	free garage space	DD telephone	sauna + jacuzzi
ornamental gardens	beauty salon	outdoor or indoor swimming pool	gift shop
live entertainment	tea/coffee-making facilities	disco	newspapers

Language Focus

Adjectives and word order

Adjectives can be divided into a number of categories:

1 Qualitative: these adjectives identify a quality that someone or something possesses.

   an **attractive** area   a **famous** hotel   a **cheap** room   a **pleasant** stay

2 Classifying: these adjectives are used to classify the following noun.

   a **double** bed   a **separate** entrance   a **single** room   a **bridal** suite

   Classifying adjectives are not normally gradable. We cannot say *a very separate entrance* or *a very double bed*. An entrance is separate or it isn't; a bed is a double or it isn't.

3 The normal order for adjectives is:

   1 qualitative   **2** classifying:

   a **small furnished** apartment   a **special free** offer   a **pleasant rural** setting   a **large double** bed

4 If there are more than two adjectives in a phrase, the order is:

   1 subjective opinion   **2** qualifier (size, age, shape)   **3** colour   **4** origin   **5** what the noun is made of   **6** what kind? what for?   **7** head noun

   an **exquisite Ming-dynasty porcelain** vase   a **beautiful antique china rose** bowl

5 Compound adjectives are formed by joining two (or more) words with a hyphen:

   an **up-market** hotel   **self-contained** accommodation   **well-appointed** rooms   an **out-of-the-way** resort

Practice

1 **Put the words on the right into the correct order to complete these sentences.**

a We ate some — local excellent dishes seafood

b One of the guests stole our — pot antique silver pepper

c In the lobby there was a — writing Flemish heavy sixteenth-century desk

d The cook's looking for a — bowl large red salad plastic

e Each room has a — red-and-white enormous superb bedside Japanese lamp

2 **Match the words below to make compound adjectives. Then add a suitable noun of your choice to each one.**

air-	season
well-	minute
self-	time
audio-	new
cut-	equipped
last-	built
part-	contained
off-	visual
purpose-	conditioned
brand-	price

3 **Write a short description to be included with each of these photographs in a leaflet publicising the hotel.**

Speechwork

Stress in compound adjectives

⊙ 5 **If an adjective is used before a noun, the stress is usually placed on the first part of the adjective. Listen.**

a '**self**-contained flat   a '**well**-furnished lounge

But if the compound adjective is used after a verb the stress is on the second part:

The flat is self-con'**tained**.   The lounge is well-'**furnished**.

⊙ **Where is the stress? Say these phrases and sentences. Then listen to the tape to check your pronunciation.**

a much-travelled woman
a newly-wed couple
a world-famous brand
an easy-going atmosphere
The bar is air-conditioned.
The conference room is well-equipped.
The furniture is old-fashioned.
The food is all home-made.

Reading 2

6 **Mrs Adams is planning to visit Berlin for the first time and has written to four hotels asking for information. Here are the four replies. Which hotel do you think she is most likely to be interested in? Give reasons for your choice.**

Lindenbaum Hotel
Tel: 27 82 21 93
Fax: 27 82 21 16

Mrs Adams
44 Cyprus Street
London
N1 1ST
England

Sehr geehrter Mrs Adams,

ich freue mich, daß Sie unserem Haus so großes Interesse entgegenbringen.

Gern übersende ich Ihnen unseren Hausprospekt.

In der Hoffnung, Sie bald als Gast in unserem Haus begrüßen zu können.

Mit freundlichen Grüßen,

Angela Badel

Angela Badel
Reservierung/Verkauf

G
G R A N D · H O T E L
B E R L I N

Mrs Adams
44 Cyprus Street
London N1 1ST

Dear Mrs Adams

We refer to your kind letter and thank you for your interest in the GRAND HOTEL BERLIN.

Enclosed please find the requested brochures about the GRAND HOTEL BERLIN.

Please do not hesitate to contact me personally if you have any questions or if we can be of any assistance to you and we would be very pleased to welcome you at the GRAND HOTEL BERLIN in the near future.

Yours sincerely,
GRAND HOTEL BERLIN
Maria Wamneboldt
Reservations Manager

Great Eastern Hotel
Toleranz Str., Berlin

Dear Mrs Adams,

Thank you for your letter and your interest in our hotel. Enclosed we send you our hotel brochure with the price list.

The Great Eastern Hotel is situated at the famous corner Toleranz str. and Unter den Linden near the Brandenburg Gate. We have 320 rooms, one restaurant, 3 meeting rooms for up to 45 persons and a lobby bar.

For your reservation you can call our booking office by phone 6743 281 or you can send a fax to the number 6743 678.

We would be happy to welcome you in our hotel.

Kind regards

Morgan Althaus
Sales Manager

Goethe Hotel

Goethestraße 197, 10713 Berlin Telefon: (030) 87 97 19 Fax: (030) 87 01 36

Mrs Adams
44 Cyprus Street
London N1 1ST

Dear Mrs Adams,

Thank you very much for your interest shown in our hotel. Enclosed you will find our hotel brochure and the room rates.

Inside the brochure you will find the restaurant, but this is closed. We do only serve drinks at the reception.

You asked about other facilities such as fitness room, conference halls and restaurants. But we have none of these. We are a middle-class hotel with 40 rooms and we don't need these facilities.
I am not sure, if you really mean our hotel? Because your questions look like you expected a first-class hotel.

Anyway, I hope to welcome you in our hotel,

with kindest regards,

Clara Karge

Writing 1

Describing hotel facilities

7 **You are the Reservations Manager at a large hotel in Berlin. You have received this letter. Reply using the information below.**

School of European Studies
5, Rolfe Street
London
WC2 12X

2 December

Dear Sir/Madam,

The above-named institute is intending to hold its forthcoming conference on "The Secret Services of Post-Communist Europe" in Berlin from 27–30 November next year.

I would be grateful if you would let me know whether your hotel would be in a position to host this conference and provide me with a description of your facilities and tariffs for approximately 100 delegates.

I look forward to hearing from you.

David Murray
Conference Coordinator

FREDERICK HOTEL

BANQUETING AND CONFERENCE FACILITIES

- 17 air-conditioned conference rooms (1400 m²)
- simultaneous translating/interpreters' booths
- 7 seminar rooms
- single and double rooms and suites, all air-conditioned with en-suite facilities
- views over gardens/historic sites
- swimming pool, sauna
- 4 restaurants and bars
- multi-storey car park (240 cars)
- price for 100 delegates (full board + conference facilities) x 3 days = DM72,000

Listening

Pricing policies

8 **Work with a partner. At the beginning of this unit you read about two different hotels – Sandy Lane and Hilton International. Discuss these questions.**

a Which do you think was the most expensive to stay in? Why?

b Do you think the price of a night's stay is the same for all guests?

c How does a hotelier fix the price of a room?

9 **Listen to Nick Patterson, who is Manager of a large London hotel, and answer these questions.**

Section 1

a Nick mentions four different rates. What are they?

b Under what circumstances will he allow a discount?

Section 2

c How do British tour operators do business with overseas hoteliers?

Section 3

d If overseas tour operators cannot fill their allocation, what does Nick do?

Section 4

e What do British hoteliers do to maximise sales?

Vocabulary 2

10 At one point Nick uses the expression *supply and demand*. There are many fixed expressions in English which have two words linked by *and*. The order is fixed – we cannot say **demand and supply*. Read these sentences and decide if the two words linked by *and* are in the right order.

a It takes us three months to negotiate all the **terms and conditions**.

b The contract hadn't been signed so it was **void and null**.

c The carpet in the lobby has to be of good quality to stand up to the **wear and tear** of continual use.

d A whisky, please, and a **tonic and gin**.

e There are no **hard and fast** rules on discounts; they vary according to the type of clientele.

f It's not easy to open a hotel; there are so many **regulations and rules** to comply with.

g I don't have all the **figures and facts** with me but we had an occupancy rate of about 90 per cent last June.

h I have to get out of the city from time to time to get some **quiet and peace**.

i We have to keep the reception area looking **neat and tidy** or it creates a bad impression.

j Every year the auditors check our **profit and loss** accounts.

k Our reservation system isn't scientific. It works more by **error and trial** than by anything else.

Speaking 2
Negotiating a group booking

11 **Work with a partner. Student A looks after the business travel arrangements for an international organisation called ATLAS. Student B works in Reservations at the Maple Leaf Hotel. Student A read the text below. Student B turn to page 113.**

STUDENT A
Read the information below and then phone your partner at the Maple Leaf Hotel to make a booking. Make notes.

You want to book rooms at a hotel for a company meeting and trade presentation involving a number of executives from your overseas subsidiaries.

You have recently seen an advertisement for the Maple Leaf Hotel and are going to phone the hotel to make a booking, provided that the facilities meet your expectations.

In all, seven members of staff will need accommodation for five nights from Monday 10 July. Three of them will be accompanied by their wives.

You will also need to book a conference room, including lunch, for twenty-five people for 11 and 12 July.

Your basic requirements are that:

- the hotel should be close to public transport.
- the rooms should be of a good standard with private bath and so on.
- the staff should be able to relax in pleasant surroundings.
- the business facilities should be spacious, professional and hi-tech.

The trade presentation on 11–12 July is very important as ATLAS wishes to show potential customers from all over the world that the company is successful and knows how to treat clients well.

You want to know the price of rooms, group discounts, the charge for the hire of business meeting facilities and the method of payment.

The names of the personnel to stay at the hotel are:

Ms Patty Bowen, Mrs Maria Spada, Mr Philippe Trudeau, Mr Stig Johansson, Mr and Mrs Böhler, Mr and Mrs Akira Nakamura, and Mr and Mrs Andreas Gryllakis (not arriving until 8 p.m.)

Your address is 101 Wellington Street, Ottawa, Canada, K 1P5TI Tel: (613) 238 5347

Your credit card number is: 4531 7862 9413. It expires in April next year.

Writing 2
STUDENT A
12 **Write a memo to your boss outlining what has been agreed with the Maple Leaf Hotel.**

STUDENT B
Write a letter confirming the details of the reservation made by ATLAS.

Selecting
Locations

1
2
3
4

Assessing new ventures

Promoting hotels

Preview

1 Work in groups and discuss this question. What factors does a hotel chain take into account when choosing a site?

Listening 1

2 Kelly Cooper, who works for Austral Tours, is at the World Travel Market in London and has stopped in front of a stand promoting holidays on the island of Tioman, Malaysia.

Listen and take notes on accommodation and facilities. Use these headings:

> LOCATION
>
> TRANSPORT
>
> ACCOMMODATION
>
> FACILITIES
>
> ACTIVITIES

Writing 1

3 After speaking to Ludwig Szeiler, Kelly Cooper sent a fax to the CEO of Austral Tours. Here is the beginning of the fax. Complete it.

FAX

To: Cathy Mays, CEO, Austral Tours

From: Kelly Cooper

Date: 07/11

No. of pages: 1

Subject: Tioman

Dear Cathy,

This morning I met LS from Tioman Promotions. What they have to offer is as follows:

1:

Speechwork

Pronunciation of the letter *i*

4 Work with a partner. Decide if the letter *i* in each of the words below is
pronounced / ɑɪ / as in *time*, / ɪ / as in *rich* or / ɪː / as in *key*.

Put the words in the box into three columns (according to the pronunciation of the underlined sounds).
Then listen and and check your answers.

island	massive	tropical	site
franchise	mini-bar	village	prestigious
prestige	biplane	Sri Lanka	sign
private	heritage	signature	skiing

5 Read this postcard aloud paying particular attention to the pronunciation of the underlined words.
Then listen and check your pronunciation.

Dear Joyce,

I'm staying here on a <u>minute</u> tropical island off the coast of Fiji. It takes ninety <u>minutes</u> to get here by biplane and is very remote. People come here for a few days to <u>wind</u> down and relax. It's very hot with very little <u>wind</u> or shade to keep the temperature down. I spend most of my time sunbathing.

Every evening they organise <u>live</u> entertainment at the hotel which is very enjoyable but I wouldn't want to <u>live</u> here permanently – there's nothing to do!

See you soon. Love, Monica.

Ms Joyce Lee
91, Bognor Road
Newtown
NT31 5SX
England

Speaking 1

London: an established tourist destination.

6 Work with a partner and discuss these questions.

a Why do tourists want to go there?
b Where do they want to stay?
c What factors do they take into consideration when booking a hotel?

7 Work with a partner. Look at these possible locations for a new hotel. Discuss the advantages and drawbacks of each site. Decide where you would build your new hotel in London. Then compare your ideas with others in the class.

Established central tourist area

New commercial development site

Suburban residential area

77

Reading

8 **Read this article about Docklands and answer these questions.**

a What are Docklands' strengths and weaknesses for tourism development?
b Would you advise a hotel chain to invest there? Why? Why not?

Docklands turns its attention to tourism growth

DOCKLANDS, DOMINATED BY the mighty Canary Wharf Tower, is the new face of tourist London. The London Docklands Development Corporation, through which the Government's grant funding for the area is channelled, is "extremely supportive of the London Tourist Board initiative" according to Sunny Crouch, its director of marketing and public affairs.

"London is the premier gateway for visitors to this country – and we must make sure we do not lose that position," she says. "Docklands are not top of the attractions visitors want to see, although English Tourist Board surveys show us to be about number six on the list of priorities, a place visitors go to on their second or third trip. What we have to offer is a new face.

"It is fascinating to show groups of overseas visitors, who have come to London with images of ancient heritage and tradition, something that is new and modern. Canary Wharf, for example, is probably the world's largest urban development project.

"Docklands is an area that is dynamic, changing, as it has been over the centuries – and there is plenty for visitors to see. There is Tower Bridge, of course, with its walkways, and the new Design Museum on the south side of the river. On the north side, there is the Tower itself and St Katherine's dock.

Our communications links with the rest of London are also good. We have the Docklands Light Railway, buses and, by next May, we will have completed our road programme when the Limehouse link is opened. And the DLR, which now operates between Mondays and Fridays, will open at weekends from next summer."

Airport success

And, of course, there is London City Airport, which now has connections with seven major European cities. Its popularity is rapidly improving – but we British seem slow to realise its advantages, as some 80 per cent of its passengers are inbound.

Previous criticisms that there are few shops, restaurants, pubs, wine bars and so on in the area are no longer valid, adds Sunny Crouch. "Terence Conran now has three restaurants on the south side and in the newer area there are at least twenty-one shops, plus half a dozen pubs, restaurants and other places to eat and drink," she says.

Furthermore, there are now more than 1,000 hotel beds in Docklands, including the new Scandic Crown and International Britannia hotels. "Docklands attracts over 500,000 visitors a year," says Sunny, "and, in tourism terms, we have an important cluster of attractions. We are finding that visitors pick up the Docklands Light Railway at Tower Bridge, take it right through Docklands to Island Gardens, then walk through the foot tunnel to Greenwich and take the boat back. That way, they get the best possible view of what we have."

The Docklands development story is far from over. "We have plenty of land in the Royal Docks area and we are looking for tourism/leisure type developments for this because we feel that in the present climate we don't need any more office schemes," says Sunny. "For example, there is the London Dome project, to create a magnificent covered bowl for sporting events, conferences, concerts and so on."

Finance, it seems, is almost in place for this ambitious project – with the backers undeterred by the failure of Olympia & York, developers of Canary Wharf, where, until it was temporarily closed following an attempt to plant a bomb there, the tower (the tallest office building in Europe) was attracting 5,000–6,000 visitors every weekend, eager to see the unique panorama of London from its top floor.

(from **Tourism Enterprise**)

Vocabulary

Formal and informal language

9 In formal situations *big* and *a lot of* are often replaced with other expressions.

Choose words or phrases from the box to replace *a lot*.
For example: a lot of facilities = extensive facilities

substantial	a great deal of
a wide range of	widespread

a a lot of land
b a lot of growth
c a lot of tourist attractions
d a lot of interest in the area

Choose words from the box to replace *big*.
For example: a big bill = a hefty bill

radical	handsome
spacious	large-scale

a a big refurbishment
b a big change in market demand
c a big lobby
d a big profit

10 Work with a partner. Which sentence in each pair would be more suitable for a formal report?

1 a You asked us to look into the idea of putting some money into a hotel development.
  b We were asked to investigate the potential of investment in a hotel development.

2 a Our preferred location is in close proximity to Canary Wharf.
  b The place we liked best is very near to Canary Wharf.

3 a Lots of hotels in the suburbs had to let people pay very low rates to get enough business.
  b A substantial number of hotels in the suburbs were obliged to charge exceptionally low rates in order to achieve an adequate volume of business.

4 a Demand has begun to improve and increased revenues are beginning to compensate for the lean years.
  b Demand has begun to pick up and bigger revenues are beginning to make up for the bad years.

5 a This section is about the way we worked out the figures, the things we took into account and the way we went about getting an approximate idea of profits in the future.
  b This section details the calculations, assumptions and methodology which form the basis of estimated profit projections.

Listening 2

11 The Far East Investment Group is looking at hotel investment opportunities in London and has recently commissioned a survey from Lewis, Dupont & Kruger, a firm of independent consultants for leisure and tourism. Read the letter that accompanied their findings.

LEWIS, DUPONT & KRUGER

Forth Street, London

9 September

Dear Mr Pang,

We are pleased to present our study of the proposed FEIG hotel development in London.

As is customary with market studies of this nature, our findings are only valid for a limited period of time. The estimates are based on the most reliable evidence available at the present time.

We look forward to presenting the study to you as arranged at the Hilton Hotel on 27 September.

Yours sincerely,

Milton West

Listen to the representatives of Lewis, Dupont & Kruger presenting their findings to a meeting of the FEIG and take notes based on these headings.

REASONS FOR CHOICE OF AREA

COMMUNICATIONS

PROPOSED SITE

TYPE OF HOTEL

FACILITIES

DEMAND PROFILE

Language Focus

Conjunctions

Read this extract from the study you commissioned concerning the construction of a new hotel in London. Note the way in which the underlined words are used.

> In recent years, hotel development in central London has been hindered by restrictive planning policies, lack of suitable sites and high building costs. <u>However</u>, there is now growing pressure from hotel chains wishing to develop, and several sites have been earmarked for consideration. <u>Furthermore</u>, the British Tourist Authority has forecast a shortfall in hotel accommodation by the end of the decade.
>
> <u>As a result</u>, it is our opinion that the time is ripe to invest in the construction of a 300 bedroom, three-star hotel to meet what is forecast to be a significant shortage of bed space.

1 **Which of the underlined words:**

   – introduces a contrasting point of view?
   – shows a consequence?
   – introduces a new piece of information?

2 **Group the following words into the above three categories.**

despite this	what is more	hence	in addition
on the other hand	yet	nevertheless	consequently
besides	thus	therefore	

Practice

Complete the extract using the following words:

secondly	first of all	as a result	yet
while	furthermore	on the contrary	however

WHAT ENABLES BUDGET hotels to offer extremely competitive tariffs and (a) ...... make a profit? There are a number of answers. (b) ...... , such hotels, all built on the same pre-fabricated model, can make savings in construction costs. (c) ...... , by keeping staffing to a minimum, using automatic check-in and providing self-service breakfasts, there are economies to be made in operating costs. (d) ...... , budget hotels have standardised furniture and fittings which can be bought cheaply in bulk.

(e) ...... , the market for budget hotels includes many people with limited financial means such as low-income families, retired people or touring sports teams.

The growth of budget hotels has been the cause of some concern in the hotel market as many traditional one- and two-star establishments are unable to compete. (f) ...... , this concern is probably unjustified. Budget hotels have an educational role to play in introducing new sections of the population to the habit of staying in a hotel. And (g) ...... budget hotels will continue to influence the market place and possibly take some custom away, quality hotels offering a high level of service should not see these "competitors" as a threat but, (h) ...... , as an opportunity to expand the hotel-staying public.

Speaking 2

12 Work in two groups: A and B. Group A works for The New London Hotels chain. Group B works for Peake, Jones and O'Hara Investment Bank.
The New London Hotels chain would like Peake, Jones and O'Hara Investment Bank to invest in their projected new hotel in Docklands. Both sides have agreed to meet to discuss the viability of the project.
Look at the papers for the meeting and answer these questions.

a When do Peake, Jones and O'Hara forecast that the restaurant will be making a profit on lunches and dinners?

b Why does the hotel need such a large restaurant?
c How soon will they achieve a satisfactory room occupancy rate?
d How do they hope to pay for the maintenance of the health club facilities?

13 Discuss the arguments you will present in the meeting.

14 Meet with the other group to discuss the project.

Projected New Hotel in Docklands

- No. Rooms: 100 – all doubles with en-suite facilities.
- Restaurant covers: 250 – to allow for special functions.
- Residents' Bar.
- Fitness and health club: free to residents and open to non-residents.
- 2 private rooms for functions.

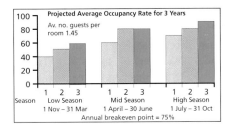

Restaurant

The plan is to develop special events banqueting facilities for local corporate entertaining. The restaurant will be partitioned and partially closed when not in full use.

Health Club Revenue

To cover costs of equipping, maintaining and staffing, the health club membership will be offered to the local community and businesses.
ESTIMATED ANNUAL COST OF STAFFING AND MAINTENANCE OF EQUIPMENT = £150,000 PER YEAR.

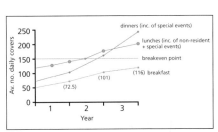

Membership	Fee	Projected no. yr. 1	Projected no. yr. 2	Projected no. yr. 3
single	£350	100	125	150
joint	£600	80	85	100
family	£700	30	40	50
corporate	£1,500	20	22	25
	(per 6 members)			
Total revenue		**£134,000**	**£155,750**	**£185,000**

Writing 2

15 Write a report outlining the decisions made at the meeting between The New London Hotels chain and Peake, Jones and O'Hara.

Follow-up

16 Work in groups. You work for a consultancy group. You have been asked to look at the hotel investment opportunities in your area.

Discuss:

a where it would be feasible to build a new hotel.
b what kind of establishment it would be (category, number of rooms, etc.).
c its facilities.
d your anticipated clientele.
e how you would advertise and promote the hotel.

17 Write a full-page advertisement about your hotel for the local paper.
Write and tape a radio commercial for your hotel.
Write a report on new hotel investment opportunities in the area.

13

Things
to Do

Giving tourist advice on local attractions and events

Preview

1 Look at the map and discuss what visitors to Portsmouth, New Hampshire in the USA can do there.

Reading

2 Read these extracts from a guide to leisure pursuits in New Hampshire and choose one of the places in the box to complete each gap in the text. Note that there are more places listed than gaps.

1 Wentworth by the Sea Golf Club	**4** Seabrook Greyhound Park	**7** Water Country	**10** Portsmouth Maritime Museum
2 Salmon Falls Stoneware	**5** Whale Excursion	**8** Harbor Cruise	
3 Science and Nature Center	**6** Strawbery Banke	**9** The Children's Museum	

THE CHARMS OF NEW HAMPSHIRE

Think of New Hampshire's Seacoast and what comes to mind? Welcoming sandy beaches and warm summer sun? Or do you picture ocean cruises, deep-sea fishing, family attractions, and an abundance of tax-free shopping? Perhaps it's a fair, a jazz festival, or charming antique shops, fascinating museums, historic homes and a glimpse into this country's beginnings? Picture all these things, and you've only begun to picture what the Seacoast region offers.

Portsmouth was the first colonial capital of New Hampshire and its appeal is immediate. The city includes a ten-acre outdoor museum known as (a) ...... , so-called because in 1630 the first English settlers chose the site for their new plantation, naming it for the abundance of wild fruits they found along the shores of the Piscataqua river.

The spirit of early American crafts is captured in (b) ...... , produced at the Engine House in Oak Street. Each pot is hand-made and individually decorated with a traditional or country design.

(c) ...... is open all year round and is packed with amusing hands-on activities for toddlers, including the Yellow Submarine, the Computer Center and Arts Area.

Why not bring your family to (d) ...... for the best family outing ever? Over twenty acres of rides and exciting attractions plus the huge wave pool, adventure river and octopus blue lagoon.

And if you want to combine blues and greens come to the (e) .... This is more than a succession of fairways, putting greens and bunkers, it's a whole series of scenic experiences. The fifteen holes present a unique challenge and an absolutely fantastic view of the spectacular coastline.

Follow Route 1 to Odiorne State Park, the site of the (f) ...... at Seabrook Station. The more than thirty exhibits and displays focus on the Seacoast environment, and how Seabrook Station safely uses uranium to produce electricity. Take a fascinating imaginary journey nearly 260 feet below sea level to Seabrook's cooling tunnels. View local marine life in the touchpool and ocean aquariums – all this, and much more besides.

No visit would be complete without a cruise on the open waters of the Atlantic Ocean. Sail out on a (g) ...... and get a close-up of the ocean's great giants with expert commentary by an experienced naturalist.

Speaking

Holding a public meeting

15 **You are going to take the roles of different people and debate the pros and cons of a major tourism development in an area of outstanding natural beauty. First read this newspaper article and summarise the main points.**

Ambitious plans to spend £100 million on a disused slate mine in north Wales are causing a fierce dispute among locals. The tourist development is planned to centre around a "Quarrytorium", with a guided visit down the mine, and a residential complex built around eight dry ski slopes, a tropical park with illuminated waterfalls, lasers and holograms and an adventure playground.

The disused mine is at Glyn Rhonwy, less than a mile from the village of Llanberis, on the northern edge of the Snowdonia National Park. It has been bought by Arfon Borough Council which has asked several developers to come up with plans for redeveloping the site.

Recently a company called LeisureLand has come up with a project which, besides the Quarrytorium, also includes hotels, conference facilities, shops and restaurants, and a sports centre. Most controversially, there are also plans for thirty "holiday farmsteads", each consisting of about twenty farm-type cottages.

However, since the proposals were published in the local paper, people have started objecting. A protest group has been formed, headed by Gwynneth Jones, whose house overlooks Glyn Rhonwy. Although careful to give credit to the council for buying and trying to develop the area, the protest group feels that the scheme would overwhelm the village and be alien to the natural beauty of the region.

The matter is now being debated at an extraordinary council meeting in the town hall at which a decision on the future of Arfon must be reached. Representatives of all the viewpoints of the local community have been invited.

(extract from *Holiday Which?*)

16 **Work in groups. Your teacher will choose a chairperson who should use the role card below. Your teacher will tell the other people where to find their role cards. You can add your own ideas to the suggestions on the cards.**

Meetings Tip

The chairperson

Your role is to make the meeting go smoothly and let everyone have their say. Discussions can get heated and you may have to remind participants to remain polite, not interrupt, not monopolise the discussions and so on.
Here is some useful language:

Opening a meeting	*Right, shall we get started?* *The first thing we have to discuss / decide is …*		*Could we stick to the subject under discussion, please?* *Perhaps we could come back to that later.* *I'll come to you in a minute.*
Inviting comments	*I'd like to give the floor to …* *Mrs Olsen, is there anything you would like to say?* *Does anyone have any further comments?* *Would you like to come in here?*	**Closing the meeting**	*Are there any further points anyone wishes to make?* *To sum up, …* *Are we all agreed on this?* *Shall we take a vote? All those in favour? All those against?* *I declare this meeting closed.*
Directing the proceedings	*We seem to be losing sight of the main issues.* *With respect, I don't think that is entirely relevant.*		

Writing

17 **Write a 250-word press release reporting what was said at the public meeting about the development at Glyn Rhonwy.**

9

Transport

Analysing transport requirements
Planning a transport network

Preview

1 **Work in groups and list some different means of transport. Then discuss these questions.**

a What are the advantages and disadvantages of each one for long or short distances?

b How do you prefer to travel? Why?

1   2

3   4

Listening 1

2 **Susan recently went to the USA for three weeks. The map below shows the places she stayed in or visited during her trip. Listen to Susan making the final arrangements for her trip and answer these questions.**

a What is an open-jaw ticket?

b Why doesn't Susan want to use the Greyhound bus?

c Why doesn't she want accommodation booked in Las Vegas or LA?

3 **Listen again and follow Susan's route. Write the dates, times and means of transport.**

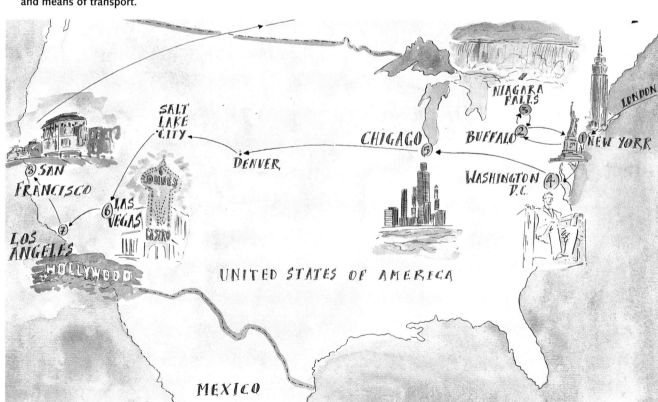

Vocabulary

Words ending in *-ing*

3 **Can you name these activities?**

4 **In the passage we read of *exciting* attractions and *amusing* hands-on activities. Work with a partner and think of some more activities that you could describe as *relaxing, entertaining* and *exhilarating*.**

5 **We play *tennis* on a *tennis court* and *swim* in a *swimming pool*. Match the activities in A with the places in B.**

A			
golf	bowling	football	volleyball
ski	athletics	camp	ice-skating

B			
pitch	course	site	court
rink	track	alley	run

Writing

6 **Design a leaflet for a local Tourist Information Centre, describing in English what visitors can do in your area.**

Include information on:

- museums, art galleries, monuments.
- places of outstanding natural beauty or historic interest.
- local amenities and facilities.
- eating out.

Speechwork

Pausing and stress

7 Listen to the message which has been recorded on an answerphone. Is it easy to understand? If not, why not?

8 Now read the text of the message and place a line (/) where you think the speaker should pause, and underline any words you think should be stressed. Then listen to the second version of the message and check your answers.

> *Thank you for calling SELEKTABED hotel reservations. Unfortunately, no one is available to take your booking at the moment. Please note that office hours are 9 to 5.30 on Mondays to Fridays except for Wednesdays, when we are open from 9.45 to 5.30. On Saturdays we are open from 9 o'clock in the morning to 1 o'clock in the afternoon.*
>
> *If you would like information on hotel availability outside office hours you can call 0891 211 402.*
>
> *For reservations, please call us during office hours. Thank you.*

Speaking 1

Answerphone messages

9 Work in groups. You work for a local Tourist Information Centre. Your manager has asked you to write an answerphone message for when the office is closed. He wants the message to include general information about the office and he would also like it to be possible to contact out-of-hours callers the next day.

Decide what information you will need to give and how you will ask for the information you require.

Write the message and practise reading it aloud.

Then record it on to a cassette and play it to the rest of the group.

As you listen to each message, make notes on the information and instructions given.

Which message (other than your own!) did you find the clearest?

Language Focus

Conditionals

1 Which of the following conditional sentences:

a describe a usual state of affairs?

b talk about the past?

c make an offer?

d make a recommendation?

e make a polite request?

f describe situations which are unlikely or impossible?

1 If you buy a travel pass, you pay less.

2 If you go to the Natural History Museum, you'll be able to see the special exhibition on dinosaurs.

3 If I were you, I'd avoid the crowded areas.

4 If you had a car, you'd be able to visit the safari park.

5 If you'd been here last week, you'd have seen the carnival.

6 If I'd known you wanted a theatre ticket, I'd have got one for you.

7 If you have enough time, you might want to visit the old mill.

8 If you're looking for something really exciting, you should go to the Museum of Horror and Torture.

9 Should you have any problems, please let me know.

10 If you'd like me to phone them, I'll do it for you now.

11 If you'll just fill in this registration form, I'll make the booking for you.

12 If you want a cheaper place to stay, you'd be better off at the Dolphin Hotel.

13 If you hadn't made the booking in advance, you'd be without a bed for the night.

14 If they hadn't created the proper infrastructure beforehand, they wouldn't be hosting the next Olympics.

15 I'd be grateful if you could fill in this questionnaire before you go.

2 To sum up, which of these is correct?

a In English there are strict rules for the sequence of tenses in conditional clauses and main clauses.

b The sequence of tenses is not absolutely fixed and depends on what you want to say.

c You can use any sequence of tenses in conditional clauses and main clauses.

3 Other ways of making a conditional:

Unless you've other plans, you could visit the Museum of Science and Technology.

You shouldn't get lost **providing / provided (that)** you take a map.

Anyone is allowed into the casino **on condition that** they are over 18.

Practice

1 Fill in the gaps appropriately. There may be more than one possible answer.

a If you ...... modern art, you ......

b The old Town Hall ...... if it ...... a tourist attraction.

c If you need any more advice, ...

d If you ...... just come this way, ... you where it is on the map.

e If I ...... you, I ...... travelling in the rush hour.

f I ...... told them that you ...... coming if I ...... beforehand.

g You won't be able to hire a car ...... you've got a valid driving licence.

h There shouldn't be any difficulty getting to Göteborg ...... that the ferries run to schedule.

i If you ...... now, you ...... there before the match starts but I doubt if you ...... time.

j If you ...... stay for more than a week, you ...... better off getting a cheap rail pass.

2 If you were the mayor of your town/city what would you do to make the place more attractive to tourists? If it did become more attractive, how would you control the extra influx of people?

Listing

10 **Listen to a conversation recorded in a tourist office in Venice and find the places that are mentioned on the map.**
Listen again and write down the intensifier which is used before each adjective.

INTENSIFIER	ADJECTIVE	REFERS TO
......	cheap	
......	popular	} places to stay
......	convenient	
......	expensive	} transport
......	reasonable	
......	amazing	building
......	useful	guidebook
......	good	} restaurant
......	recommended	
......	out-of-this-world	meal

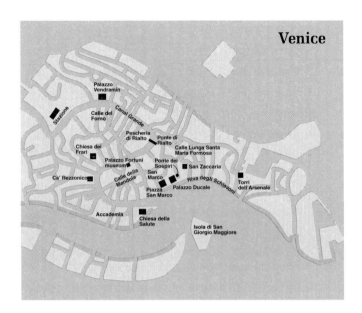

Venice

Speaking 2

11 There is a Portsmouth in New Hampshire, USA, and there is a Portsmouth in Hampshire, England.
Work with a partner. Take turns to be tourist information clerks. Student A look at the map and information below. Student B turn to page 114.

STUDENT A
You are a tourist information clerk in Portsmouth, Hampshire, England. Read the information here and on page 87. Note the important points. Then answer your partner's questions. He/She is a tourist.

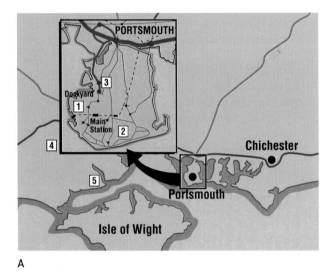

A

PORTSMOUTH'S HISTORIC DOCKYARD

Traditional home of the Royal Navy, now a world-famous centre of maritime heritage

THE MARY ROSE
Henry VIII's Mary Rose sank in 1545 and was raised in 1982
– over 20,000 artifacts recovered
– hull restored and conserved

HMS VICTORY
Lord Nelson's flagship at Trafalgar, 1805

THE ROYAL NAVY MUSEUM
tells the story of the sailors who manned these ships through the centuries
– the latest aircraft carriers and missile-carrying destroyers
– The Museum is open daily, except Christmas Day

Closing times: 5.30p.m. March to October; 6.45p.m. July to August

B

Natural History Museum

- Wildlife dioramas and geology of the Portsmouth area
- Full-size reconstruction of Iguanadon (our local dinosaur)
- Riverbank scene and audio-visual displays
- From May to September see British and European butterflies flying free

Opening times:

April – October 10.00 a.m. – 5.30 p.m.
November – March 10.00 am – 4.30 p.m.
Closed 24 – 26 December

C

CHARLES DICKENS'S BIRTHPLACE

Charles Dickens was born here on February 7th 1812 to John and Elizabeth Dickens. House is furnished in the Regency style (1812) See:

- the parlour where friends were received.
- the dining room .
- the bedroom where Charles was born.

A small exhibition room shows a range of prints illustrating the works of Charles Dickens and memorabilia: a signed cheque, a lock of his hair, waistcoat buttons and the couch on which Charles Dickens died.

Opening times

April – October   10.00 a.m. – 5.30 p.m.

E

BUCKLER'S HARD

18th century village on banks of Beaulieu River
Recreated as 18th Century ship-building village
Tells the story of village life
Nelson's ships built here

River cruises
Picnic areas and riverside walks

Transport: buses from Portsmouth bus station

D

THE NEW FOREST

Relax in the forest
See the wild ponies and deer roaming free. The medieval hunting preserve of the Normans.

Transport
local buses from Portsmouth bus station to Lymington.

12 Change roles. Student B is a tourist information clerk in Portsmouth, New Hampshire, USA. You are Professor Pitruezzella from Bologna University in Italy. You and your colleagues have just attended a conference on pollution and the environment.

Ask the tourist information clerk if he/she can suggest things to do during the day and evening in Portsmouth. You have heard that you can see whales off the New Hampshire coast. Ask if this is right. Ask if there are any good restaurants in Portsmouth, or must you make do with hamburgers till you return home to Italy?

14

Marketing
the Past

Guiding tourists round places of interest

Preview

1 **Work in groups and discuss these questions.**

a When was the last time you visited a museum?
b What did you see there?
c How was it displayed?
d Why do we keep things from the past in museums?
e What is the role of a museum in society today?

Reading

2 **Read the introduction from a guidebook to the Louvre and answer these questions.**

a What was the aim of the Grand Louvre project?
b What was it that made people very angry?
c What is the purpose of a museum according to Ieoh Ming Pei?

Listening 1

3 **Listen to an expert talking about the reconstruction of the Neues Museum in Berlin and answer these questions.**

a What are the choices facing the architects?
b How do the expert's views on the design of a museum compare with Ieoh Ming Pei's?

4 **Work with a partner and discuss how a museum can encourage visitors to keep coming back.**
Then listen to how the Neues museum intends to deal with tourists, and answer these questions.

a How does the museum intend to encourage the frequent visitor?
b What will the museum do for the groups on a thirty-minute tour?
c How will this help the individual visitor?
d According to the speaker what are the disadvantages of museums like the Louvre?

Do you agree with the speaker's view of how a museum should be organised? Give your reasons.

1

2

3

4

THE DECISION TO turn the Louvre into the world's biggest museum was taken in the autumn of 1981 by the French President François Mitterand. The challenge lay in turning what was basically a nineteenth-century museum into a modern museum equipped to handle the ever-growing number of people anxious to see and learn about art. The first step towards creating the "Grand Louvre" was to create more exhibition space and to reorganise the collections, so that works could be presented both more logically and with more breathing space.

According to a number of experts the most rational way to reorganise the museum was to use the area beneath the courtyard itself. This is just what the Chinese-American architect Ieoh Ming Pei decided to do. He had been named to design the project, without a prior competition being held, in March 1983.

The architect's choice of a 71-foot high pyramid, albeit of glass, created a storm of protest. Many believed that this historic site was already "saturated with architectural styles…" I.M. Pei, who designed the striking East Wing at Washington's National Gallery, wanted to turn this historic palace into a modern museum. He wanted to create something alive and welcoming, without destroying the history of the place, and he succeeded in persuading the authorities to accept his transparent, reflecting prism.

Pei is convinced that museums should play a role in educating the public. With competition from so many other forms of recreation, museums must be inviting enough for people to want to spend the day there. At the same time, the architecture must be functional, so that museums can offer better service in more comfortable surroundings. Even more important, museums should not only be a place to see art but, thanks to their architectural quality, should be an aesthetic experience in themselves.

Speaking 1

5 **Work in groups. Describe your favourite museum or art gallery to your group.
Tell them:**

- why you like it.
- how the museum attracts tourists.
- how it copes with large groups.
- how the architecture of the building is used to show off the exhibits.

Have you ever taken a party round a museum?

Vocabulary

6 **The guides at both the Louvre and the Neues Museum need specialised vocabulary to describe the artefacts.
Work with a partner. Put these words into logical sets. Give each set a title. Add three words to each set.
Which sets would a guide describing Ancient Egyptian exhibits in the Neues Museum need?
Which sets would a guide in the National Gallery in London need?**

arch	necklace	shield	portico	facade
gateway	statue	fresco	sculpture	gable
coronet	spire	mural	frieze	spear
mosaic	gold	bronze	etching	pistol
helmet	chariot	cloak	watercolour	carriage
copper	carving	bracelet	column	cart

Writing 1

Descriptions of artefacts

7 **Use the words in the box to complete this short description of the bust of Nefertiti.**

The bust of Nefertiti. Look at the faultless symmetrical face enhanced
by make-up tastefully applied to brows, …

ribbon	necklace	neck	lips	flowered
flat-topped	eyelids	crown	graceful	

8 Write a short description of one of these paintings.

a

Christina of Denmark by Hans
Holbein the younger (1538)

b

Lord John and Lord Renard
Stuart by Anthony van Dyke
(1638)

c

Madame Moites Sier by Ingres
(1856)

Learning Tip

When you visit a museum,
monument or art gallery it is a
good idea to pick up leaflets,
or buy the guidebook, in your
own language *and* in English.
Then you can study the
quality of the translations
(they're not always good!)
and also learn any new
vocabulary.

Listening 2

9 Listen to the guide describing artefacts in the Pergamon Museum. As you listen find Athena, Zeus and Alkyoneus in the pictures on the right.

10 Are these statements true or false?

a Pergamon was the name of a man.
b The monument was built 2,000 years ago.
c It has always been considered one of the wonders of the world.
d The Gauls had come from Europe.

e The frieze symbolises two victories.
f The giant attacks Athena with his serpent.
g The whole frieze is painted in bright colours.
h You will see another monument.

Speechwork

Pausing and stress

11 Why is the speaker in Listening 2 easy to understand?
Listen to another part of his tour and mark where he pauses.
Mark a short pause with / and a long pause with //.

Now let's follow the path of the gods and walk up the processional avenue towards the great gate ahead of you. Remember as you go past these lions that they were not only admired as wild, noble and free animals but that they also represented Ishtar, the goddess of love, the sky and of war. Ishtar was the patron goddess of the Babylonian army and the enormous gateway that you are now approaching was named after her. The original decorations revealed much about the religious life of the city. They showed that the avenue was decorated during the time of King Nebuchadnezzar II to mark the path of the annual new year procession when statues of the gods were carried with great ceremony from a special banqueting house to the main temple of the city. As the gods were believed actually to inhabit these statues it was very important that whatever they saw should please them and so a great deal of effort was lavished on this processional avenue.

12 In spoken English we use stress, pauses and pitch to draw our listeners' attention to what we want them to know.
New information is announced by a change in the pitch of the voice.
Look at the following excerpt from a guided tour of Prague.
Mark your own pauses / and draw an arrow above the words where the pitch rises.
Practise saying the excerpt aloud. If possible, record yourself. Then compare your voice patterns with those on the tape.

Good morning, ladies and gentlemen. My name is Teresa. Let me first welcome you to our tour of The Kralovska Cesta or Royal Mile. This was the route which was taken by the Kings and Queens of Bohemia on their way to coronations or to festivities in Prague. We start here at the Powder Tower. It is so-called because it served as a gunpowder store in the seventeenth and eighteenth centuries. It had originally been a tower of the town palace during the Middle Ages. Let us now walk through the archway and into Celetna street which is named after the bread – the calt – that was baked here in the Middle Ages. On your left is the old mint where Bohemian groschen and ducats were coined. A little further down we will pass two houses that are part of Charles University, which was founded in 1348. It's the oldest university in Central Europe. Now we enter the Old Town Square. In the centre you can see a memorial to Jan Huss, the reformer.

Language Focus

Relative clauses

1 **Relative clauses are used to make two separate statements into one sentence. For example:**

This is what the Chinese architect, Ieoh Ming Peh, decided to do. Ieoh Ming Pei had been named to design the project in March 1983.

This is what the Chinese architect, Ieoh Ming Peh, **who** had been named to design the project in March 1983, decided to do.

2 Relative clauses can be *defining* or *non-defining*.

The pyramids **which/that** were built up until the Third Dynasty were made of mud and brick, not stone. ("which/that were built up until the Third Dynasty" identifies and defines a particular kind of pyramid.)

The Rosetta stone, **which** was found in 1799, enabled Champollion to decipher the hieroglyphics. ("which was found in 1799" is *extra* information – it does not define the Rosetta stone. "That" is not possible in a non-defining relative clause.)

3 **Which of these is defining and which is non-defining? How do you know?**

a The Greek goddess who represented war was called Athena.

b King Charles IV, who was a Czech king and built the famous Charles Bridge in Prague, must have been a good military commander.

Practice

1 **Make sentences with these words. You will have to add extra words.**

For example:
Aphrodite/Greek goddess/represented love and beauty
Aphrodite was a Greek goddess who represented love and beauty.
Alexander the Great/born 356 BC/father/King Philip of Macedonia
Alexander the Great, whose father was King Philip of Macedonia, was born in 356 BC.

a Tower of London/11th century/built by William the Conqueror/ both prison and palace

b Statue of Liberty/American Museum of Immigration in base/seen by all visitors arriving in New York by sea

c Taj Mahal/outside Agra/built as a testimony to love

d Catacombs/early Christians buried/a maze of underground passages

e Assyrian King Nebuchadnezzar/ built the Hanging Gardens of Babylon/one of the Seven Wonders of the Ancient World

f Mozart/father a violinist at Archbishop of Salzburg's court/learnt to play the piano/three years old

2 **Work with a partner and use the notes to write a tour of Prague. Practise giving your tour and if possible, record it and listen to yourself. Begin your guided tour 'Good morning ladies and gentlemen. We're starting our tour of Prague today in the Old Town Square ...'**

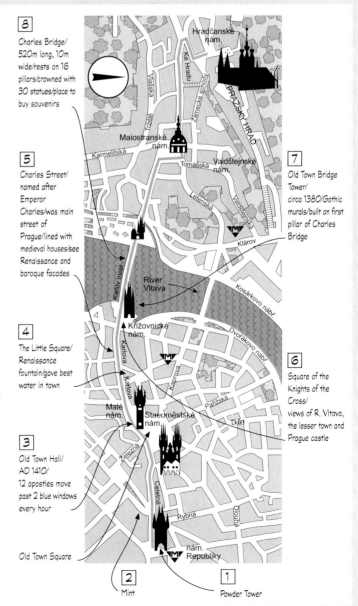

8 Charles Bridge/ 520m long, 10m wide/rests on 16 pillars/crowned with 30 statues/place to buy souvenirs

5 Charles Street/ named after Emperor Charles/was main street of Prague/lined with medieval houses/see Renaissance and baroque facades

7 Old Town Bridge Tower/ circa 1380/Gothic murals/built on first pillar of Charles Bridge

4 The Little Square/ Renaissance fountain/gave best water in town

6 Square of the Knights of the Cross/ views of R. Vltava, the lesser town and Prague castle

3 Old Town Hall/ AD 1410/ 12 apostles move past 2 blue windows every hour

Writing 2

13 You work as the local representative for Skyways Holidays in Sorrento, Italy.

Your boss has left this message on your desk.

You have the poster below on your wall. Use it as an example to design and write a similar poster.

Please design a poster to be put up in the hotel advertising Saturday's guided tour of Pompeii.
Make it as appealing as you can. Be sure you include the following information!

Leave 9 a.m. from The Royal Hotel; return 6.30 p.m.

cost 15,000 lire per person

visit: Pompeii / covered in lava in 63 AD / at foot of Mount Vesuvius / finest example of a Roman city.
Picnic Lunch (provided) in foothills of Vesuvius overlooking the bay of Sorrento.

Saturday 6th May

Join us on

A day trip to Tivoli and the gardens of Villa d'Este

Scenic drive through the Sabine Hills with panoramic views of Rome

Lunch at a small trattoria in the hills

Afternoon in the magnificent Renaissance gardens built in 1549 by Pirro Ligorio

Marvel at the cascades and fountains. Relax in the cool cypress avenues.

Depart 8 a.m. - Return 6.30 p.m.   18,000 Lire

See Viki at Reception for tickets

Speaking 2

14 Work in two groups. Group A look at the text below. Group B turn to page 115.

GROUP A

You work as tour guides at the conference centre in Graz, Austria. You have been asked to plan a two-hour walk round Graz.

Read your information. Plan your route. Prepare your talk. Give your talk to someone in Group B.

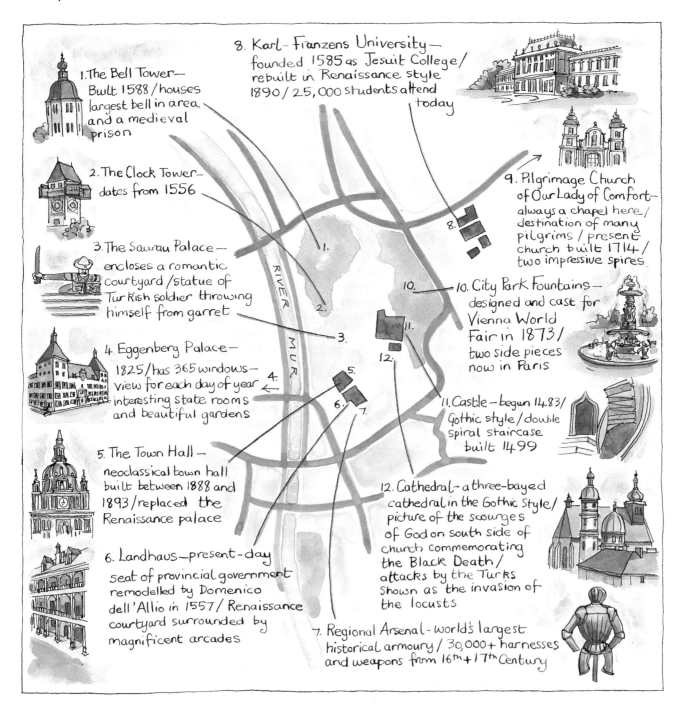

1. The Bell Tower — Built 1588 / houses largest bell in area and a medieval prison

2. The Clock Tower — dates from 1556

3. The Saurau Palace — encloses a romantic courtyard / statue of Turkish soldier throwing himself from garret

4. Eggenberg Palace — 1825 / has 365 windows — view for each day of year / interesting state rooms and beautiful gardens

5. The Town Hall — neoclassical town hall built between 1888 and 1893 / replaced the Renaissance palace

6. Landhaus — present-day seat of provincial government remodelled by Domenico dell'Allio in 1557 / Renaissance courtyard surrounded by magnificent arcades

7. Regional Arsenal — world's largest historical armoury / 30,000+ harnesses and weapons from 16th + 17th Century

8. Karl-Franzens University — founded 1585 as Jesuit College / rebuilt in Renaissance style 1890 / 25,000 students attend today

9. Pilgrimage Church of Our Lady of Comfort — always a chapel here / destination of many pilgrims / present church built 1714 / two impressive spires

10. City Park Fountains — designed and cast for Vienna World Fair in 1873 / two side pieces now in Paris

11. Castle — begun 1483 / Gothic style / double spiral staircase built 1499

12. Cathedral — a three-bayed cathedral in the Gothic Style / picture of the scourges of God on south side of church commemorating the Black Death / attacks by the Turks shown as the invasion of the locusts

Follow-up

15 Collect information about your local area and design a guided tour for a group of foreign students visiting your town. Or choose a museum you would like to visit and give a talk on one of its exhibits.

15

Business
Travel

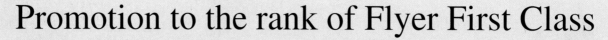

Describing and promoting business and conference venues

Preview

1 **Work with a partner and discuss these questions.**

a How are business travellers different from other travellers?
b How can an airline cater for their special needs?

Reading

2 **Read this article from the business travel section of a British newspaper and answer these questions.**

a What is it that airlines cannot "have both ways"?
b How easy is it to get an upgrade?
c Why will it "count as nought" if a traveller is wearing jeans and a T-shirt?
d How can a business travel agent help?
e How could a business person try to get on the 7 p.m. Concorde flight from London to New York?
f Why should a business traveller try to sit next to noisy children?

Promotion to the rank of Flyer First Class

HOW EASY is it to get an airline upgrade? Obviously it is happening all the time – how else would business and sometimes first class cabins be full so often? Airlines cannot have it both ways: they cannot bemoan their low yields and losses yet claim that the cabins up front are full of bona fide full-fare paying travellers.

But when the cheapest economy ticket price on the transatlantic route is between nine and ten times cheaper than for a business class ticket, many executives have no option but to fly economy and hope for an upgrade.

Some carriers are known for their stringent approach to upgrading. Most Far Eastern carriers, such as Singapore and Malaysian Airlines, are loath to upgrade unless there is no other option. UK travel agents suggest this is due to the importance of status in the Far East and the granting of it to those who have earned it, i.e., paid the fare.

On the very competitive transatlantic routes, however, it is a different story. Both US and British carriers – and certain European ones – are keen to win business, albeit not at any price, but at a cost which might encourage you to fly with them again. There is no more powerful incentive for a business traveller than the lure of an upgrade up the aircraft or the Holy Grail – an upgrade to Concorde. BA knows full well the drawing power of Concorde and does upgrade certain executives when appropriate to this speedy, if not exactly comfortable, sovereign of the skies.

But while transatlantic upgrades are sought for the comfort they provide, upgrades to business class flights are more status symbols than of real practical benefit on short-hop European flights. So what strategy should the savvy business traveller adopt? A seven-point programme could be:

1. Dress smartly – the single most important rule. You may feel it is more comfortable to travel in

trainers and tracksuit – and it is, if you are sitting in economy. But whatever else you may have going for you at the check-in it will count as nought if you are wearing jeans and a T-shirt. For men this means wearing at least a jacket and tie at the check-in. For women, a smart suit or dress is required. Once you are on the plane with your upgrade it does not matter what you wear.

2. Join a frequent-flyer programme. This is the simplest and most painless way to get an upgrade. US carriers, saddled with many millions of unclaimed mileage points, are happy to let you use some of them on an upgrade. BA always gives first upgrade priority to its silver and gold Executive Club members. These cards are only gained if you are a frequent flyer anyway and so BA recognises you deserve any upgrades going. If upgrades rather than free flights are important to you, join a scheme that is most likely to hike you up the cabins.

3. Use a business travel agent. Earlier this year Wagonlits Travel ran a special promotion with United Airlines which meant that all United flights booked through the travel agency were automatically upgraded. It is worth checking with your business travel agent to see if any similar deals are in the offing.

Booking through a big agency, moreover, should give you a better chance. Given the volume of business that the multiple travel agencies place with the airlines, then they are usually willing to give priority to their clients when space is available. Not always though, since if an upgrade was always automatic, then clients would always book the cheapest flights.

4. Shop around. With or without the help of a specialist business travel agent, there may be deals that offer effective upgrades. Airline Ticket Network (0800 727747) can often find business class flights at the same price as you would pay economy on another airline, though you may have to fly Air India or Iceland Air.

If your company will pay for first class travel but not the supplement for Concorde, try Air France Concorde instead: the fare is equivalent to BA's first class price, although you have to fly to Paris (flight included) to catch the supersonic jet.

5. Check in late. Experienced users of this system arrive just within the allowed check-in time in the hope that full economy or business class cabins might get them either into business (with someone else bumped up to first) or into first class itself. Some very experienced and determined upgraders try this with BA's 6.30 p.m. daily flight to New York from Heathrow Terminal 4 on the possibility that they may get onto the 7 p.m. Concorde flight.

6. Be confident. Those executives arriving at the check-in desk brimming with confidence will often give the aura that they should be upgraded. Unfortunately for women, this is more of a sexist male ploy to predominantly female check-in staff.

7. Keep trying. Even if you fail to be upgraded at the check-in, the savvy traveller knows that all is not lost. It helps sometimes to be seated next to noisy children in economy. Get out some work or, better still, a portable computer and look busy. Then, while people are still being seated, ask a flight attendant if you can speak to the senior steward or purser. If you are smartly dressed and look like an obvious business traveller then many flight staff will be sympathetic and move you up.

(from **THE SUNDAY TIMES**)

3   Work with a partner and discuss this question.
    What advice can you now give to a business traveller who wishes to fly in comfort without having to pay for it?

Speaking 1

4   Work with a partner. Role play this situation. Student A works as a check-in clerk for an international airline. Student B is an economy class passenger. Student B would like an upgrade to business class.

Speechwork

Sound and spelling

4 Some words have silent letters – letters which are not pronounced. For example:

business / bɪznɪs /   guarantee / gærəntɪː /

How are these words pronounced? Say them aloud. Then listen and check.

exhibition	guide	flight	receipt
vehicle	subtle	registered	debt
buoyant	half	sovereign	foreign

5 Some words are pronounced in different ways even though they are spelt the same. Look at these pairs of sentences. Where is the stress in the words in italics? How would you say them?

1 a He was *presented* with a gold watch when he retired from the company.

   b He thanked the company for the *present*.

2 a This year they have sold a *record* number of package holidays to the Seychelles.

   b The highest temperature was *recorded* yesterday in London.

3 a Please allow me to introduce my business *associate*, Mr Riley.

   b Our company does not like us to *associate* with employees from rival operators in the resort.

4 a Immigration officers *refuse* admission to anyone travelling without a passport.

   b All *refuse* must be put in the bins.

5 a The bank agreed to *transfer* £1.4m from the tour operators' New York account to their bank in Switzerland.

   b The *transfer* from the airport to the hotel will take fifty minutes.

Listen and check your pronunciation. Then practise saying the sentences.

6 How are these words pronounced?

suit	suite	
desert	dessert	
price	prize	
island	Iceland	Ireland
career	carrier	
lose	loose	

Read the words aloud. Then listen and check.

Language Focus

Possibility and certainty

1 **There are many ways of indicating how sure we feel about an event. For example, we use modals to make predictions of varying degrees of certainty. Read these sentences and match them with the descriptions 1 – 3.**

a He'll have got there by now.

b He must have got there by now.

c He should have got there by now.

d He could have got there by now.

e He might have got there by now.

f He can't have got there by now.

g He won't have got there by now.

1	a possibility
2	a certainty
3	an expectation

2 **We also use phrases to express degrees of probability and certainty. Most of these sentences contain *will* but the degree of certainty is determined by the words printed in italics. How certain do you think these statements are? Give each sentence a % score. 0% = impossible; 100% = certain. The first one has been done for you.**

a The results of the enquiry are a *foregone conclusion*. They'll refuse all planning permission. `100%`

b *There's no way* they'll agree to build a new airport so near to the city.

c *I doubt very much* whether the company will pay the supplement for Concorde.

d *In all likelihood*, you'll get an upgrade if you book through a business travel agent.

e *It's just possible* that we'll make a profit next year.

f *It's a safe bet* that they'll try to force us out of the market.

g *The chances are* that you'll be able to get a better seat provided that you're smartly dressed.

h *In all probability*, share prices will continue to rise.

i *There's a slight chance* that the project will attract more foreign investment.

j *There's a distinct possibility* that the air traffic controllers' dispute will be settled soon.

k *There's little likelihood* of their allowing us to hire extra coaches.

l They're *bound to* increase their prices next year to allow for inflation at the very least.

Practice

For each of the sentences below, write two sentences which keep the original meaning. Use the words in capitals in each sentence. The first one has been done for you.

a In all probability we'll be able to catch the 10.15 train.

    CHANObS   *The chances are we'll be able to catch the 10.15 train.*

    CHANCES   *The chances are we'll be able to catch the 10.15 train.*

    SHOULD   *We should be able to catch the 10.15 train.*

b I hardly think she'll want to hang around for a stand-by flight.

    DOUBT

    LIKELIHOOD

c I'm sure they've left by now otherwise they'd have answered the phone.

    MUST

    BOUND

d It's impossible for them to have arrived – they only left an hour ago and it takes at least two hours, if there's no traffic!

    CAN'T

    WAY

e If we're lucky, we may well be able to charter an aircraft for an early morning flight.

    POSSIBILITY

    JUST

Listening

7 You will hear Agnes Johnson talking about how they promote The Manor Hotel as a business venue and conference centre.

Decide if these statements are true or false.

a The Manor uses the services of over 500 conference agencies.

b The standard rate of commission is 8 per cent.

c The agency always takes the client to visit the hotel.

d Making company contacts is a complicated process.

e Corporate clients tend to make rapid decisions on their choice of conference venue.

f The Manor relies far more on direct sales prospecting than on printed advertising.

g The sales staff are authorised to negotiate conference rates.

h The local Shakespeare festival is popular with delegates.

Vocabulary

8 Look at this meeting room in The Manor Hotel.
Match the words in the box with the objects in the room.

flip chart	PC	screen
LAN	plug	slide projector
lectern	podium	socket
marker pens	pointer	
OHP	remote control	

Speaking 2

9 Work with a partner. Student A look at the text below. Student B turn to page 115.

STUDENT A

1 You work for Albatross Engineering plc and have been asked to find a suitable local venue for a full-day seminar. Professor Markowitz will be giving a lecture on new techniques in electrical engineering in the morning, and this will be followed by your annual general meeting in the afternoon.
You require a lecture theatre for fifty people. Ring The Manor Hotel and find out what they have to offer.

2 You work for The Manor Hotel in the venues department. You receive a phone call from Tangerine Computers of New York. On the right you have information on day and 24-hour conference rates. You will not need to pay agency commission so you can be flexible in pricing.

Day delegate rate:	£57	includes coffee, lunch, afternoon tea, cordials, conference equipment and room hire – minimum 25 people
24-hour residential rate:	£169	inclusive of mid-morning coffee, lunch, teas, cordials, room hire, conference equipment, dinner, deluxe bedroom and country house breakfast

Writing

10 You work for an international hotel and have recently received this memo from a member of the Senior Management Team. Work in groups and brainstorm your ideas, then write your response to Graham Whittaker's request.

MEMO

FROM: Graham Whittaker

TO: Marketing Dept.

DATE: 11 October

RE: Circular letter promoting business travel

As you know, last year saw increased competition from within the trade and we feel that the time is ripe to look at some fresh ideas in an attempt to capture a larger market share than we have so far been able to do.

I would be grateful if you would draft a convincing letter which can be mailed to the managing directors and business travel managers of organisations likely to be interested in offering travel as a means of motivating and rewarding their staff.

Would you please:

– include information about the kind of facilities we are able to provide

– outline a package we can market

– include itinerary, special events and attractions

– state why our area is the ideal place for them to come.

Scenario 3
Organising Excursions
Organising an excursion programme

Work with a partner. You both work as resort representatives for the same tour operator. Your teacher will tell you which one.

STUDENT A: You are the new resident Resort Representative in Lakesburgh, a thriving cosmopolitan city on the shores of Lake Aurora. This is your first job. You were appointed last night when the local rep suddenly resigned to go and work for a rival operator.

STUDENT B: You are the new Tour Representative in Lakesburgh, a thriving cosmopolitan city on the shores of Lake Aurora. You have just arrived in the resort, a few hours ahead of the tourists. This is the first time you have been there.

Today is the first day of the holiday season.

Your company specialises in short city-break holidays, two- and three-night stays. The brochure promises a full optional excursion programme with evening activities.

Your first plane-load of package tourists arrives this evening at 6 p.m. local time. They will be staying from tonight, Friday, to Monday morning on half board. Before 6 p.m. you must both find out what there is to do. You will need to know times, prices and discounts for your clients.

You will be interested in any commission you can get for yourselves, since your pay is not very good. The previous reps left you a tourist guide in the hotel which they have annotated with their comments.

1 Look at the guide together and design the itinerary.

2 You would like to be able to repeat this itinerary weekly throughout the season. Approximately how much commission will you receive if thirty people go on most of your excursions?

3 Compare your itinerary and your commission levels with other tour operator representatives.

Shopping

The area is known for its local blue crystal and distinctive ceramics.

The main shopping centre is in the Glasshouse Centre, a pedestrianised area where you can find stores of international renown. — *great shops* *No commission*

There also are many souvenir shops in and around the Old Town Square. — *friendly, helpful owners*

✻**THE ARCADE**
for all your pottery and glassware!
Gifts for all the family.
54, Old Town Square

— *Take them in: get extra 5% com.*
— *good selection*
— *pricey*

✻**CRYSTAL'S GLASS FACTORY**
Guided tours
Free entrance
Factory shop
28, The Esplanade

✻ *NB: collect vouchers + GIVE to all guests.*
VOUCHERS = 5% discount on marked price for them
= 15% commission to ME

✻**THE CERAMIC GROTTO**
Come and watch your gifts spin into shape.
Open daily 10–5.
73, New Crescent

worth chatting up

THE EMPORIUM
Renowned the world over for pottery and glassware.
20, The Glasshouse Centre

go in occasionally – give reps good presents

Restaurants

THE ARPEGGIO
traditional cuisine in pleasant surroundings
table d'hôte from £10.00 per head
98, The Esplanade
tel: 876 439 8876

— *nice place, gd. food 5% com.*

THE LEMON TREE
guéridon service
à la carte from £30.00 per head
19, Circus Road
tel: 192 834 7459

20% com. but pricey for guests

HAMBURGER PALACE
American restaurant
open 11.00 a.m.–12 a.m.
10, The Esplanade
tel: 129 485 7694
Set meal: £12.50

Best hamburgers ever!! V. pop. with locals 5% com.

THE BLUE VISTAS
live band
private room for parties
42, Mount Hadrian
tel: 128 394 8576
traditional cuisine from £20 a head

eaten better school dinners! 15% com. take 1 party a week

Bars

THE CAPTAIN'S TABLE
904, The Esplanade

THE JOLLY ROGER
784, The Esplanade

TERRY AND JUNE'S CAFF
39, The Old Town Square

THE THREE FISHERMEN
8, Jetty Point

[handwritten] 15% com.
bad-tempered landlord – hates tourists

[handwritten] gd. watering hole, v. friendly 10% com.

[handwritten] gd. place to end an evening

Night Clubs, Casinos and Discos

THE COTTON CLUB
open nightly
9 p.m.–3 a.m.
£10.00 per person

[handwritten] great!!
lively
girls get in free before 10
10% com.
+ free eats & drinks

THE NEW YORKER
open Thursday–Sunday incl.
black tie
£30 a couple

[handwritten] 5% com. on reservations only

WHISKY GALORE
open nightly
10 p.m.–2 a.m.
£20 per person

[handwritten] no male gps 15% – must accompany

THE GOLDEN WHEEL CASINO
black tie optional
8 p.m.–4 a.m.

[handwritten] v. upmarket no com.!

THE SILVER SWORD CASINO
open 12 p.m.–3 a.m.

[handwritten] min. stakes £5 free £25 chips if take gps of 10+

Tours

Walking tours of old town:
visit this picturesque quarter with medieval houses and cobbled streets.

[handwritten] sturdy shoes!

Tours depart every two hours from 10.00 a.m. to 4.00 p.m.
£3.50 per person

[handwritten] 15% com. on 2 p.m. tour only

[handwritten] Take on to shops and cafés

Hourly boat trips on lake:
£2.50 per person.

[handwritten] beautiful views easy on feet 5% com.

Theatre, Concerts, Ballet

THEATRE PRESIDENT
classical plays
Box office: 8394 5783 4867

[handwritten] 2 for the price of 1 seats £10, £15, £20
boring! tourists love it £3 pp on gps of 25+ £1 pp on gps of 12-24

HADRIAN'S CASTLE
son et lumière nightly
all seats £12
Tel: 876 9212 387

PALACE THEATRE
ask for details
Tel: 876 94987 982

[handwritten] good deals from time to time

Sightseeing

IMPERIAL PALACE AUTO COLLECTION
over 200 antique, classic and special interest cars on display at this spectacular automobile collection
£5.00
53, Aurora Boulevard

[handwritten] where did they find them! 10% com.
worth every penny!

WORLD OF RECORDS MUSEUM
See the amazing videos, life-sized replicas, unique displays that will entertain the whole family for hours.
£7.50
79, Lakesburgh St.

[handwritten] v. pop. no com.!! 5% discount on gps of 15+

HERITAGE MUSEUM
County history museum with exhibits, restored historic structures and ghost towns
£10.00
435, The Mall

[handwritten] new, partially open 20% com.

NATIONAL ART MUSEUM
Houses three galleries, changing monthly with local and national artists
£5.00

[handwritten] who? 25% com.

MUSEUM OF NATURAL HISTORY
Journey through time from dinosaur age to present-day wildlife
£8.00

[handwritten] 5% if lucky v. pop. v. interesting

DISCOVERY CHILDREN'S MUSEUM
designed for hands-on, interactive, fun learning about the arts, sciences and humanities.
£6.00

[handwritten] need to book full of school parties no com.!

GOVERNOR'S PALACE
A baroque masterpiece housing 18th to 19th century watercolours
£7.50

[handwritten] stuffy!
gd. gardens/great views 15% com. gd. teahouse – great for some peace and quiet

Groupwork / Pairwork B Texts

① Types of Holiday

16 Writing (page 11)

You work for a travel agency which belongs to a group called Europa Tours. You have
received a letter from a potential customer.

This extract from your catalogue shows the kinds of things you have to offer.

Write a suitable personalised reply and send it back. If necessary, refer to the **Writing tips**
on page 11.

GRAND COACH TOUR OF FRANCE

Duration	12 days
Departure day	Monday
Return	Friday
Mar. 27	$270
Apr. 3, 10, 17, 24	$280
May 1, 8, 15, 22, 29	$290
June 5, 12, 19, 26	$300
July 3, 10, 17, 24, 31	$300
Aug. 7, 14, 21, 28	$300

Price includes 11 nights
accommodation in twin rooms
with en-suite facilities, 11
continental breakfasts and 6
dinners. $5 single supplement
per night.

No child discounts.

Touring: by modern air-
conditioned cruise-liner coach.

No overnight travel.

❷ A Career in Tourism

Reading (page 13)

6 STUDENT B

Tell your partner what recommendations "The Write Way to Find a Job" makes about:

- personal information and experience.
- layout, language and style.

Which of the fifteen points (a–o) in exercise 5 (page 13) are mentioned in the article?

The Write Way to Find a Job

ANSWERING advertisements is one way of finding a job. But there is a big gap between the number of vacancies filled and those advertised. So writing on spec. to employers can often be a good idea.

The object is to get the employer to see you – no more, because the best you can hope for from such an approach is an interview. Asking straight out for a job is fatal because it invites a yes or no response. As no one will offer a post to an unknown quantity the answer will always be negative.

There are a number of golden rules:

- Try to research the name (spelt correctly!) of a specific person to write to.
- Put yourself in the employer's shoes. Think of what you have to offer.
- Try to keep your CV brief – one page is enough; perfect prose isn't expected – note form is acceptable.
- Gear your CV to the job and organisation. No two CVs should be exactly alike.
- If you've been in work, explain your duties and how your work has evolved. Demonstrate on paper that you are a potential asset.
- List your outside interests and skills. Don't forget your language abilities. Participation in sports can show your capacity for team work.

If your covering letter is in English it should be checked by a native speaker. You should state at the beginning why you are writing and then try to keep the reader interested. You must establish that you would like an interview. Edit ruthlessly. Go over your letter as many times as necessary. Search out and get rid of all unnecessary words and sentences.

(adapted from an article by
Geoffey Golzen in **THE TIMES**)

Speaking 2 (page 17)

17 STUDENT B

Work in a group. You are recruiting employees for one of the posts described on page 15 (your teacher will tell you which one).

Write a short profile of what you expect a good applicant to be and prepare a list of questions to ask the candidates you have short-listed. Make notes under these headings:

APPEARANCE

QUALIFICATIONS

LANGUAGES

TRAVEL

ADAPTABILITY

PERSONALITY

SALARY EXPECTATIONS

18 Now work with the others in your group and interview candidates from Group A for the job. When you have seen all the candidates make your final selection.

❽ Responsible Tourism

Speaking (page 55)

A1

G. Jones

Leader of the local protest movement

Views on the proposed tourist development:

- tourism creates mainly temporary, seasonal employment
- the few permanent jobs unlikely to go to locals
- community will not benefit overall
- will create land speculation, causing house prices to rise and forcing more young people to leave the area

Suggestion:

- Develop the area into a high-tech business park

Advantages:

- permits the area to be levelled and landscaped
- area would blend in with the surrounding countryside
- creates wealth in the area
- creates a permanent and stable workforce in the region
- avoids the inevitable congestion and disruption caused by excessive tourism
- sustains local culture and language

❸ Trends in Tourism

Speaking 2 (page 23)

16 TEAM B

Look at the map and read the fact file.
Discuss tourism in Egypt.
Decide what you will tell Team A.
Make notes and plan your talk.
When you are ready, give your talk.

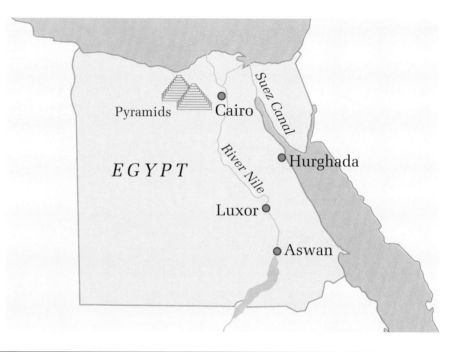

Egypt fact file

History	Recent developments	The present situation
tourist attraction since "the dawn of time"	1963/4: Ministry of Tourism set up	visitors: 43% ◄── Arab world 57% ◄── Europe & N. America
1798: Napoleon's Egyptian campaign ──► new interest in Egyptian culture	1960s: > 1m tourists / yr.	av. stay: 8½–9½ days
1869: 1st Thomas Cook tour	gradual increase in no. of carriers and hotels ──► 3.6m arrivals in 1992	attractions: classical tour (Pyramids, Luxor and Aswan) Nile cruises
Nov. 1869: opening of Suez Canal; 2nd Cook tour	1992–94: adverse publicity ──► fall in arrivals	package charters (Hurghada on the Red Sea)
1950s: tour operators and hoteliers in place		

❽ Responsible Tourism

15 Speaking (page 55)

B3

M. Jones

Owner of small gift shop and restaurant

Views on the proposed tourist development:

- welcome influx of tourists
- valuable business opportunity
- unemployment in the area: 10.1% (recently son had to leave home to live and work in London)
- Greens are in a small minority – should not be allowed to influence such an important decision
- wildlife has never been in danger
- derelict mine an eyesore

④ Where People Go

Speaking 1 (page 27)

GROUP B

Discuss what should go in the gaps in the grid. Then work with a partner
from Group A to check your answers.

COUNTRY	CAPITAL	LANGUAGE	CURRENCY
	Buenos Aires	Spanish	
Austria			Schilling
		Portuguese	Real
The Czech Republic	Prague		
	Cairo		Pound
Greece	Athens		
	Budapest	Hungarian	
Italy			Lira
	Tokyo	Japanese	
	Nairobi		Shilling
Malaysia			Ringgit
Spain		Spanish	
	Bern	Swiss German, French, Italian, Romansh	
		Arabic, French	Dinar
	Ankara	Turkish	
The Ukraine			Karbovanet

Speaking 2 (page 29)

STUDENT B

14 Ask your partner for the information which is missing from
the table and answer his/her questions.

THE MOST VISITED MONUMENTS AND MUSEUMS IN THE EU (NUMBERS PER YEAR)		
RANK	PLACE	NO. OF VISITORS
1		
2	The Louvre	4.0m
3		
4	The Eiffel Tower	3.6m
5	The National Gallery	2.8m
6		

Listen to your partner talking about the value of tourism to
the UK and complete the pie chart below. Then present the
figures in the pie chart on page 106 to your partner.

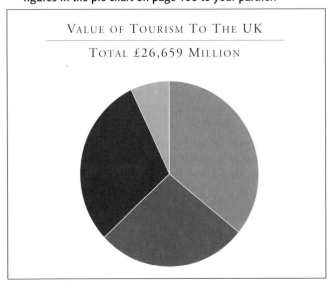

VALUE OF TOURISM TO THE UK

TOTAL £26,659 MILLION

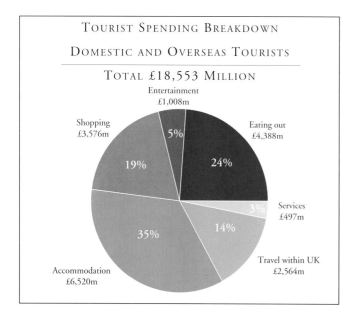

TOURIST SPENDING BREAKDOWN

DOMESTIC AND OVERSEAS TOURISTS

TOTAL £18,553 MILLION

Entertainment
£1,008m

Shopping
£3,576m

Eating out
£4,388m

5%

19%

24%

Services
£497m

3%

35%

14%

Accommodation
£6,520m

Travel within UK
£2,564m

⑧ Responsible Tourism

15 Speaking (page 55)

B1

M. Hamilton

Leisureland's vice-chairman

Views on the area:

- the Llanberis area: tourism potential
- work in shops and cafés is seasonal
- in summer the Snowdon mountain railway, which runs from the village, takes over 150,000 people to the summit, and has to turn many away
- during the winter, Llanberis is dead
- area losing valuable human resources (exodus of Welsh-speaking people to the big cities)
- improvements to the main roads from England into North Wales – more people coming into the area
- if there is nothing for the extra number of tourists to do, they will wander round the National Park, causing unnecessary damage

LeisureLand will:

- establish a year-round tourist attraction
- create 300–500 temporary construction jobs
- create 1,000 permanent full-time jobs for local Welsh-speaking population
- create controlled entertainment for the day trippers
- save the National Park from damage

⑤ Travel Agents

Preview (page 30)

2 STUDENT B

Tell your partner your name, address and phone number (on the business card), and write down your partner's name, address and phone number.

Speaking 2 (page 31)

8 STUDENT B

1 Your name is Penelope McBain. Telephone Skyways Holidays for information about holidays to Puffin Island. Ask to speak to the sales department. If no one is available, leave a contact number.

2 You will recieve a telephone call from Skyways Holidays. You require brochures and prices on holidays to Puffin Island. Your address is 6 Leybourne Crescent, Bristol, Avon, BS24 9EA.

JJ

Jamien Jansen

Mauritskade 63

8606 AP Sneek

The Netherlands

Tel: (31) 5150 54761

Speaking 4 (page 35)

20 STUDENT B

You will receive a phone call from a client interested in a tour of Cefalù in Sicily. Reply to his/her enquiries and take down their details. Charge the full amount of the holiday to his/her credit card.

Departures: June 16   July 14

Cefalù: situated on the northern coast, 1 hr from Palermo. Picturesque Arab-Norman town dating from 5th century BC.

A Norman cathedral in the town square contains some of the finest mosaics in Italy. The town sits under the Rock of Cefalù on which the Temple of Diana was built.

All Sicily's classical and medieval sites are within driving distance. There is also a sandy beach near the town centre.

Programme: Included in the price are scheduled Alitalia flights from London LHR, transfers and accommodation at the ***Kalura Hotel (half board). The hotel is situated in a quiet bay 20 mins from the centre. All rooms are decorated in Mediterranean style and have private bathrooms. Typical Sicilian cuisine. Activities include creative writing, painting, photography, a Sicilian folk night, trips to Palermo and Agrigento and a country lunch including wine and a picnic with a walk up Cefalù Rock.

Price: £579 for 1 week. £180 for a second week. Insurance £19.

You want to go on a holiday called "Venice and the Verona Opera" in June or July. You have two weeks' holiday. Ring up to make a booking and check the details.

Venice & the Verona Opera
Dates?
Things to see and do?
Accommodation?
Cost?
Insurance?

J. WILKES

computer consultant

2 Kingston Avenue
Manchester
M20 8SB
Tel: 0161 434 3591

Credit Card

6289 0150 6885 8372

Expiry date: J. WILKES
06/2006

Writing 2 (page 35)

21 STUDENT B

Write a letter of confirmation to M. Figuereido, enclosing the tickets and the details of the holiday in Cefalù.

8 Responsible Tourism

15 Speaking (page55)

A2

B. Hall

Chair of Snowdonia National Park Society

Views on the proposed tourist development:
- people come for natural beauty and tranquillity

- area would be spoilt by: heavily congested roads, day trippers, litter
- local infrastructure could not cope with the coachloads from Manchester and Liverpool

- too great a burden on local hospitals and the police

Suggestion:
- if people want the sort of tourist attraction being proposed they should go to the seaside

Scenario 1 Advising a Client (page 36)

GROUP B

Activity 1

You are trainee tour operator sales staff for Dream Holidays Inc., an American tour operator. Today you are attending a training session. You are learning about the amenities and facilities at a new resort.

Work with a partner from your group. Read the brochure extracts about Steamboat, Colorado, on page 109 and follow the instructions below.

1 Answer these questions:
a Where is the resort?
b How long is each holiday?
c At what time of year can you go?

2 Note the important facts about the resort and the hotel under these headings:

THE RESORT	THE HOTEL
• location	• facilities
• amenities	• cuisine
• climate	• rates
• transport	• discounts
• activities	
• souvenirs	

3 Discuss and answer these questions:
a Which are the most popular weeks?
b What type of client is attracted to this type of holiday?

Activity 2

Now work with someone from Group A.

You are a travel consultant working for a large bank. One of their staff has asked you to research a winter-sun holiday in Goa for herself and some colleagues.

They have set aside about £500 per person per week.

Your client wants to find out about:
- a good resort.
- a good hotel.
- if there are things for her teenage children to do.
- how the hotel will cater for them.
- if there are any child discounts.

You have recently heard about a hotel there but you cannot remember the name. It was something like "Eden".

Ring up your partner who works for Paradise Holidays plc and find out about:

THE HOTEL	THE RESORT
• precise location	• transport to and from the resort
• facilities	• leisure activities
• rates and discounts	• shopping
• hotel amenities	• the climate
• cuisine	

Activity 3

Change back to the role you had in Activity 1, working for Dream Holidays Inc. Keep your partner from Activity 2. He/she is now an independent travel consultant and he/she will telephone you.

Use your notes from Activity 1 to answer the caller's enquiries.

Activity 4

Change back to your role for Activity 2, working as a travel consultant. Work with other people from Group B.

You have now gone back to your consultancy offices. Were you impressed by Paradise Holiday's description of the package holiday to Goa? On the basis of what you have heard, will you want to recommend this Goan hotel and the resort?

Discuss your recommendations with your colleagues. What will you tell your client?

Activity 5

Write to your client to give your opinion of the hotel and the resort in Goa.

STEAMBOAT
Colorado, USA

Après-ski and Eating Out

The ski resort and old town of Steamboat boast more than sixty restaurants offering a cosmopolitan selection of Cajun, Italian and even Vietnamese dining. There are Steamboat favourites like Old West Steak House and gourmet mountain dining at Ragnar's where you'll enjoy a starlit sleigh ride before a fabulous dinner with the lights of the valley set out below. Away from the mountain, Steamboat again scores high. Take your pick from a morning hot air balloon ride with celebratory champagne, snowmobiling, ice skating and shopping (jeans and Western boots are real bargains).

Prices include round trip air travel by scheduled airline to Steamboat.

Accommodation for the stated number of nights on the basis shown.

Airport and hotel taxes.

Child reductions for children under 12 sharing with two adults.

Transportation

Daily flights London–Denver connecting with domestic flights Denver–Steamboat Springs, a mere 5 miles from the resort. Regular resort shuttle.

Ski Facts

Average annual snowfall: 325 inches
Trails: 106 over 50 miles
Ski lifts: 20
Vertical drop of 3,600 ft
Longest trail: 3 miles
Slopes face: N, NW, NE
Cross country: 12.5 miles
Ski school: 200 instructors
Mountain restaurants: 6
The Billy Kidd Centre for performance skiing is a unique programme for intermediate and advanced skiers only.

Climate

Average temperature in the resort at 6,900 ft is 28F. Colder on the peaks (10,600 ft). Steamboat has a dry, pleasant and invigorating climate with little wind, so little wind chill effect.

Activities off the slopes: ice skating, indoor tennis, dog sledding, sleigh rides (including mountain dinner tours) ballooning, shopping, horse riding, thermal hot springs

Facilities for Children

Nursery/childcare: for children aged 6 months to 6 years. Provides games/puppet shows/arts and crafts for non-skiing children.

Kids' Vacation Center: for children aged 2½ to 4 years. Ski instruction and supervision in a special area with a ski-lift just for children.

Rough Riders: ski instruction and supervision for ages 5–15 years.

K.C.'s nite club: evening childcare for children. Advance reservations required.

Resort Shuttle

Runs regularly from Steamboat Springs to Steamboat Ski area until late at night.

The Hotel

Sheraton Steamboat Resort ★★★★ Genuinely ski-out and ski-in, the Sheraton enjoys an ideal location adjacent to the Silver Bullet Gondola. Within yards of the hotel are numerous shops plus the ski school and lift ticket office. Accommodation: spacious guest rooms have two double queen size beds, private balcony, cable TV & movies (charge), private bath /shower.

* 300 rooms and suites
* hot tubs and jacuzzis
* sauna and massage
* fitness and games room
* valet service
* concierge
* ski storage
* ski rental/shop

HOTEL	SHERATON STEAMBOAT RESORT			
Room Type	Double Queen			Child Price
Basis	Room only			All holidays
no. of nights	7	10	14	
no. of adults sharing	2	2	2	
from 23 Nov to 07 Dec	715	829	955	370
from 08 Dec to 14 Dec	1065	1299	1669	496
from 15 Dec to 21 Dec	1265	1599	1929	496
from 22 Dec to 03 Jan	1095	1299	1555	370
from 04 Jan to 01 Feb	925	1125	1369	370
from 02 Feb to 08 Feb	1029	1315	1669	370
from 09 Feb to 15 Feb	1059	1299	1599	370
from 16 Feb to 15 Mar	1019	1259	1489	370
from 16 Mar to 22 Mar	945	1125	1259	370
from 23 Mar to 29 Mar	789	899	N/A	370
All prices in £ sterling.				

⑧ Responsible Tourism

15 Speaking (page55)

B2

F. Evans

Town councillor for twenty years and vice-chairman of the Snowdon National Park committee

Views on the proposed tourist development:
- ridiculous to turn down an opportunity to create 1,000 jobs
- without jobs, the language and culture of Wales will be lost
- no additional financial burden to the community – grants can be obtained from the Welsh Tourist Board, the Sports Council and the EU

Suggestions:
- Arfon Borough Council owns the land – can insist that the 600 new houses are not sold outright or as timeshare apartments, but rented strictly on a weekly or weekend basis
- the council can make sure that the Welsh language and culture are promoted, e.g. hold festivals of Celtic music and Welsh arts and crafts festivals

⑥ Tour Operators

Reading (page 38)

2 **STUDENT B**

Before you read, check you know these words in the box. Use a dictionary if necessary.

frosty	outstanding	to hold down (prices)	to cover (overheads)	a brand name
ailing	to be out of pocket	to settle up	sluggish (business)	to go bust

Read "When the welcome is frosty" and answer these questions:
a To what extent can a hotelier trust a tour operator?
b How do tour operators attempt to persuade hoteliers to take less money?
c How did a hotelier in Spain react?

Tell your partner about how hoteliers work with tour operators.
Make notes before you begin.

WHEN THE WELCOME IS FROSTY

If holidaymakers get a cool reception in some holiday destinations it may have more to do with the practices of some tour operators in the UK than with the hospitality of the local hoteliers.

Many hotel owners and local agents feel badly treated by British tour operators. Some of them have lost a small fortune when unsecured trade creditors have gone bust. They feel especially bitter when an ailing competitor is taken over: the new owners may continue to do business under the same brand name, and yet are under no legal obligation to settle any outstanding debts. As a result, hoteliers may be out of pocket when a tour operator ceases trading, even though the same company, now under new ownership, is sending its customers to the same destinations.

So it comes as no surprise if hoteliers accuse tour operators of sharp practice. For example, allegations have been made that tour operators use their position to force down the rates for which hotel rooms were originally contracted. Sales may be booming but the tour operators will tell the hotelier that business is sluggish and that the rooms can only be filled if they discount their prices.

Another tactic is to claim that competitors are holding down their prices and that the only way to remain in business is to do likewise. The hotelier can do nothing to prove the contrary. Hoteliers also suffer from cash flow problems through delays in payment. Although most settle up within a couple of months, some operators have been known to request a fresh allocation of bed-nights when they still have not paid for the previous season.

So if you're going on a package don't be surprised if the welcome you receive is less than enthusiastic – the chances are that the room was contracted at a rate that will barely cover overheads. But you would still be in a better position compared to some unfortunate holidaymakers in Spain last year. One British operator had forced a reluctant hotelier to accept a greatly reduced rate with the result that when the tourists arrived their rooms had been re-allocated to a foreign operator offering a better deal.

Speaking (page 43)

Negotiating an Agreement

11 TEAM B: VISTAS

Look at the agenda on the right. You have just finished discussing item 2. Read and discuss your negotiating position on the remaining items with your partner:

Item 3
You would like to receive commission of at least 13.5%. You realise this is optimistic; your average is 12%.

Item 4
You can guarantee eye-level racking in larger agencies, but smaller shops will display brochures at their own discretion.

Item 5
As an incentive to sales staff you would like to see a payment of £1.25 per person paid to the consultant who confirms the booking. This would be paid monthly working from the departure date.

Item 6
You feel that any customer complaints should be dealt with in writing by the operator within a week. Customers need to feel that their complaint is getting somewhere.

Item 7
You would like educationals for your agency staff.

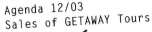

Agenda 12/03
Sales of GETAWAY Tours
1 Minutes ✔
2 Review of forecasts for next season ✔
3 Commission levels
4 Racking
5 Incentives
6 Policy on complaints
7 Educationals

Before you start negotiating with GETAWAY you should decide:

- what you want to achieve.
- your order of priorities.
- what you think GETAWAY will want.
- how much you are prepared to accept.
- what you think GETAWAY will be prepared to accept.

If neccessary refer to the Language Tips on page 43.

Decide who will say what. Then negotiate with the GETAWAY representatives.

❼ Promoting a Destination

Speaking 1 (page 46)

9 STUDENT B

Tell your partner about the itinerary below in your own words.

ICELAND *Outline itinerary*

Thursday: evening flight from London Heathrow to Keflavik. Transfer on arrival to Hotel Island in Reykjavik.

Friday: morning City Sight-seeing Tour and afternoon to explore or shop at leisure.

Saturday: (New Year's Eve): late morning excursion to the Blue Lagoon to bathe in its milky blue waters. Evening Viking-style banquet. Just before midnight firework display. See the New Year in with a celebratory glass of Brennivin (Icelandic schnapps).

Sunday: (New Year's Day): The Golden Circle – a full day tour. Leaving Reykjavik we travel over Hellisheidi Pass to Hveragerdi, the "greenhouse village" where fruit, vegetables and flowers are grown in greenhouses heated by geothermal water. Visit to the Great Geysir, after which all others are named. Drive to Gullfoss, considered by many to be Iceland's most beautiful waterfall. Cascading in two stages into a spectacular 15 km gorge, the falls are often partly frozen at this time of the year.

Stop at Laugarvatn, where steam emerges at the edge of a lake, forming a natural sauna. Optional swim in the lake! Head back to Reykjavik and listen to a few sagas on the way. Dinner in the evening.

Monday: Return to London

⑩ Customer Relations

Reading 1 (page 62)

STUDENT B

4 **Read this case study about an unfortunate incident in a travel agency and answer the questions.**

a Who was involved?
b Were the travel agency staff experienced?
c What kind of mistake did the staff make?
d How do you think the customer felt?
e How would you describe the staff and their behaviour?

Tell your partner what happened.

What lessons can be learnt from the two situations?

Speaking 1 (page 65)

10 STUDENT B

Situation 1   You are a hotel receptionist. A customer has just come into the lobby and wants to speak to you.

Situation 2   You are staying at a beach resort. The hotel room is fine, but outside at certain times of day there is an unpleasant smell coming from the local municipal rubbish dump down the road. You ask to speak to the manager.

Situation 3   You are a resort representative. Someone has asked to speak to you.

Situation 4   You bought a return airline ticket from a travel agency but the wrong time was written on the return ticket and you missed your flight. You had to purchase another ticket for a later flight (which, to make matters even worse, was delayed), and as a result you missed a very important business meeting. You want to know what the agency is going to do about it.

WHEN I FIRST started in the travel industry, I worked in a small retail agency which was owned by a very pleasant and knowledgeable man who was liked and respected by all of his customers. One day I was listening to him dealing with some customers who wanted flight seats to Malaga at very short notice, and I learned a valuable lesson which has held me in good stead in my dealing with customers. The incident occurred in the days before travel had become fully computerised and so my boss found himself telephoning a number of companies to check availability for the customer, and this was taking some time. While he was waiting to get through to operators, he struck up a conversation with the customers which eventually led to their asking his opinion on the merit of the huge choice of charter airlines operating on that route. This happened to be a pet subject of his, and he went into graphic detail about the merits and pitfalls of each carrier. Finally, he said, "The worst flight I ever had was with B...B airlines. The staff were rude, the food was awful and they even ran out of duty-frees."

The customer thanked him for his advice and then attention was switched back to the call that was being answered by the tour operator. Up to now, no availability had been found, but on this occasion a flight with suitable timings was available. The customer was quite satisfied with the price and decided to book straightaway. As my boss and the tour operator began to process the booking, the customer said "Oh, by the way, which airline are we flying with?"

My boss asked the operator, looked very sheepish, then looked up at the customer and quietly said, "Uhh ... it's B...B Airlines."

RICHARD WILLIAMS TALKS ABOUT SANDY LANE

HIS HOTEL: It's a very special place – Barbados as a destination is easy to reach so people can decide on a whim to come here to relax. People have so little leisure time now, it is important to have somewhere like Sandy Lane which is easy to visit. We also have a huge advantage because of its location on easily the best beach surrounded by elegant private homes in a private estate. The hotel owns 400 acres but has only 120 rooms so it never seems busy even when we are full. People also like the elegance of the hotel, the coralstone which changes colour from white to pink as the sun sets, and the theatre of mahogany trees around.

STAFF: We have just under four staff, about 3.8 to every guest room, which is a nice ratio because it allows us to be very attentive. Training is very dear to my heart – about 25 per cent of our training budget goes on technical skills as the rest is on attitude and motivation. We send staff overseas to work in hotels such as the Savoy in London and their staff come here so they are always learning. But what impresses me the most is the friendliness of the staff. Where else does a maid come in on her day off to bring fruit from her garden for a guest who does not feel well?

RATES: We think our rates are good value. In the summer the rates are lower which we think is spectacular value because you get exactly the same service and facilities as in the winter. We also consider families very important and have just built a children's village in the grounds and offer adjoining rooms for US$100, complete with soft drinks and cookies instead of a minibar. Our dominant market is still couples aged forty or over.

GUESTS: Our dress code sometimes causes problems because we will refuse entry to dinner if someone is not smart enough. Sometimes celebrities will try to bend the rules which is a shame because other guests don't like it if exceptions are made.

FAVOURITE STAY AT A HOTEL: Galley Bay in Antigua. We go there quite a lot because I can really relax there after the formality of my hotel. I can go to dinner in shorts and without shoes. The atmosphere is relaxed, but the service and the food are excellent. I like not having any air conditioning and being able to virtually roll out of bed into the sea. A lot of places you can unwind, but you don't get the good service – here you get both.

DISLIKES: What I particularly dislike are city hotels where the management and owners don't bring any sense of caring. They give you a bed in a box and sterile, unoriginal surroundings. You don't have to spend a fortune on a room to find good places so it's not just a question of price.

ONE WISH FOR THE INDUSTRY: That we could get over the problem of seasonality. I wish I could somehow get across the message that the Caribbean is a beautiful place in the summer.

(from Travel Trade Gazette)

⑪ Hotel Facilities

Reading 1 (page 70)

2 STUDENT B

When you have finished reading the text on the opposite page, ask Student A questions to find out about:

- the good features of Tommaso Zanzotto's hotels.
- the staff.
- the room-pricing policy.
- his favourite stay at a hotel.
- what he dislikes at a hotel.
- what he would like to see happen in the industry.

Answer your partner's questions about Richard Williams.

Speaking 2 (page 75)

11 STUDENT B

Student A will phone you to make a booking. Use the information from the brochure to answer his/her queries. Make notes.

You have no single room accommodation free as from 12 July but you can be flexible on pricing.

Make sure when taking any booking that:

- you have the names of all the guests and their requirements.
- you have a forwarding address and telephone number.

⑧ Responsible Tourism

15 Speaking (page55)

A3

B. Morgan

Local teacher

Views on proposed tourism development:

- would result in cars coming over Llanberis Pass at the rate of one every four seconds on a summer holiday weekend
- would create havoc on the roads
- Welsh language and culture would be severely affected by the number of holidaymakers from England – already difficult to keep the ancient language and culture of Wales alive
- this new housing estate will be used by people from the North of England as second homes
- they will be a separate community giving nothing to the area
- the 600 houses will be empty for most of the year

Maple Leaf Hotel

The Maple Leaf Hotel is conveniently located five minutes from the L.B. Pearson International Airport and downtown Toronto. The Maple Leaf overlooks an eighteen-hole golf course.

Rates

Single $95–$125 (Canadian) Weekend $75–$95
Double $115–$135 Suites From $265
Check-in 3 p.m.; check-out 12 noon.
Group discounts: see residential delegate rates below.
All major credit cards accepted

Room guarantee policy

First night's deposit is required to guarantee a room if arrival after 6 p.m.
Cancellation must be made prior to 6 p.m. on arrival date to receive a full refund.

Room facilities

Color TV, in-room movies, DD telephones, mini-bar, soundproofing, hairdryer, all rooms en suite.

Business Center

The Maple Leaf has a fully-equipped business center with six private meeting rooms and three offices, offering its guests a comprehensive range of services, including 24-hour facsimile and telex, photocopying, word processing, e-mail, interpretation and translation.

Conventions and meetings

Meeting rooms	Theatre	Classroom	Conference	U–shape	Size (sq.ft.)	Rate full day
Delaware	100	55	40	40	1144	$200
3 Peaks	45	25	20	20	572	$150
Pine View	30	20	20	20	486	$120

Lecterns, flip charts, slide projectors, OHPs, white boards and stationery supplied at no extra charge. Audio-visual assistance available.

Daily delegate rate

Includes morning tea and coffee, hot and cold buffet lunch, afternoon tea, main meeting room hire, $32 per delegate.

24-hour residential delegate rate

Includes above, plus three-course table d'hôte evening meal, overnight accommodation, full American breakfast. $110 per delegate single occupancy and $90 per delegate double occupancy.
Clients must be able to guarantee at least fifteen delegates per day to be able to benefit from the daily or residential delegate rates.

Restaurant

A la carte three-course menu from approx. $35 per person.

⓭ Things to Do

Speaking 2 (page 86)

11 STUDENT B

1 You are P. Frumkin, a modern historian from Boston University. You are staying in London. You have hired a car and come down to Portsmouth for the day together with your nine-year-old daughter, Caroline.

As a modern historian you are particularly interested in sailing and maritime history. Caroline doesn't have a long attention span and tends to get bored quite easily.

Ask the tourist information clerk if he/she can suggest what you can do for the day.

2 Now change roles. Student A is a tourist and you are a tourist information clerk in Portsmouth, New Hampshire, USA.

Read the leaflets. Note the important points. A tourist has just walked through the door. Answer his/her questions.

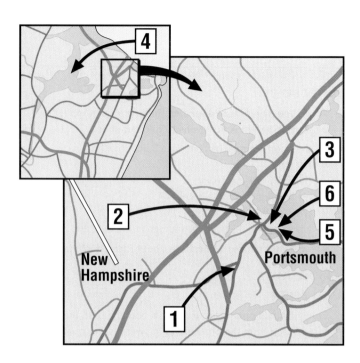

1

John Paul Jones House

Guided tours of the house and museum by attendants
in period costume

Built in the mid-18th century
Home of Captain John Paul Jones for a time during the American
War of Independence

Now the home of Portsmouth
Historical Society

Open:
Weekdays 10.00 a.m. – 4.00 p.m.
Sunday 12.00 p.m. – 4.00 p.m.

2

PORTSMOUTH HARBOR CRUISES
Discover the River Piscataqua's heritage and the adventure of sail aboard the Pisces:

A. Inland River Cruise
through a peaceful world of winding rivers and the expanse of Great Bay.
A great cruise for naturalists.
In the fall, see an abundance of migratory bird life.

B. Evening Cruise
Enjoy a jaunt around the harbor for our version of Happy Hour.
Or relax with your favorite drink and take in sunset over the harbor.

C. Isles of Shoals
Visit nine windswept islands just six miles off-shore.
These islands have played a vital role in the legendary folklore of the seacoast, with a history spanning nearly four centuries.

3

Blue Strawbery Restaurant

Founded 1970, overlooking Portsmouth's historical harbor, serves a 6-course, gourmet dinner by reserved seating.

4

Great Bay National Estuarine Research Reserve

• comprises 4,471 acres of tidal waters
• 48 miles of inland Atlantic bays

Estuary habitat includes tidal creeks, woodlands and open fields

Experience the natural fauna and flora of the area.

5

Whale Watch Expedition

All trips guided by naturalists.
Data collected is sent to New England
marine research centers.
We have access to three whale zones.
Humpback, fin, right, minke, sei whales, as
well as whitesided dolphins can be seen.

6

THE OAR HOUSE

Traditional foods, uniquely prepared. Located on Portsmouth's historic waterfront. A favorite among locals, and a find for visitors. This is a truly relaxing gourmet experience in an atmosphere reminiscent of days gone by.

⑭ Marketing the Past

Speaking 2 (page 93)

14 GROUP B

You work as tour guides for Summer Tours of Switzerland. You have been asked to plan a
two-hour walk round Rapperswil. Read your information. Plan your route. Prepare your talk.
Give your talk to someone in Group A.

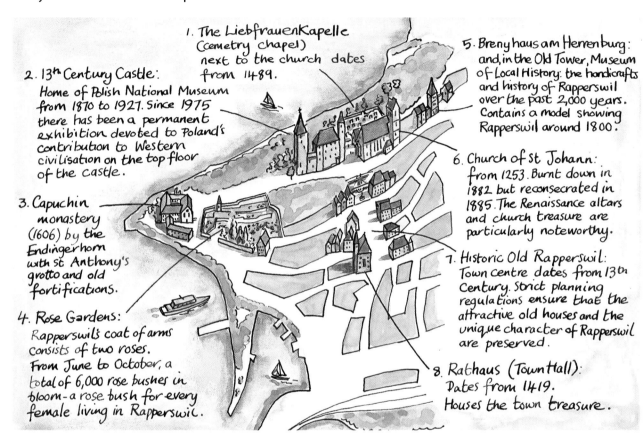

1. The LiebfrauenKapelle (cemetry chapel) next to the church dates from 1489.

2. 13ᵗʰ Century Castle: Home of Polish National Museum from 1870 to 1927. Since 1975 there has been a permanent exhibition devoted to Poland's contribution to Western civilisation on the top floor of the castle.

3. Capuchin monastery (1606) by the Endingerhorn with St Anthony's grotto and old fortifications.

4. Rose Gardens: Rapperswil's coat of arms consists of two roses. From June to October, a total of 6,000 rose bushes in bloom – a rose bush for every female living in Rapperswil.

5. Breny haus am Herrenburg: and, in the Old Tower, Museum of Local History: the handicrafts and history of Rapperswil over the past 2,000 years. Contains a model showing Rapperswil around 1800.

6. Church of St Johann: from 1253. Burnt down in 1882 but reconsecrated in 1885. The Renaissance altars and church treasure are particularly noteworthy.

7. Historic Old Rapperswil: Town centre dates from 13ᵗʰ Century. Strict planning regulations ensure that the attractive old houses and the unique character of Rapperswil are preserved.

8. Rathaus (Town Hall): Dates from 1419. Houses the town treasure.

⑮ Business Travel

Speaking 2 (page 99)

STUDENT B

1 You work in the venues department of The Manor Hotel. You receive a telephone call from Albatross Engineering. Using the information below, answer the enquiry. Find out what equipment the client requires. All equipment is provided free of charge if you have prior notice.

	U-SHAPE	CLASSROOM	THEATRE
The Bishop Fortescue Room 15.9 x 8.5 m £150/day	52 people	64 people	150 people
The Brittany Room 6.4 x 7.3 m £75/ day	30	32	50
The Gurney Room 8.5 x 9.2 m £100/day	42	42	75

2 You work for Tangerine Computers of New York. You are interested in holding a three-day business seminar in the UK for local businesses on the benefits of your new software packages. You will be sending a team of eight senior employees who will require accommodation for four nights. You expect there to be some thirty local people attending on each of the three days. They will not require accommodation.

Ring The Manor Hotel and find out what they can offer.

Will they provide OHPs, flip charts and so on? Do they have a local area network you can demonstrate your software on?

Tapescripts

❶ Types of Holiday

Listening

6 Conversation 1

Travel consultant: Hello, can I help you?

Woman: Um … well, yes perhaps. Last year we went to Italy in December and stayed at a small, relatively cheap hotel in Rome and it was very nice, and the year before that we spent the New Year in the Canary Islands, but this year – well, we're sort of looking for something a bit more exciting and adventurous – something that'll give the kids a treat for Christmas.

Travel consultant: Well, how about this, there's a very reasonable and successful package put together by … (*fade*)

Conversation 2

Young man: Hello, we saw your notice in the window and we'd like to find out a bit more about what it includes.

Travel consultant: OK. What exactly is it you want to know?

Young woman: Er … well, we're getting married in three months' time and we've decided we want to go somewhere exotic – you know, the holiday of a lifetime sort of thing, not just Benidorm or the Algarve.

Travel consultant: Oh well, I think it's definitely Bali for you. There's a special offer at the moment with three extra nights free on the island of Lombok … um … which is about twenty minutes' flight off the coast of Bali itself.

Young man: Lombok. I've never heard of that.

Travel consultant: Well, that's one good reason for going there. It's completely unspoilt.

Young man: And how much does it cost?

Travel consultant: Well, it's very competitive. Would you like a brochure?

Conversation 3

Travel consultant: OK sir, I've booked you into a three-star hotel and I'll make out the flight ticket now. So that's Alitalia flight number AZ1621 and then there's a train connection to Florence. Right. And how are you paying?

Man: American Express.

Travel consultant: Fine. Can I have your card? Thank you.

Man: Oh by the way, I'd like to hire a car and make my own way on to Perugia. Is that possible for you to do from here?

Travel consultant: No problem, sir. What kind of car do you require?

Man: Oh, the most economical.

Conversation 4

Woman: And so could you tell me what the price includes?

Travel consultant: Well, the price is inclusive of air travel, ten nights on the MV Kirov, full board and all the excursions except the one on Day 2 which is optional.

Woman: What's that exactly?

Travel consultant: Um … I think that's a guided tour round St Petersburg, just let me check in the brochure. Yes, that's right.

Woman: Actually, on second thoughts, I think it's a bit expensive.

Travel consultant: Well possibly, but on the other hand it is excellent value for money. (*pause*) No? Well, what about going … (*fade*)

❷ A Career in Tourism

Listening

3 1 I've been working in the local office of a major travel agency group in the United States for the last three years. I … er … I have to try to find corporate clients who will regularly use us when their personnel has to come for a meeting or a conference or a negotiation – something like that. It's a pretty competitive market because when a company is going through a bad patch then travel is often one of the first things that gets cut. So we try to include a number of incentives, but of course that cuts our own profit margins.

2 I'm on a programme where every month or so I change departments, so I started off in the restaurant and then spent some time in the kitchen and went into the reception and at the moment I'm working in one of the offices and learning accountancy and financial management, and then … er … at the end of that I hope I'll get a job in a position of responsibility either generally or in a particular department.

3 I basically have to be friendly to passengers, make sure everyone is in the right seat, then show them the safety procedures and serve drinks and a snack. It's not easy to combine this job with a social life because I'm frequently away from home. This week we're stopping over in Dubai so we won't be back for another couple of days. But I enjoy the contact with people and we're part of a good team.

4 I have a checklist of points which I go over beforehand to make sure that everything is ready. I check that the equipment is in the right place and in working order, that all the catering has been looked after, that the hotel reservations have been made and things like that. Then when people arrive I welcome them and give them their badges and information folders. Next week we're having a big do with about 600 participants so … (*fade*)

5 I have to deal with the public and take their bookings for flights, hotels, tours, car hire and that sort of thing. It's quite hard work and the basic salary isn't brilliant, but I get a performance-related bonus and commission so I don't do too badly. I'm doing a training course at the moment because I'd like to specialise in incentive travel. In fact I have an interview next week.

6 What I have to do is to plan ahead so that in two or three years' time we have another destination or resort to offer in the catalogue. This means that I have to visit and travel around the region, contract with hoteliers and service providers and so on. Obviously, I have to deal with a lot of money matters and negotiate terms and conditions. At the moment we're thinking of opening up a resort in Albania.

Speechwork: Word stress

reliable	sociable
available	suitable

❸ Trends in Tourism

Listening 1

3 Interviewer: Dr Alberto Garcia works for the World Tourism Organisation in Madrid and has come into the studio to talk to us about developments in the modern tourist industry. Dr Garcia, how can we actually determine what a tourist is?

Dr Garcia: Good question. We have now, in fact, adopted a kind of common language – a set of definitions if you like – so that when various countries collect statistics on tourism they are all measuring the same thing. And so the WTO now classifies all travellers under various headings. The most important of these for statistical purposes is that of visitors. But obviously, for tourism purposes, we don't count people such as temporary immigrants, border workers, nomads and other groups like diplomats, members of the armed forces and people like that. And then visitors are broken down into two separate groups: tourists who are overnight visitors – that is, people who stay for at least one night in some form of accommodation in the country they're visiting and same-day visitors who do not stay the night. For example passengers on a cruise stopping over in a port or people simply on a day trip.

Interviewer: How long can tourists stay in a country without ceasing to be a tourist and becoming a resident?

Dr Garcia: Not more than a year. And the reason for the visit must be different from the kind of activity he or she is usually employed in. So the purpose of the visit has to be for leisure and recreation, for business and professional reasons, VFR …

Interviewer: VFR?

Dr Garcia: Yes, that is: visiting friends and relatives. Or perhaps people are travelling for health reasons to a spa or somewhere like that or going on a pilgrimage to places like Mecca, or Lourdes in the south of France.

Interviewer: OK, so we know what tourists and visitors are, but we still haven't actually defined the word tourism!

Dr Garcia: Well, I can give you the official definition – it's the activities of persons travelling to, and staying in, places outside their normal environment for not more than one consecutive year for purposes such as leisure or business. And this definition can be further subdivided so that we can distinguish between the types of tourism. There's domestic tourism, that's where the residents of a country travel within their national borders. And then there is inbound tourism, that's when people who live in another country come to visit the country where you live. And finally outbound tourism which involves the residents of a particular country going abroad for one of the reasons which I mentioned earlier.

Interviewer: Right, so we have domestic, inbound and outbound. And I suppose you can also … (*fade*)

Listening 2

***Summer holiday* by Cliff Richard**

We're all going on a summer holiday
No more working for a week or two
Fun and laughter on our summer holiday
No more worries for me or you
For a week or two.
We're going where the sun shines brightly
We're going where the sea is blue
We've seen it in the movies
Now let's see if it's true.
Everybody has a summer holiday
Doing things they always wanted to
So we're going on a summer holiday
To make our dreams come true
For me and you.

Listening 3

15 Interviewer: Can you tell me something about when and how tourism actually began in Singapore?
Christopher Keoh: Tourism in the strictest sense began a long time ago when people from the east and the west were travelling and trading. Singapore began its existence, owes its existence actually, to trading. It started off as a trading port, a harbour for pirates actually, but more significantly when trading developed between the east and the west, from China, from India into Europe or intra-Asian travel, then most of it went through Singapore. So Singapore started as a trading nation between the Spice Islands and Europe. Now that naturally gave birth to what we would call the tourism industry, with inns, hostel keepers, restaurants – well that's how I think tourism started. A lot of travel between the UK and Australia would stop in Singapore back in the days of steamers and the romantic days of travel. Of course now, very few people – about 3,500 out of a total of about 225,000 – come by sea. The vast majority fly directly into Changi airport. Right now tourism in Singapore has become a major industry attracting people from all over the world into South-East Asia through Singapore and also features very prominently on the UK–Australia routes.
Interviewer: If we look at the kind of modern tourism of the last twenty to thirty years what patterns do you think have emerged?
Christopher Keoh: If we were to take 1965 as the benchmark, because 1965 was the year Singapore gained its independence, arrivals into Singapore then numbered 90,000 a year and the bulk of that travel actually came, like we said, from the steamers and ships coming through the port of Singapore. So, from very humble beginnings since 1965 tourism has taken off in a very big way and, if we take 1993 for example, we welcomed 6.4 million arrivals from all over the world.
Interviewer: These 6.4 million, about how long did they stay?
Christopher Keoh: The average length of stay is 3.8 days in Singapore and we from the Singapore Tourist Authority, believe that there is more to see and do in Singapore and should justify it being a business destination.
Interviewer: How are these visitors broken down?
Christopher Keoh: If we were to talk about the breakdown of arrivals on a worldwide basis we are talking about 15 per cent of our arrivals coming in on business. Holidaymakers account for well over 60 per cent, the rest of them would be visiting friends and relatives, in transit, on their way to other spots in South-East Asia, or else going for an educational purpose. But the two main blocks would be holidays 60 per cent and business a little in excess of 15 per cent.
Interviewer: And those holidaymakers – what do they do in Singapore? What do you encourage them to do, to see?
Christopher Keoh: Well, we believe that Singapore is an excellent introduction to Asia, speaking from a European or non-Asian point of view. We see Singapore as the springboard to the rest of South-East Asia, where they should come into Singapore first to be acclimatised, to get used to the culture, to explore a little bit of what the rest of Asia holds in store for them.

❹ Where People Go

Listening 1

4 Interviewer: Penny Goodman and her husband, Charles, with their son Harry, an advertising salesman in Los Angeles, and his wife Olivia, who is from Maryland, are on the last day of the Tornado Tour. They have visited seven countries in twelve days, a total distance of 2,750 miles. This is their first trip to Europe. I asked them what their impressions were.
Interviewer: Can I ask a few questions?
Penny: No problem.
Interviewer: Have you honestly got to know the real Europe in twelve days?
Olivia: Of course not. Seven countries – 2,750 miles. That's why our tour's called the Tornado Tour!
Interviewer: Isn't it ever annoying when you can't get off the bus because you absolutely have to see Rome in two hours?
Penny: Well, I would've kind of liked to stay longer at a couple of places. But it was the first time I've been to Europe and so this was the right trip for me to get an impression of Europe, just to whet my appetite.
Interviewer: Where would you like to go back to if you had the chance to spend just another five minutes in Europe?
Harry: Paris, the Trocadero by night.
Olivia: Florence. To see Michelangelo's David again.
Charles: Those castles. All those wonderful castles on the river. Where was that now … ?
Penny: Germany – between Heidelberg and Bonn.
Interviewer: How was the food?
Harry: Swiss chocolate. Fantastic! I always get an allergy from American chocolate. But in Switzerland I could eat white chocolate for the first time in my life. Nestlé's Galak. That's one name I'll never forget.
Penny: And you could eat cheese.
Harry: That's right. I have this allergy to chemically-treated food. In LA you can spend hours trying to find cheese or an apple that hasn't been sprayed with something or other. It's great just to be able to go into a shop and not spend hours researching what is in the apple.
Penny: And the herbs … Have you ever had a pizza with fresh herbs? The difference is like night and day.
Interviewer: Did you miss anything?
Penny: Sure did, ice cubes. I can't understand how you can serve a cola in the summer without ice cubes. Two minutes in the sun and the stuff is cooking.
Interviewer: Did you go to a McDonald's here?
Olivia: Once, in London. But we have McDonald's in the US too. We came to learn about European culture.
Interviewer: Did you pick up any souvenirs?
Olivia: I picked up two outfits in Rome.
Harry: For a mere 600 dollars!
Charles: Come on, we've all spent a fortune.
Interviewer: On what?
Penny: Oh, crystal in Venice, a cuckoo clock in Geneva, leather bags in Florence. Did I forget anything?
Charles: Silver spoons from almost everywhere.
Penny: Well, my Mom will appreciate them. Anyway, I think it's good to go shopping even if you don't buy anything. It's good to know what everyone else has got. Just to compare.

Interviewer: Has twelve days really been enough to see Europe?
Penny: My son and Olivia – like most Americans – only had two weeks' vacation so there was no choice.

Speechwork 1: The schwa sound

6 again   another   monitor   certificate   internal   culture   manager   salesman   Switzerland   Piccadilly Circus

Listening 2

12 a Of the six and a half million visitors last year, about two thirds stayed in hotels.
b We're working on a thirteen point five commission basis at the moment.
c The revenue forecast for July at the full rate is £145,205.
d "Could you please quote your booking number?"
 "Yes, it's AS stroke oh two one nine seven eight."
e Your flight number from Hong Kong to Guilin is CZ three zero three two.
f The rate of inflation has gone up by over 2 per cent, that is from 6 to 8.15 per cent.
g There'll be seventeen extra guests arriving on 30th July.

❺ Travel Agents

Listening 1

7 Call 1
Agent 1: Yeah, what is it you want?
Caller 1: I'd like to speak to Monsieur Duprès, please.
Agent 1: Who did you say?
Caller 1: Monsieur Duprès in financing?
Agent 1: He doesn't work here any more.
Call 2
Invicta Press: Hello, Invicta Press, can I help you?
Agent 2: Good morning, this is Sunrise Tours. Can I speak to Mrs Sharp, please, on extension 452?
Invicta Press: Hold the line, I'm putting you through.
Mrs Sharp: Hello, Mrs Sharp speaking.
Call 3
Caller 2: Hello, can you tell me what currency I'll need to go to the Ukraine?
Agent 3: Yeah, hold the line please and I'll find out for you.
Caller 2: Yes … (noise of conversation in background)
Agent 3: Hello, are you still there?
Caller 2: Yes.
Agent 3: It's the karbovanets.
Caller 2: The what?
Agent 3: The karbovanets.
Caller 2: Never heard of it!
Agent 3: Me neither! (more background noise)
Caller 2: Well … er … thank you.
Agent 3: Jane! Stop it! Thank you. (hangs up)
Call 4
Tour operator: Hello, reservations.
Agent 4: Could you check me something on an invoice please?
Tour operator: An invoice. I'll put you through to the accounts department.
Agent 4: Well, er … no it's … (pause)
Accounts: Hello, Accounts.
Agent 4: Sorry, but I didn't want Accounts, could you transfer me back to Reservations please?

Accounts: To Reservations? No, I can't. All their lines are engaged. You'd better call back later.

Call 5

Agent 5: Funtours, can I help you?

Caller 3: Could I speak to Mr Poynter, please?

Agent 5: No, I'm sorry, he's in a meeting at the moment.

Caller 3: Sorry, I didn't quite catch that?

Agent 5: I said he's in a meeting.

Caller 3: Oh … um … OK, um … thank you.

Call 6

Customer: Can you tell me how much that'll be?

Agent 6: Yes, that's £375 plus a £5.50 sea-view supplement and that's per person per night, so that comes to £452 and another twice £38 flight supplement charge.

Customer: Oh.

Speechwork: Intonation in tag questions

11 **a:** You went for two weeks last year, didn't you?

b: The 10.35 flight is fully booked, isn't it?

c: You're returning alone, aren't you?

d: Your husband isn't going with you, is he?

e: There is a guided tour, isn't there?

Practice 2

A: Good morning. Would you like some help or are you just looking?

B: Good morning. Well, I was considering taking a short skiing trip. You don't happen to have any bargain packages, do you?

A: Ah well. As it so happens, yes. But could you first give me some idea of where and when you'd like to go?

B: Anytime between now and mid-March really but the sooner the better.

A: Would you prefer to ski in Europe or America?

B: I was thinking of Switzerland or Austria but it's more a question of cost and good skiing. Could you suggest where we can find good intermediate to advanced ski runs?

A: Mm, well … we have a seven-night self-catering deal to Verbier in Switzerland and that's £259 and one to Alpach in Austria for £169. Both leave this Saturday. That's not too short notice, is it?

B: No, that's fine. Um, my partner prefers Switzerland so I guess I'll take that one. Er, could you tell me which airport the flight leaves from?

A: Yes, Gatwick.

B: And the plane comes back to Gatwick, does it?

A: That's right.

B: Fine.

A: Right, well, let me take a few particulars. Could you tell me what your name is?

B: Yes, Bogdan Kominowski.

A: Um … yes … er, would you mind spelling that for me?

Listening 2

15 **Travel agent:** Good morning, Intourist, can I help you?

Mr Maughan: Hello, er yes, can I speak to Natasha, please?

Travel agent: Er, yes, who's calling?

Mr Maughan: I spoke to her last week about a holiday in the Ukraine and I'd like to make a booking.

Travel agent: OK, could you hold on please? I'll put you through to her desk.

Mr Maughan: Thank you …

Natasha: Hello.

Mr Maughan: Is that Natasha?

Natasha: Speaking.

Mr Maughan: Um, I visited your agency last week and we talked about the tours you organise in the Ukraine. You said I should get in touch with you if I'd made up my mind.

Natasha: Oh yes, I remember. Have you decided where you'd like to go?

Mr Maughan: Yes, I'd like to make a booking if that's OK.

Natasha: Fine. I'll just get a booking form. Hold the line … Right. Could you tell me which tour you've decided on?

Mr Maughan: The one – sorry, I haven't got the reference with me – the ten-day one to Moscow via Odessa. We fly from Gatwick.

Natasha: OK, I'll look up the reference number later. Can you tell me what date you want to leave on?

Mr Maughan: The thirteenth of July.

Natasha: Fine. So would you mind giving me your name, please?

Mr Maughan: It's for me and my wife – Mr and Mrs Maughan.

Natasha: How is that spelt?

Mr Maughan: M - A -A -U -G -H -A -N.

Natasha: And please could I have your first names?

Mr Maughan: Linda and Kevin.

Natasha: Is that Linda with an i or a y?

Mr Maughan: An i. It's L - I - N - D - A.

Natasha: Thank you, and I'll need your home address.

Mr Maughan: Certainly. That's 41, Swynford Hill, Temple Fortune, London NW11 7PN.

Natasha: 41, I'm sorry, could you please spell Swynford for me?

Mr Maughan: Of course, S-W-Y-N-F-O-R-D. Then Hill, Temple Fortune. London NW11 7PN.

Natasha: And the telephone number?

Mr Maughan: 0181 392 4535.

Natasha: And do you have a number at work?

Mr Maughan: Yes, 0171 274 0083, extension 32.

Natasha: Thanks. And are you both British?

Mr Maughan: I am, my wife has an Irish passport.

Natasha: Right, now do you mind if I just check the details? It's Mr Kevin Maughan spelt M-A-U-G-H-A-N and Mrs Linda Maughan of 41 Swynford Hill, Temple Fortune, London NW11 7BN.

Mr Maughan: Sorry, could you repeat that?

Natasha: Mr Kevin M —

Mr Maughan: No, the last bit of the postcode. Did you say P or B?

Natasha: B. B for Bravo

Mr Maughan: No, it's P for … for er … Peter.

Natasha: Sorry, thanks. So it's London NW11 7PN. Telephone number 0181 392 4535 and at work 0171 274 0083, extension 32. Departure date 13th July. Now, there's the insurance which is … er … is compulsory on this kind of tour. Would you like to make your own arrangements or would you rather take out the standard insurance policy?

Mr Maughan: Oh … I guess the standard one. It saves a lot of trouble.

Natasha: Yes. OK well the insurance premium is – wait a minute I'll look in the brochure … um (*reads to herself*). It's for ten days, isn't it? "Up to eight days, £19. Nine to twelve days £22 per person". Right, so that's £22 per person. And … um … you'll need a visa as well.

Mr Maughan: OK, um … do you know how much that costs?

Natasha: Yes, that will be an additional £17 per person. Shall I look after that or would you prefer to get it yourself?

Mr Maughan: No, no, you do it! I haven't got time!

Natasha: Right, so I'll need you to fill in an application form and I'll also need three passport size photos and a copy of the inside cover of your passport, so if you bring those in the next time you drop in I'll send everything off with the confirmation.

Mr Maughan: OK.

Natasha: And I'll also need your deposit which is £100 a head.

Mr Maughan: Right, well I'll drop by at the beginning of next week and make you out a cheque then.

Natasha: Good, thank you for calling. Goodbye.

❻ Tour Operators

Listening

5 **Maria:** OK, let's get down to business, shall we? You know the situation, don't you? We've been approached by Sky Air who have some spare capacity on their transatlantic 767s and they've asked us if we're interested in chartering aircraft to Cuba. So I've been out to look at some sites and I've negotiated rates and come to an agreement with some hoteliers and I think we have a good price because obviously everyone in Cuba desperately needs foreign currency at the moment. Now David, what about you, what's the position exactly with Sky Air now?

David: Well, they've given us their seat rates and we've negotiated a discount by taking a time slot they wouldn't've been able to fill. So we've got 270 seats at approximately £250 each for twenty-five weeks in rotation. And I'm told by the marketing people that we'll probably be working on load factors of about 80 per cent – so we should be doing OK.

Maria: Right, that's good news. Shirley, how much do you think we'll be able to charge for the whole thing?

Shirley: Well, taking into account overheads like travel agents' commission … um … transport charges for local tours and other things like … um … the salaries of local reps and so on, I think £550 for two weeks is about right.

Maria: OK, and after taking into account commission, transport and salaries, what profit margin does that leave us?

Shirley: Eight per cent. It's low I know, but even just £5 or £10 will persuade people to go elsewhere. But I do think we'll be able to sell more local tours. I'm told that there's likely to be a 15 per cent take-up on the tour to Havana, which is very encouraging. Also I've made a comparison with our competitors in the Dominican Republic and we're about 10 per cent cheaper than they are.

Maria: Good. And what about the brochure? Richard?

Richard: Well, we've started to write the copy and I've had a lot of photos taken of the resort and I must say it looks pretty good. If you can give me your final prices I can update the figures.

Maria: What kind of time scale are we working in?

Richard: Well, we're having this brochure printed by a different firm and we have to meet a deadline for 1st September so, if all goes according to plan, the brochure should be published in October.

❼ Promoting a Destination

Listening 1

4   Interviewer: So what kind of people come to Barbados?

Ann Trevor: It's a great spread – it runs from the very upmarket – people who will spend £5,000 for a week, fly here by Concorde and, you know, stay in Sandy Lane which is probably one of the best hotels on the island – it's on the west coast which is the most prestigious – all the way through to the budget end of the market; now you can get some pretty good deals – a lot of the hotels on the south coast do special packages, so we really target the whole range, but in terms of what this office does, this office will really try to pinpoint the upper end because Barbados is an aspirational island, if we advertise or target in our PR the top end it'll bring the rest with them …

Interviewer: Yes.

Ann Trevor: … and that's our strategy.

Interviewer: Could you explain what you do at International Trade Fairs – because you have a stand at most of them?

Ann Trevor: We go to a majority of the big ones – World Travel Market in the UK, the big one in Germany that's just happened, the … um … the ITB, we go to that one. It's really to establish – our main objective is to establish and keep our name in front of the trade – and these shows are very trade-orientated – and at these exhibitions you can't do too much else, there's no point in setting up a series of meetings because everybody gets delayed, everybody gets very busy so it really is a PR exercise to let people know that Barbados is still there, still on the map, and it's still an island they can send their clients to. And obviously we give out information and we have ground tour operators and hoteliers with us. If any of the trade wants to ask a specific question about a hotel, who better to have it from than the mouth of the actual owner, so they will come over as well and help us to generally spread the gospel.

Interviewer: What's your relationship with your tour operators?

Ann Trevor: Our tour operators are pretty aggressive and they're also pretty specialised, either in the Caribbean or long-haul. There are certain tour operators who deal with honeymoons, certain tour operators who deal with just the very, very exclusive upmarket areas – so we can target them pretty closely to promotions. So if we are doing a promotion there's only probably two or three that we can talk to and they know now that if we approach them it'll be pretty worthwhile, but if it's not worthwhile we wouldn't do it anyway.

Interviewer: How would you go about setting up a new area or destination?

Ann Trevor: Well … I can use Almond Beach Village as an example of that. They've just launched a new hotel and had a press launch and some of our staff took part, and they'll be making a number of marketing efforts and sales calls to help them on, but they're actually putting their own people on the road. Anywhere we go obviously we'll promote it and our sales team is out three times a week actually selling Barbados – if there's something specific that needs pushing then we will push.

Listening 2

8   Helen Lee: Good morning everyone. My name's Helen Lee and I'm going to describe the itinerary to you and tell you a little bit about what you'll be seeing. It's a fifteen-day tour which covers the main tourist spots and also goes down to Hong Kong as well, so it gives you a good introduction to China if you've never been there before.

Easter's quite a good time to go; the weather's getting a bit warmer then in the north of China. It'll be quite pleasant in the south … but really the best times to go are May to June and then in the autumn, but obviously they're the times when there are going to be more people around. But we start our tours going just before Easter.

You'll be flying London to Beijing to start with and staying for three nights and doing the most famous places like the Forbidden City where the Emperors used to live, the Summer Palace up in the west of the city, the Temple of Heaven, and just time to stroll around, have a look at the streets, go shopping, and so on.

You'll have the experience of two guides with you, a national guide who'll stay with you all the way through the tour and a local Chinese guide – both trained, English-speaking guides so you'll have the benefit of their knowledge.

And then from Beijing we go by coach to a smaller city in the north called Chengde which is – or rather was – the summer resort of the Emperors and there's a pretty park there and we visit three temples. One of them is very reminiscent of the Potola Palace in Lhasa. And on the way there we stop at a certain part of the Wall called Jinshanling and have a picnic on the Wall – it's slightly quieter than the other places on the Wall which tend to be packed with tourists, so this is nicer.

And then from Chengde we go back to Beijing and then connect with a flight to Xian which is the beginning of the Silk Road and famous for the Terracotta Warriors that everybody's heard about, and we lunch at the Warriors and go on to the Banpo Neolithic Village, the Huaquing Hot Springs and other sightseeing spots.

Then we go down to Shanghai for one night, and a couple of hours on a train to Suzhou which is known as the Venice of the East because it's a canal city and it's where a third of the silk is actually produced in China, so it's quite an interesting place. And it's famous for its gardens so we go there too to see the gardens. And there'll be a visit to a silk factory as well.

And then go back to Shanghai, another night there, and the following day go down to Guilin which is a very well-known city – more in the countryside than other places you'll be visiting … for its river, the Lijang River, and its magnificent limestone formations along the river bank. So there'll be a river trip all the way down to the small town of Yangshuo where there's an interesting market which sells wild animals, flowers and plants and herbal medicines, and then back up to Guilin afterwards. There's also an optional excursion you can take in the evening to see cormorant fishermen at work – they have rafts and they have their own private cormorant and the birds dive down and bring the fish up to the surface and it's quite fascinating to see that.

OK, are there any questions so far?

Travel agent: Yes, when do we get to go to Hong Kong?

Helen Lee: Well, we're flying there the following day – it only takes an hour. Your guide will actually leave you in Guilin, and in Hong Kong you're basically left to do your own thing – there's no sightseeing included. You'll be staying at the Metropole Hotel which belongs to our group and you can book onto tours there. And then the final day, we fly back Cathay Pacific. So, by the end of the tour, hopefully you'll have learnt a lot about China.

❽ Responsible Tourism

Listening

6   Interviewer: I know you're very concerned about environmental issues at Overland Encounter, but, in practical terms, what can a tour operator do to make sure that tourists don't destroy the beauty of the thing they came to see?

Michael Leech: Well, I think you have to get involved in what we call "low impact tourism". You can't deprive people of their interest in wanting to travel. But what you can do is to set up patterns of behaviour which will introduce them to a country in a responsible way. That means, for example, making sure that, on an adventure holiday, no detergents are used in springs or streams and that no rubbish is left behind after camps. It means, if you're visiting a protected area like the Antarctic, that people must respect the rules and not damage fragile plants or go too near the penguins. It means providing travellers with a pack with instructions on how to behave and what to do to best preserve the cultures and places visited.

Interviewer: Do you think that many people will in fact not listen and will just ignore whatever guidelines you give them?

Michael Leech: Perhaps, but the key factor in minimising damage through tourism is to keep groups to a manageable size and then you can control how they behave. Thirty on a safari is an absolute maximum.

Interviewer: Are operators now putting things back into the environment instead of just taking from it?

Michael Leech: Very much so. There are schemes to protect wildlife habitats in Kenya and Tanzania, to save the rhino, veterinary programmes and so on. People now go on holiday to restore ancient monuments or clean up beaches. Things have changed and the model of Mediterranean tourism of high-rise concrete, sun, sea, sand and sex is not the one most people now want. And another thing, in some places the environment *is* tourism and national parks have been created by it. Without tourism, the animals would have gone. I think the environment is strengthened by sensitive tourism – look at the preservation of the gorillas, for example. And you never know, tourism might save the tropical rainforest in a place like Madagascar. I think most countries go through several phases in their tourism development and hopefully, in the best scenario, the local people not only share the income and foreign exchange generated by tourism but also use the amenities.

❾ Transport

Listening 1

2   Travel consultant: Good morning. Can I help you? (**Susan:** Yes, I …) Oh sorry, I didn't recognise you. You came in the other day about a trip to the

States, didn't you?

Susan: That's right and … er … if it's OK by you I'd like to sort out the final itinerary. I've rung up some of my friends and relatives over there and so I've pretty well worked out what I'll be able to do while I'm there.

Travel consultant: Good. Do you still plan to start off in New York and come back via San Francisco?

Susan: Er … yes. Last time you mentioned something about an open-jaw ticket. Could you tell me what …?

Travel consultant: Oh, an open-jaw … yeah, you'll fly out from Heathrow to Newark International and come back to London from San Francisco. That means you pay half the return fares on both routes added together.

Susan: And do I get my student discounts on those flights?

Travel consultant: Yes, no problem.

Susan: OK. So I'll set off on 1st September and fly to Newark, and return on the 21st from San Francisco.

Travel consultant: Fine. Do you need accommodation in New York?

Susan: No, thanks. My uncle will be picking me up from the airport and putting me up for a few days in Manhattan. I was thinking of visiting Ellis Island and of course the Empire State Building and … I guess it's pretty easy to travel around New York.

Travel consultant: Well, there are guided tours of the city but you can get around quite easily on the subway, and if you want to look around Ellis Island and Liberty Island there are regular ferries. You don't need to take the guided tours if you want to go around on your own.

Susan: Right. And … um … about my trip to Niagara. I've looked at what's available and I've decided to take the Grayline one-day tour.

Travel consultant: Um … yes, it's a bit pricey you know. Are you sure your budget will run to that?

Susan: Um … well I know it's expensive but, well, I've been saving up for this and I really don't want to miss out on seeing the Niagara Falls.

Travel consultant: OK, fine. Well that's $290 and for that you have to pay in advance. Er … they pick you up at the Sheraton and you go by coach to Newark International Airport, fly to Buffalo and then on to the Niagara Falls by coach. There's a guided boat tour and then you drive over to the Canadian side, then back to Buffalo and the plane to New York, to arrive back at about 6.30 p.m.

Susan: Right, and the next day I was planning to go to Washington.

Travel consultant: By Greyhound bus or by rail?

Susan: Well, I was told that the bus can be dangerous for young women travelling alone so I thought … well … could you get me an Amtrak fifteen-day travel pass?

Travel consultant: Sure. But I need to know your times and routes before I can book everything.

Susan: Right, so on the 5th I'll take the day trip to Niagara and on the 6th I'll take the train to Washington … spend some time there before going on to Las Vegas. And then on the …

Travel consultant: Hang on a minute. Here we are, New York to Washington on the Capitol Ltd.

Susan: Sorry?

Travel consultant: The Capitol Ltd. All Amtrak trains have names. So that leaves at 07.23 and arrives at 11.05 on 6th September.

Susan: Fine.

Travel consultant: And then your best route would be to take the Capitol Ltd. on to Chicago and then get on the Desert Wind for Las Vegas. The only problem is that you'll have to hang around in Chicago for a few hours.

Susan: Well, that doesn't matter.

Travel consultant: So if you took the 16.40 from Washington on the 7th you'd arrive in Chicago at 09.10 on the morning of the 8th and have until 15.05 to have a look around Chicago.

Susan: OK.

Travel consultant: So I'll book you on the Desert Wind to Las Vegas via Denver and Salt Lake City, arriving in Las Vegas at 07.45 on the morning of the 10th.

Susan: Then I want to leave Las Vegas on the 12th for Los Angeles. I'll want to spend a few days there.

Travel consultant: OK, so that's the Desert Wind again for Los Angeles.

Susan: And then I'll need to reserve a seat from LA to San Francisco on the 17th.

Travel consultant: Will you be wanting accommodation in Las Vegas or Los Angeles?

Susan: No, I really need to cut down on costs so I'm hoping to be able to look up some old friends and ask them if they can put me up.

Travel consultant: OK. So we'll book those trains for you, the excursion to Niagara and of course the international flights. I'll draw up the itinerary for you, make a note of the check-in times for the flights and so on and make out the tickets for you.

Susan: Great. And just one more thing. While I'm in Los Angeles I want to be able to see Disneyland, Hollywood, and so on and so I'd like to hire a car while I'm there. Can I do this through you?

Travel consultant: Yes, I've got a brochure here in fact. You have a choice of … *(fade)*

Listening 2

6 a The next stop will be Terminal Two.

b Would all foot passengers please proceed to the disembarkation point on B deck.

c Mind the doors!

d Would Mr Vince Chung, a passenger on British Airways flight BA 755 to Hong Kong, please go to the Flight Information Desk?

e The train arriving on platform four is the 10.13 for London Victoria, stopping at Rochester, Chatham and Bromley South.

f UK 700 to Edinburgh. Passengers are advised pre-flight checks are being carried out. Departure will be delayed for approximately half an hour.

g In the unlikely event of an emergency, all passengers should proceed to the nearest muster station where a member of crew will issue everyone with a lifejacket.

h Good morning, passengers. Captain Nolan and his crew would like to welcome you on board this airbus number 820 to Hamburg.

i Would Miss Andreas please report to the Purser's Office next to the duty free?

j Good morning, ladies and gentlemen. The maître d'hôtel will be coming to your compartment in a few minutes' time to take orders for brunch.

k We regret to announce that there is an industrial dispute on the Italian railways, therefore the transfer between Innsbruck and Venice will be by coach.

l We'll be flying over the Atlantic at thirty-five thousand feet.

m Ladies and gentlemen, as we drive round the corner, here in the main square, if you look to your right you can see the famous Leaning Tower.

n Passengers are advised not to leave their luggage unattended.

o We're now approaching Pigeon Point, Tobago, where passengers can disembark.

❿ Customer Relations

Listening

5 **Melanie:** Well, it was three or four years ago when the boys were still very young. Oliver – that's our youngest – was only three and a half. Anyway, we'd arrived at Heathrow in good time for our scheduled flight for Dallas, only to find that they weren't willing to give us our seat numbers. Instead we were told to wait on one side. Well, quite a queue was developing – middle-aged couples, students, families like us, and then, as the time of the flight approached, a couple of staff in suits appeared and eyed us all up and down. It was very unpleasant really. And then we were addressed by the older, I suppose the senior, member of staff who apologised for our delay and explained that they'd overbooked on economy class and that they were doing all they could to make sure that we'd be given seats on this flight – or another.

Friend: With the stress on another!

Melanie: Well, we didn't know that at the time. Needless to say, the boys were getting a bit impatient and wanted to get on the plane, but then after a while some people started to be singled out and disappeared towards passport control with relieved expressions. Eventually we were left standing there on our own! My husband was getting more and more impatient but then an officious-looking lady came up to us with new tickets. She told us it'd been impossible to allocate five seats together in any one part of the plane and so we were to travel to the States on another airline. The plane would leave in two hours and, instead of flying direct to Dallas, would take us to Houston. There we'd be met at the airport and taken to a good hotel – a luxury hotel, they said – for the night and then shuttled back to the airport the next morning for the connecting flight to Dallas.

Friend: What did you think about that? I don't suppose you were all that pleased.

Melanie: Pleased – we were furious, but there was very little we could do. Anyway, when we did arrive in Houston, late that night, no one was there to meet us, no one knew why we were there, nor anything about a hotel and connecting flight. So, after several very angry telephone calls to the airline's Dallas office, we were finally booked into a very shabby downtown motel and told that a taxi would pick us up at seven next morning.

Friend: And that was the end of it?

Melanie: No, it wasn't. When we got home I wrote a letter to the airline and in fact they refunded most of the fare.

Friend: So you ended up with a cheap holiday!

Melanie: Cheaper perhaps, but it was a catastrophic start and nearly ruined it completely. But one thing – it taught us a lesson.

Friend: What's that?

Melanie: To kick up a fuss. The same thing nearly happened again, not in London this time but in San Francisco. This time we weren't on holiday, we were on business. So we were looking pretty smart, not like your usual holidaymakers but more like VIPs. Anyway, same thing, kept hanging around, told to wait in line and this time we complained – boy did we complain, we would never travel with the airline again, we wanted compensation, etc. And so we were asked if we wouldn't mind travelling club class …

Friend: Mm.

Melanie: And we said – not club class – first class.

Friend: And they let you?

Melanie: They sure did. And I saw a programme the other day on TV and someone from a British carrier was explaining how they cope with overbooking. Apparently a lot of travellers don't show up and the airline stands to lose money. So they overbook their seat allocations. But in the summer, most people do show up so they have problems. So when it happens they watch check-in. And if they think some people look as if they will make a fuss they get preferential treatment.

Friend: So it pays to be aggressive.

Melanie: Yeah, well, not so much aggressive as assertive, polite – and well-dressed.

⑪ Hotel Facilities

Listening
9 Section 1

Interviewer: How do you actually cost the rooms in your hotel?

Nick Patterson: Well, we have the commercial sector and the leisure sector. Within the commercial sector there are various subsections – there are those that come in and will pay the published tariff, the rack tariff and there are no discounts involved. There are those people who, because they say "we've got 100 people a week in the area who will stay with you for, say, forty-eight weeks a year", they will come in and negotiate a price – a corporate rate and most hoteliers will try to hold that to a 10 per cent discount, but clearly, depending upon the importance of the contract to the hotel, the rate can be either 8 per cent or up to 15 per cent.

Interviewer: And what other rates are there?

Nick Patterson: Well, we have a conference rate and there's a standard retail travel agency rate, because sometimes the retail agent will book direct – we're giving them a straight 10 per cent and we subdivide that into special schemes as well … um … because someone might come along and say "if you wish I can take 20 per cent of your total occupancy every night, can I have a special deal?" But as a hotel manager I have to be careful because I might say to my boss, "I'm full," and he might say, "Why are you full at this rate? It's appalling," and so I have to do a balancing act and try to eradicate the cheaper business and slowly build it back up to the more realistic room rate.

Section 2

Interviewer: What sort of contacts do you have with foreign travel agents?

Nick Patterson: Well, that's interesting because wholesale operators working out of this country and going to a place like Spain or elsewhere will contract a number of bedrooms – say 5,000 rooms for this summer – and they'll bargain very hard with the hotelier who will have to work out his own break-even point and decide whether there is enough demand for his rooms to hold out for a bigger price.

It's the usual situation – if there are six wholesalers from Germany, Scandinavia, Britain and so on competing for this same block of rooms then the overseas hotelier can hold out for a higher price – it's a question of supply and demand.

Interviewer: So there the rooms are contracted for and the operator will pay for them whether or not they are actually filled?

Nick Patterson: That's right.

Section 3

Nick Patterson: But the foreign travel agents sending visitors to London and the UK rarely, very rarely, contract in the same way. In other words, we will agree to hold a block of rooms and give the foreign agent, say, thirty every night, but normally there is a cancellation or release date so you will sell your thirty rooms. And so a party of four might book and they will notify us that Señor and Señora Gonzales and two kids are coming and they will be entered into our reservation system, and we will know they still have twenty-six to sell. But three weeks out or four weeks out – and that's subject to negotiation – I will cancel the rooms that he has not sold and he will be under no obligation to pay for those rooms. And that's a totally different way of contracting than the other way round, where, if you took thirty rooms, you'd have to pay for the whole lot whether you'd filled them or not.

Section 4

Nick Patterson: So you see incoming tour operators to Britain have a much easier deal.

Interviewer: Why is that?

Nick Patterson: Well, that's just the way it has developed. But there's another trick of the trade in Britain because we will then overbook; so if I've got 100 rooms to sell I'll give each agent fifty a night because I know they won't fill them. But, I mean some operators are so small that they only have a freesale facility for two or four or six, and so a hotel with 300 bedrooms in London works with 100 people with two or three or four rooms on freesale, and so they can sell them without reference to the hotel and simply post-notify us that Mr and Mrs Gonzales are coming. But there comes a cut-off point when those rooms are no longer available and so the hotelier is at the same time selling into other markets, into other segments, so we allocate some rooms on a freesale basis to the in-coming tour operators but retain rooms for our rack-paying business sector, other rooms for the 10 per cent business people, the 15 per cent discount people, the conference allocation, and the weekend traffic for short break programmes, and so on. You really have to invent ways of balancing all the balls in the air at the same time.

⑫ Selecting Locations

Listening 1

2 Kelly: Hello, can I introduce myself? My name's Kelly Cooper from Austral Tours in Sydney.

Ludwig: Pleased to meet you. I'm Ludwig Szeiler. Austral Tours, you say?

Kelly: That's right. I'm looking into the possibility of taking Australian travellers to Malaysia for tropical breaks and er … well your resort here looks very attractive. I see you have a leaflet about Tioman Island. Where is Tioman exactly?

Ludwig: It's just off the eastern coast of Malaysia, forty-three nautical miles to be exact.

Kelly: And how do you get there?

Ludwig: Well, there's a daily ferry service from Mersing which can carry 200 people and also a catamaran service which takes about 250 passengers from Singapore, and that leaves every day from the Singapore World Trade Centre. That takes about four and a half hours. Otherwise we do ten flights a day on nineteen-seater biplanes belonging to Berjaya Air from Singapore.

Kelly: Oh, so you're part of the Berjaya group?

Ludwig: That's right. It's Malaysian-owned and based in Kuala Lumpur. And we also have hotels in other parts of Malaysia and Sri Lanka, Mauritius, and the Seychelles.

Kelly: And what exactly do you have on offer?

Ludwig: Well, if you look in the brochure here, the hotel complex consists of basically chalet accommodation. There are 480 double rooms, and about a third of these have an extra bed and so we can accommodate about 1,000 people at any one time. And each chalet gives onto a courtyard which is named after a flower. We try to keep the gardens beautiful because if people come to a tropical destination we reckon it's because they want to see colour and variety. And in the resort itself we have a lot of activities like scuba-diving and snorkelling, golf, swimming, horse riding, jungle trekking and live entertainment in the evenings.

Kelly: It looks a very attractive site. And what are the rooms like?

Ludwig: They're all very luxurious with private shower and a hair dryer, a telephone, colour TV and – what else? – oh yes, a mini bar.

Kelly: Looks good. I'll have a word with our Chief Executive, I think she'll be interested. And … um … how is business going at the moment?

Ludwig: Well, at present we're doing very well but we're always trying to improve. At the moment we're putting in snooker rooms, a badminton and volleyball court and a karaoke lounge. And we're offering special deals for retired people.

Kelly: I see. That sounds interesting. Can I give you my card – and your name again is?

Ludwig: Ludwig Szeiler. Let me give you my card.

Kelly: Thank you. So I'll tell our Chief Executive that I've spoken to you, … *(fade)*

Listening 2

12 Speaker 1: So, as you can see from the documents in your folders, ladies and gentlemen, the first part of the report deals with the siting of the proposed development. The obvious candidate is the Docklands area to the east of London. There are two main reasons for this. First is the fact that there has been a shortage of suitable sites in London, and the Docklands development represents a unique opportunity for expansion. Secondly, many hotels in the city centre – that is the area known as the West End – have been upgrading recently and have correspondingly more expensive. As the demand for hotel accommodation has increased there has been a shortfall in supply of more price-conscious, three-star accommodation, and this is the sector we recommend you should invest in.

Thirdly, this area of London represents a unique investment opportunity. The English Tourist Board surveys show that it's about number 6 on the list of things to see in London and it'll probably develop as a tourist destination in its own right. And with the City so close it's also the main business area and particularly well served by London City Airport to which about 80 per cent of passengers are inbound. And communications with the rest of London are good with the Docklands Light Railway and the Thames River Bus. Hopefully, we'll also see the completion of the London Dome Project, which will be a major venue for sports events, concerts, conferences and so on.

Speaker 2: Have you been able to identify a suitable site?

Speaker 1: Yes, we've made enquiries with a number of agents and we've earmarked a site in the Port East development – this is on the North Quay of the West India Dock and we'll be visiting it this afternoon.

Speaker 3: Fine. So this is described in section 1, is it?

Speaker 1: Yes, and well, as you will see in section 2 of the report we feel that you should aim for a 300 bedroom hotel in the three-star category so the guest rooms would obviously reflect that standard – so … should have private bathroom and shower, colour TV, in-house video films, direct dial telephone and so on. And we think that, because there's bound to be some noise from road traffic, the rooms should be sound-proofed.

As far as the restaurant is concerned you'd probably need about 150 covers and even that number may be too small at peak times. So you would be well advised to use the conference and banqueting facilities as an additional breakfast room, or give tour groups continental breakfast as room service.

Speaker 3: What about the location of the restaurant?

Speaker 1: Well, it should really look out onto the river to maximise its appeal for both residents and non-residents. The same goes for the bar and lounge area. It would be a shame if they didn't. Um … other things we deal with are, section 2.3, the conference room which should be really for quite small events, say a maximum of ninety to 100 people.

Speaker 2: Why so small?

Speaker 1: Because most of the office sites have planned their own in-house conference and meeting facilities and, as we said before, there will be conference centres in the area. 2.4 deals with the health and fitness club and possibly a swimming pool, which is actually very important because if you have club membership it could well be of considerable appeal, not only to guests but to office workers and local residents. This could generate quite a substantial additional revenue for the hotel. And another thing we feel is important is the provision of a car park for about 100 cars – possibly with some kind of security system – and also space for half a dozen coaches for the tour group business.

Speaker 2: OK, so that perhaps brings us to the anticipated demand for the hotel. What would be the mix of guests?

Speaker 1: George, that's your speciality.

Speaker 4: Yes, well, we surveyed other hotels in the region and found that there's an average mix of 58 per cent tourist demand and 42 per cent business, but there are wide variations as there are some that have a 75/25 business / tourist split and others with a 20/80 split. But, from our contacts with both tour operators and business houses, it would seem that, given that Docklands is a secondary location, it would be more price sensitive than the West End

and could therefore attract tour groups for whom the centre of London is too expensive.

⑬ Things To Do

Listening

10 Tourist: Hello … um … do you speak English?

Information officer: Yes, how can I help you?

Tourist: Well, we've just arrived and we're planning on staying three or four days, and we were wondering if you could give us some advice about where we can stay and some of the things we should do while we're here.

Information officer: OK, well if you're looking for relatively cheap accommodation you could try the Locanda Silva which, if you look at the map, is here on the Calle del Forno. It's a kind of bed and breakfast and costs 60,000 lire a night. It's an extremely popular place to stay.

Tourist: Uhuh … and do all the rooms have a bathroom?

Information officer: Um … no, so if you want a better class of hotel then you might like to look at the San Giorgio which costs 110,000 lire. If you're interested in art it's especially convenient because it's just next door to the Palazzo Fortuni museum and a couple of minutes from the Accademia museum.

Tourist: Well, that sounds quite good. Where is it?

Information officer: That one's here on the Calle della Mandola.

Tourist: OK, we'll try there. Could you tell us a bit about the water taxis?

Information officer: If I were you I'd forget about the speedboat taxis because they're horrendously expensive – it's best to stick to the vaporetti, the water buses. If you get a tourist pass you can use them as often as you like.

Tourist: How much is it?

Information officer: I'm sorry, I can't tell you offhand, it depends on the number of days – but they're pretty reasonable.

Tourist: Right. What about things to do?

Information officer: Well, you can't miss the Piazza San Marco and the Palazzo Ducale – er, the Doge's Palace, which is absolutely amazing. And there's the Ponte dei Sospiri – the Bridge of Sighs – and the Ponte di Rialto. But the best thing is probably for you to take one of these guidebooks so you can plan your own sightseeing depending on the kind of thing you're interested in. There's one here in English which is very useful.

Tourist: OK. And what about places to eat? Can you recommend an especially good restaurant?

Information officer: Yes, there's the Ponte Vecchio which is highly recommended. That's here on the Pescheria di Rialto. Or you could go to Al Mascaron on Calle Lunga Santa Maria Formosa. Try the spaghetti with lobster – it's absolutely out-of-this-world.

Tourist: Right. Well – thank you very much for your help.

Information officer: You're very welcome.

⑭ Marketing the Past

Listening 1

3 Interviewer: Could you tell us a little bit about the reconstruction of the museum here?

Expert: Yes, the Neues Museum was built in 1850 and was a very odd mixture of architectural styles. Then, of course, it was bombed in the second world

war and left as a monumental ruin. Art historians don't think of it as the best piece of architecture in Berlin, but it is an interesting early example of an ironwork construction. But aesthetically it's a problem. We're trying to renovate and preserve all that has been left standing of the original building but there are two choices: either we choose a modern contemporary architectural style in harmony with the still preserved parts of the ruin, or we reconstruct it as it used to be. It's funny that the avant-garde, the kind of modernist viewpoint is very much with the archaeologists – art historians tend to defend the reconstruction of the destroyed architectural heritage.

Interviewer: And what do you think?

Expert: Personally, I think if architects had always concentrated on reconstructing the past we would still be building pyramids. I would much prefer a dialogue between western art of the late twentieth century AD and Egyptian art of the twentieth century BC – it's much more constructive and creative and interesting.

4 Interviewer: And what will it look like when it's finished?

Expert: When Museum Island is complete we plan to display only a very limited number of exhibits and to keep on changing what there is to see so as to give frequent visitors, and especially the citizens of Berlin, a permanent impetus to come back again and again. I don't like museums where you show thousands and thousands of objects. The average visitor is unable to make a choice, to distinguish between what is important and not so important.

Interviewer: So how can you help visitors to choose what they should see first and what they can leave until later on?

Expert: For the six archaeological museums we'll try to separate the quick visitor groups, those coming to the museum for half an hour/forty minutes maximum; and we'll try to install on the island an intensive tour for these tourist groups with very limited time available for the museum visit. And we'll display selected representative exhibits from the different museums starting with, for instance, ancient Egypt and the most famous piece in our museum, the bust of Nefertiti, surrounded by monumental pieces of architecture – a temple gate, an obelisk, some temple statues. And this is Egypt for the quick visitor. Then the tour goes on with the Ishtar gate from Babylon as a representative example of the ancient Near East, then we come to the market gate of Miletus from Asia Minor and the famous Pergamon altar, and finally the facade of the castle of Mshatta as an example of Islamic architecture. So the quick visitor sees just a few selected examples of the great civilisations of antiquity and not the proper museum where the individual visitor is not disturbed by these visitors.

Interviewer: Right, so the rest of the museum is relatively empty.

Expert: Yes, in the rest of the museum the atmosphere is quieter and we can cater for smaller groups, smaller guided tours can go there, and I think this is how we can deal with mass tourism. We cannot change tourism for the masses, we have to accept it, we have to make the best of it. Personally I deplore that in huge museum designs, such as the Louvre for example, or in the new installations in the British Museum you have to walk enormous distances if you want to go from one famous exhibit to another. I mean in the Louvre you have to walk more than one kilometre between the Venus de Milo and the famous Mona Lisa or the famous Egyptian scribe of the Old Kingdom and you have to walk through all the art galleries that you may not want to see at all.

I think we should give people what they have really come to see and then, once a member of the group visit has seen that part of the museum, he will say, "Oh, I must come back as soon as I can and see the rest."

Listening 2

9   Guide: As you come into this first room, let me welcome you to the Pergamon museum and to the astounding monument for which this museum was built, the great altar from the ancient city of Pergamon. My name is Martin Leicester and I am delighted to be your guide on this tour of the museum's greatest treasures. Let me begin with the altar itself. While you make your way over to the massive flight of marble steps I'll give you a little background information about the city in which this spectacular monument was built over 2,000 years ago.

Pergamon was particularly famous for its sculpture and what you see in this room today are the remains of the greatest sculptural project that the city ever produced. Even in ancient times this altar was considered to be a wonder of the world. It's believed to have been built soon after 180 BC by King Eumenes II to commemorate a series of victories over Pergamon's long-standing enemies the Gauls, some of whom had migrated not long before from western Europe.

A similar struggle is shown in the frieze – the continuous band of sculptured figures that used to run completely around the altar beginning and ending at these steps. Carved in relief were over a hundred life-size figures, illustrating the mythical battle between the Olympian gods and their rivals, the giants. But these sculptures are not only symbolic of triumph in war they also represented the victory of Greek culture over barbarism. The altar and its frieze were in fact a thunderous proclamation of the glories of Greek scholarship and art and of the right of Pergamon to see itself as the new Athens.

As you look at this section of the frieze you'll see that it is dominated by two standing figures. Athena is the striding woman with the shield, Zeus is to the left with his broad bare chest. As the goddess strides forward she turns and with a serene but powerful movement lifts the winged giant Alkyoneus by his hair. The giant can only loosely clutch at her arm and, with the serpent of Athena coiled about his body, he's powerless.

Although the colour has gone from many of the objects in this room, just a few steps away there is another great monument from the ancient world that has lost little of its original brilliance. So come with me now for another unexpected delight. If you walk through the centre archway of the Miletus gate and keep going straight ahead down the long corridor you will find the walls on either side decorated with a series of lions. When you reach the last of these lions please stop and turn round.

⑮ Business Travel

Listening

7   Interviewer: So how do you go about selling this particular venue?

Agnes Johnson: Basically, the way that we sell this venue here at The Manor is we contact conference agents; in England there are a number of agencies who will book conferences on behalf of companies – in England there's about 500 agencies operating, and they usually have a computer base so they have a good knowledge of all the venues – some specialise in country house hotels like us, some specialise in chain hotels but, by and large, most of them will book any sort of hotel and what happens is, we pay them commission because they've gone to all the trouble of finding the business for us – we don't have to go out and get it, but we need to offer them incentives to use us … something that's going to attract people to use us, whether it be an additional commission or a special rate for the conference delegates.

Interviewer: How much is the commission?

Agnes Johnson: We normally give them 8 per cent, so 8 per cent of the charge goes to them for finding the conference. If a client is looking for a conference centre they'll actually pick three hotels from the computer that match what the client wants, then they'll come out and visit each hotel, then they may bring the client out to visit the hotels and then the client will make a decision based upon what he knows about them – so it's a lot of work, but, on the whole, what we try and do is get in there and try and be friends with most of the conference agents – the better we get on with them the easier it is to sell to them. And that's what you find in selling any product. If you can make your clients your friends you're going to be able to do business a lot better.

Interviewer: Can you ever sell direct?

Agnes Johnson: Well, on the one side we've got the conference agents we talk to and on the other side we go direct to the corporate clients, and there's a lot of companies out there who have requirements for meetings, for conferences, for dinners perhaps, and what we need to do is to find out who they are and if they would use us. It's a long and complicated, well not a complicated – it's a quite honestly tedious process of telesales, of cold calling, going out knocking on doors of companies, giving them our conference brochure, talking with them, asking them – you know – would they consider using us for a conference. It can take a long time. You may have talked to a corporate client six months ago and they may have said, "mm … we could use you," and then you may find two years down the track they'll remember us and use us, so it's not the kind of thing that happens overnight.

Interviewer: And what about advertising? Or do you rely just on direct sales?

Agnes Johnson: No, we also have to participate in advertising. We can't just have sales people out and about because they can't cover the huge mass that advertising through the printed word can cover. Within our advertising we use books like these, the green book and the blue book. They're bibles for people who organise conferences – most large companies will have a copy so it's vital that we be in there. There's information about the hotel and a picture so they can go through and find you and give you a call. We also advertise in a lot of smaller

publications and in the Yellow Pages – the phone book – we also often attend exhibitions where we'll put ourselves forward, make a display and tell people who come to the exhibitions about the hotel. A fair amount of our business also comes from telephone enquiries, so down in our sales office we need to have people that can answer the telephone and know exactly what the capabilities of each room are and how we can negotiate our prices.

Interviewer: What else can you do to attract potential clients?

Agnes Johnson: Well, we also have a lot of special events – the major one we do is a Shakespeare festival which has been running for forty-five years and we often do a thousand people a night. With all our guests it seems to go down like a house on fire, and so it does a lot of our hospitality and our advertising for us. And other people might come and see a play and think, "oh I need to book a conference next year".

Word List

English	French	Italian	German
accommodation	hébergement	l'alloggio, la sistemazione	Unterkunft
air traffic control	contrôle du trafic aérien	il controllo di volo	Flugleitung
aircraft	avion	l'aeromobile, l'aereo	Flugzeug
airline	compagnie aérienne	la compagnia aerea	Fluggesellschaft
all-inclusive	tout compris	tutto incluso	alles inklusive
allocation	attribution/répartition	l'assegnazione	Platzanweisung
baggage	bagages	il bagaglio	Gepäck
backpacker	randonneur	il backpacker, l'escursionista	Wanderer
balance	solde	il saldo	zu zahlender Restbetrag
bed and breakfast	chambre (petit déjeuner compris)	camera e prima colazione	Übernachtung mit Frühstück
boarding	embarquement	l'imbarco	an Bord gehen
book	réserver	prenotare	buchen
booking	réservation	la prenotazione	Buchung
booking form	formulaire de réservation	il modulo di prenotazione	Buchungsformular
break	vacances de courte durée	la breve vacanza	Miniurlaub
bridal suite	suite réservée aux jeunes mariés	la suite matrimoniale	Hochzeitssuite
brochure	brochure	il dépliant, la brochure	Broschüre
cabin crew	équipage	il personale di bordo, l'equipaggio	Kabinenpersonal
cancellation charges	frais d'annulation	le spese di cancellazione	Stornierungsgebühr
car rental	location de voitures	l'autonoleggio	Autovermietung
carrier	transporteur	il vettore	Fluggesellschaft, Reisegesellschaft
catering	restauration	l'approvvigionamento, il catering	Gastronomie
chalet	chalet	lo chalet	Chalet
charge	prix/faire payer per personne	l'addebito pro capite, l'addebito a testa	Preis pro Person/pro Kopf
charter	affréter	noleggiare	chartern
charter flights	vols charter	i voli charter	Charterflüge
check-in	enregistrement	il check-in, l'accettazione	Abfertigung
coach (Br. E.)	car	il pullman, la corriera	Reisebus
condo	appartement en copropriété	il condominio, lo stabile in condominio	Appartementhaus
consultant	expert-conseil	il/la consulente	Berater
courier	guide	il corriere	Reiseleiter
cover	assurance	la copertura assicurativa	Deckung
covering letter	lettre explicative	la lettera di accompagnamento	Begleitbrief
covers	couverts	i coperti	Gedecke
cruise	croisière	la crociera	Kreuzfahrt
currency	monnaie, devises	la valuta, la moneta	Währung
day tripper	excursionniste	il gitante	Tagesausflügler
departure	départ	la partenza	Abreise, Abflug
departure lounge	salle d'embarquement	la sala partenze	Warteraum, Abflughalle
deposit	caution/arrhes	il deposito	Anzahlung,
discount	remise	lo sconto	Rabatt, Preisnachlaß
duty free	hors taxe	duty free	Zollfreie Waren
educational	educatour	informativo	Fortbildungsreise
en-suite (facilities)	(salle de bain) attenante	en-suite (servizi)	mit Bad und Toilette
excess baggage	excédent de bagages	il bagaglio in sovrappeso	Übergewicht
exchange rate	taux de change	il tasso di cambio	Wechselkurs
excursion	excursion	l'escursione, la gita	Ausflug
familiarisation trip (fam.)	educatour	il viaggio di familiarizzazione	Eingewöhnungsreise
fare	prix du billet	la tariffa, il prezzo	Fahrpreis, Flugpreis
flight	vol	il volo	Flug
foreign exchange	devises	il cambio estero	Devisen
frequent flyer programme	programme de fidélisation	il programma per chi viaggia spesso	Programm für häufige Fluggäste
full-board	pension complète	a pensione completa	Vollpension
full fare	plein tarif	la tariffa completa	der volle Flugpreis, Fahrpreis
fully booked	complet	tutto prenotato	ausgebucht
game reserve	réserve naturelle	la riserva di caccia	Wildschutzgebiet
gift shop	boutique de cadeaux	il negozio d'articoli da regalo	Geschenkladen
guest	client	l'ospite	Gast
half-board	demi-pension	a mezza pensione	Halbpension
hiking	randonnée	l'escursionismo	Wandern
holidaymaker	vacancier/estivant	il turista	Urlauber
hotel chain	chaîne hôtelière	la catena alberghiera	Hotelkette

Spanish	Polish	Turkish	Greek
alojamiento	zakwaterowanie	konaklama	στέγαση
control de tráfico aéreo	kontrola ruchu powietrznego	hava trafiği kontrolü	έλεγχος εναέριας κυκλοφορίας
avión	samolot	uçak	αεροσκάφος
línea aérea	linia lotnicza	hava yolları	αεροπορική γραμμή
todo incluido	wliczając wszystkie koszty	hepsi dahil	όλα συμπεριλαμβανόμενα
asientos	przydział (miejsca)	yer ayırtma	καταμερισμός θέσης
equipaje	bagaż	bagaj	αποσκευή
mochilero	turysta z plecakiem	sırt çantalı turist	ταξιδιώτης περιπλανώμενος
saldo	saldo	bakiye, hesap	ισολογισμός
alojamiento y desayuno	nocleg i śniadanie	yatak ve kahvaltı	ύπνος και πρόγευμα
embarcar	wsiadanie na pokład	binmek	επιβίβαση
reservar	rezerwować	yer ayırmak, rezervasyon yapmak	κλείνω θέση
reserva	rezerwacja	yer ayırma, rezervasyon	κράτηση θέσης
solicitud de reserva	formularz	rezervasyon formu	φόρμα κράτησης θέσης
descanso corto	krótki urlop	kısa tatil	σύντομες διακοπές
suite nupcial	apartament dla nowożeńców	balayı dairesi	γαμήλια σουίτα
folleto	broszura	broşür	φυλλάδιο διαφημιστικό
camarote de la tripulación	załoga kabinowa	uçak personeli	πλήρωμα
recargo por cancelación	opłata za rezygnację z usługi	iptal ücretleri	πρόστιμο ακύρωσης
alquiler de coches	wypożyczanie samochodów	araba kiralama	ενοικίαση αυτοκινήτου
compañía de trasporte	przewoźnik	taşımacı, nakliye şirketi	μεταφορέας
catering	żywienie	yiyecek içecek hazırlama	τροφοδοσία
chalet	dziakka	köşk, dağ evi	εξοχική έπαυλη
recargo por persona	opłata za jedną osobę	kişi başı ücret	χρέωση ανά άτομο
fletar	czarterować	kiralamak, tutmak	ναυλώνω
vuelos charter	loty czarterowe	çarter seferi	πτήσεις τσάρτερ
facturar	zgloszenie się do odprawy	bileti vize ettirme	άφιξη στο γκισέ πτήσης
autobús	autokar	yolcu otobüsü	λεωφορείο
condominio	wakacyjne mieszkanie własnościowe	kat mülkiyeti	συγκυριαρχία
asesor	konsultant	konsültan, danışman	σύμβουλος
mensajero	pilot wycieczki	kurye	συνοδός
cobertura	ubezpieczenie	sigorta kapsamı ve miktarı	κάλυψη ασφάλειας
carta de presentación	list przewodni	evrakın mahiyetini anlatan mektup	συνοδευτική επιστολή
cubierto	nakrycie stolu	sofra takımı	αξεσουάρ τραπεζιού εστιατορίου
crucero	wycieczka morska	deniz gezintisi	κρουαζιέρα
moneda	waluta	para birimi	ισχύον νόμισμα
excursionista	wycieczkowicz	günübirlik dolaşan kimse	ημερήσιος εκδρομέας
salida	odjazd	kalkış	αναχώρηση
sala de embarque	sala odlotów	giden yoku salonu	σαλόνι αναχωρήσεων
depósito	depozyt	kaparo	καταβολή εγγύησης
descuento	zniżka	iskonto, indirim	έκπτωση
libre de impuestos	bez cła	gümrüksüz	αδασμολόγητα είδη
viaje educativo/ viaje de estudio	objazd trasy	eğitsel amaçlı gezi	εκπαιδευτικό
incorporado	(apartament, pokój) z łazienką	en-suite	διευκολύνσεις
exceso de equipaje	nadwaga bagażu	fazla bagaj	υπέρβαρο αποσκευών
tipo de cambio	kurs wymiany	döviz kuru	συνάλλαγμα
excursión	wycieczka	gezinti	εκδρομή
viaje de familiarización	objazd trasy	personele turizm şirketlerince yaptırılan gezi	ταξίδι εξοικείωσης
pasaje	opłata	bilet ücreti, yol parası.	τιμή εισητηρίου
vuelo	lot	uçuş	πτήση
divisas	wymiana pieniędzy	döviz	ξένο συνάλλαγμα
programa de vuelos frecuentes	udogodnienia dla pasażerów regularnie korzystających z linii lotniczych	sık uçuş yapan yolcu programı.	πρόγραμμα συχνού ταξιδιώτη
pensión completa	zakwaterowanie z pełnym wyżywieniem	tam pansiyon	πλήρης διατροφή
billete entero	bilet pełnopłatny	tam bilet parası	πλήρης τιμή εισητηρίου
totalmente lleno	brak wolnych miejsc	rezervasyon dolu, yerler dolu.	εντελώς κλεισμένα
coto de caza	rezerwat łowiecki	avı korumak için ayrılmış arazi	κράτηση για παιχνίδι
tienda de regalos	sklep z pamiątkami	hediyelik eşya dükkanı	κατάστημα δώρων
invitado	gość	misafir, konuk	φιλοξενούμενος
media pensión	zakwaterowanie z kolacją	yarım pansiyon	ημι-διατροφή
excursionismo	wędrowanie	uzun yürüyüş	πεζοπορία
veraneante	urlopowicz	tatile çıkan kimse	παραθεριστής
cadena de hoteles	sieć hoteli	otel zinciri	αλυσίδα ξενοδοχείων

hotelier	hôtelier	l'albergatore	Hotelier
in-flight	pendant le vol	durante il volo, in volo	während des Fluges
in-flight service	service à bord d'avion	servizio durante il volo	Service während des Fluges
incentive travel	voyages de stimulation	il viaggio d'incentivazione	Reisen als Leistungszulage für Personal
insurance policy	police d'assurance	la polizza assicurativa	Versicherungspolice
itinerary	itinéraire	l'itinerario	Reiseroute
jet lag	fatigue due au décalage horaire	il jet lag	Jet-lag
liner	paquebot de grande ligne	il transatlantico	Passagierschiff
load factors	taux de remplissage d'avion	i fattori di carico	Lade-Faktoren
lobby	réception	la lobby	Eingangshalle, Foyer
long-haul flight	vol long-courrier	il volo lungo	Langstreckenflug
occupancy rate	taux d'occupation	il tasso di occupazione degli alberghi	Belegungsrate
one-way ticket	aller simple	il biglietto di sola andata	einfache Fahrkarte
option	option	l'opzione	Wahl, Möglichkeit
out-of-season	hors saison	fuori stagione	außerhalb der Saison
outbound	en partance	in uscita	auslaufend
package tour	voyage organisé	viaggio 'tutto compreso'	Pauschalreise
passenger	passager	il passeggero	Passagier
passport control	contrôle des passeports	il controllo passaporti	Paßkontrolle
premium	prime	il premio	Prämie
racking	présentation de brochures	l'esposizione	Ständer/Regal für Werbematerial
reception	réception	il ricevimento	Empfang
refurbishment	remise à neuf	l'ammodernamento, la messa a nuovo	Renovierung
resort	station	il centro turistico, il luogo di soggiorno	Urlaubsort
return ticket	billet aller-retour	il biglietto di andata e ritorno	Rückfahrkarte
round trip (Am. E.)	aller-retour	il viaggio di andata e ritorno	Hin- und Rückreise
runway	piste d'envol	la pista di decollo o di atterraggio	Start- und Landebahn
safari	safari	il safari	Safari
scheduled airline	compagnie aérienne assurant des vols réguliers	la compagnia aerea di linea	Linienfluggesellschaft
scheduled flight	vol régulier	il volo di linea, il volo regolare di linea	planmäßiger Flug, Linienflug
seasonal	saisonnier	stagionale	Saison- /je nach Jahreszeit
self-catering	(appartement) indépendant	con uso di cucina	selbstversorgend
self-drive	voiture sans chauffeur	senza autista	für Selbstfahrer
shuttle	navette	la navetta	Pendeltransport
sightseeing	visiter/faire du tourisme	il giro turistico, la visita ai monumenti	Sightseeing, Besichtigungen
skiing	ski	lo sci	Skilaufen
special interest holiday	vacances à thème	la vacanza d'interesse speciale	Urlaub je nach Interessengebiet, Hobby
special offer	promotion	l'offerta speciale	Sonderangebot
stand-by (passenger)	voyageur sur une liste d'attente	in stand-by	Standby-Passagier
stay	séjour	il soggiorno	Aufenthalt
stopover	halte	lo scalo	Zwischenstation, Zwischenlandung
surcharge	surtaxe	il supplemento di prezzo, il sovrapprezzo	Zuschlag
tariff	prix	la tariffa	Tarif
tax-free	exonéré d'impôts	esentasse, non imponibile	zollfrei
terminal	aérogare	l'aerostazione, il terminal	Terminal
terms and conditions	modalités	termini e condizioni	allgemeine Geschäftsbedingungen
theme park	parc à thème/parc d'attractions	il parco tematico	Freizeitpark
time slot	plage horaire	il tempo disponibile	Zeitschlitz, Zeitspanne
time zone	fuseau horaire	il fuso orario	Zeitzone
timeshare	maison en multipropriété	il timeshare	Timeshare
tour	excursion/visite guidée/circuit	il viaggio, il tour	Tour
tourist board	office de tourisme	l'ente turistico	Fremdenverkehrsverein
Tourist Information Centre	syndicat d'initiative	Centro Informazioni Turistiche	Touristen-Informationsbüro
transfer	transférer/transfert	il transito, il trasferimento	Transit
travel	voyager	viaggiare	reisen
twin room	chambre à deux lits	la camera doppia, la camera a due letti	Zimmer mit zwei Einzelbetten
upgrade	meilleur classement	avanzamento di grado	Steigerung
valet service	ster	il servizio di guardaroba	Reinigungsdienst
window-shop	faire du lèche-vitrines	guardare le vetrine dei negozi	einen Schaufensterbummel machen
winter sports	sports d'hiver	gli sport invernali	Wintersport

hotelero	hotelarz	otel yöneticisi/sahibi.	ξενοδόχος
en vuelo	podczas lotu	uçuş esnasında	κατά την πτήση
servicio a bordo	usługi podczas lotu	uçuş sırasında sunulan hizmetler	εξυπηρέτηση κατά την πτήση
viaje incentivo	wakacje opłacone przez pracodawcę w nagrodę za wydajną pracę	başarılı personeli ödüllendirme yolculuğu.	διακοπές κίνητρο
póliza de seguros	polisa ubezpieczeniowa	sigorta poliçesi	ασφαλιστήριο
itinerario	trasa (wycieczki)	kılavuz programı, yolculuk kitabı.	δρομολόγιο
desfase horario	zmęczenie wywołane długim lotem	uçak yolculuğundan sonra 'beden saati'nin bozulması.	ενόχληση λόγω διαφοράς ώρας
transatlántico	statek oceaniczny	transatlantik	πλοίο γραμμής
factores de carga	współczynnik zajętości miejsc	bilet ücreti ödeyen yolcuların gerçekte kullandıkları yerin yüzdesi.	περιορισμοί πτήσης λόγω βάρους
vestíbulo	hall	lobi	αίθουσα αναμονής
vuelo de larga distancia	loty dalekiego zasięgu	uzak mesafe uçuşu	πτήση μακράς πορείας
tarifa de alojamiento	współczynnik zajętości	oda doluluk oranı	έξοδα ημερήσιας διαμονής
billete de ida	bilet w jedną stronę	yalnız gidiş bileti	εισητήριο μονής διαδρομής
opción	rezerwacja wymagająca potwierdzenia	seçenek, tercih	δυνατότητα εκλογής σε διακοπές
fuera de temporada	poza sezonem	sezon dışı	εκτός σαιζόν
salida/partida	tam (o kierunku jazdy)	memleket dışına sefere çıkan.	αποπλέων
viaje organizado	zorganizowana wycieczka	toplu gezi	περιοδεία πακέτου
pasajero	pasażer	yolcu	επιβάτης
control de pasaportes	kontrola paszportów	pasaport kontrolü	έλεγχος διαβατηρίων
prima de seguro	składka ubezpieczeniowa	prim	ασφάλιστρο
estante	półka	reklam rafları	θήκες διαφημιστικών φυλλαδίων
recepción	recepcja (reception); przyjęcie (party)	resepsiyon, misafir kabul töreni	υποδοχή
renovación	odnowienie	yenileme	ανακαίνηση
centro turístico	uzdrowisko	gezinti yerleri	καταφύγιο
billete de ida y vuelta	bilet powrotny	dönüş bileti	εισιτήριο επιστροφής
viaje de ida y vuelta	podróż tam i z powrotem	gidiş-dönüş yolculuğu	εισιτήριο με επιστροφή
escapado	pas startowy	uçak pisti	δρόμος τρεξίματος
safari	safari	safari	σαφάρι
linea aérea programada	regularna linia lotnicza	tarifeli hava yolları	προγραμματισμένη αερογραμμή
vuelo programado	regularny lot	tarifeli sefer	προγραμματισμένη πτήση
estacional	sezonowy	sezonluk, mevsimlik	εποχιακός
selfcatering	zakwaterowanie z możliwością przygotowania posiłków	kendin pişir kendin ye	αυτόνομη διατροφή
sin chófer	własny transport (dojazd)	şoförsüz kiralanan	αυτόνομες διακοπές
servicio de enlace	autobus, pociąg	servis otobüsü.	μεταφορά σε αεροδρόμιο
visitar lugares de interés	zwiedzanie	gezme, görülecek yerleri ziyaret etme	επίσκεψη αξιοθεάτων
esquiar	jazda na nartach	kayak yapma	σκί
vacaciones de interés especial	wakacje specjalistyczne	özel ilgi amaçlı tatil	διακοπές ειδικού ενδιαφέροντος
oferta especial	oferta specjalna	indirimli fiyatlar	ειδική προσφορά
en espera	stand-by	bekleme listesi	αναμονή επιβάτη
estancia	pobyt	kalma, ziyaret süresi	διαμονή
parada	przerwa w podróży	konaklama, mola	σταμάτημα
aplicar un recargo	dopłata	krediyi deftere kaydetmeme	προσαύξηση
tarifa	taryfa	tarife	ταρίφα
sin impuestos	bez podatku	vergisiz	χωρίς φόρο
terminal	terminal	uçak terminali	σταθμός αεροδρομίου
términos y condiciones	warunki	şartlar	όροι και συνθήκες
parque temático	wesołe miasteczko	konulu eğlence parkı	πάρκο αναψυχής
escala de tiempo	odcinek czasu	zaman dilimi	χρονική στιγμή
zona horaria	strefa czasowa	arz derecesine göre resmi saatin aynı olduğu bölge	ζώνη ώρας
multipropiedad	mieszkanie wakacyjne stanowiące współwłasność wielu osób	devremülk	θέρετρο πολλών ιδιοκτητών
gira	wycieczka	tur	περιήγηση
oficina de turismo	instytucja promująca turystykę w danym regionie	turizm bürosu	τουριστική επιτροπή
Centro de Información y Turismo	Centrum Informacji Turystycznej	Turist Danışma Merkezi	Κέντρο Τουριστικών Πληροφοριών
transbordo	transfer (n); transferować (v)	aktarma	μεταφορά - μεταφέρω
viajar	podróżować	yolculuk etmek	ταξιδεύω
habitación doble	pokój z dwoma łóżkami	iki yataklı oda	δωμάτιο με δύο μονά κρεββάτια
ascenso/aumento/mejora	świadczenie wyższej jakości	daha iyi bir hizmet sınıfına geçilmesi	αναβάθμιση
servicio de planchado	obsługa przez pokojówkę	temizleme servisi	υπηρεσία δωματίου
mirar escaparates	oglądać wystawy sklepowe	mağazaları dolaşma, vitrin bakma.	γυρνάω τις βιτρίνες
deportes de invierno	sporty zimowe	kış sporları	χειμερινά σπόρ